# *Early Childhood Administration*

# Early Childhood Administration

**Bruce D. Grossman**
Hofstra University

**Carol Keyes**
Pace University

Allyn and Bacon, Inc.
Boston   London   Sydney   Toronto

Series Editor: Jeffrey W. Johnston
Production Administrator: Jane Schulman
Production Services and Design: Total Concept Associates

Library of Congress Cataloging in Publication Data
Grossman, Bruce D.
  Early childhood administration.

  Bibliography: p.
  Includes index.
  1. Day care centers—United States—Administration.
2. Child development.   3. Community and school—United
States.   4. Education, Preschool—United States—
Administration.   I. Keyes, Carol.   II. Title.
HV854.G76   1985        362.7'95        84-14631
ISBN 0-205-08308-0

Printed in the United States of America.

10 9 8 7 6 5 4 3 2      90 89 88 87 86

# *Contents*

Preface    ix

Acknowledgments    xi

Introduction    xiii

*Part I   Creating the Center    1*

Chapter 1   Establishing an Early Childhood Center    3
Needs Assessment    3
Sponsorship and Funding    5
Community Support    10
Licensing Requirements    11
Locating the Center    12
Equipment, Materials, and Supplies    17
Suggested Activities    22
References and Further Readings    23

Chapter 2   Setting Up a Classroom    25
General Principles    25
Interest Areas    26
Arranging the Room    35
Basic Equipment and Supplies    37
Timetable of Activities    45
Suggested Activities    46
References and Further Readings    46

Chapter 3   Public Relations    47
Identifying Your Target Population    47
Reaching Your Target Population    48
Fund-Raising    52
Public Relations Assessment    55
Suggested Activities    56
References and Further Readings    56

*Part II  Working with People*     57


Chapter 4   Staff Selection     59
        Concerns in Staff Selection     59
        The Employment Process     62
        Postemployment Procedures     66
        Suggested Activities     69
        References and Further Readings     70


Chapter 5   Staff Development     71
        In-Service Staff Development     72
        Professional Growth and Development     74
        Working with Parents     76
        Curriculum Planning and Implementation     77
        Personal Needs of Staff Members     87
        Staff Development Through Observation
          and Supervision     89
        Staff Manual     97
        Monitoring and Evaluating Teacher Effectiveness     98
        Suggested Activities     101
        References and Further Readings     101


Chapter 6   The Humanistic Administrator
          and the Children     105
        Enrolling the Children     106
        Identifying the Needs of the Children     109
        Developmental Considerations     112
        Matching the Needs of Children
          with Policy and Program     116
        Evaluating the Children's Progress     123
        Suggested Activities     130
        References and Further Readings     131


Chapter 7   Meeting Children's Special Needs     133
        Different Backgrounds, Different Abilities     133
        Setting Up a Program for Infants and Toddlers     140
        Identifying and Monitoring Children's Individual Needs
          in the Classroom     151
        Suggested Activities     154
        References and Further Readings     154

Chapter 8   The Humanistic Orientation and Parents     159
        Concerns of Parents and Programs for Parents     160
        Enrollment Preparation and Process     165
        Ongoing Contact with Parents     167
        Parents and Administrative Functions     179
        Parents in the Classroom: Visitors and Volunteers     180
        Parent-Teacher Conferences     192
        A Final Note     198
        Suggested Activities     198
        References and Further Readings     198

Chapter 9   Volunteers     201
        Screening and Orienting Volunteers     202
        Health and Safety Considerations     205
        Volunteer Activities and Benefits     206
        Parents as Volunteers     209
        Conclusion     211
        Suggested Activities     212
        References and Further Readings     212

Part III   Management     213

Chapter 10   Managing the Program     215
        Characteristics of an Early Childhood Director     215
        Moving into Management     216
        Policies and Procedures     221
        Program Evaluation     234
        Outside Funding     238
        Suggested Activities     242
        References and Further Readings     242

Chapter 11   The Director as Advocate     245
        Advocacy with a Board or Sponsoring Agency     246
        Advocacy with Business and Industry     245
        Advocacy with Government     247
        Advocacy for Humanism     249
        Professional Activism     249
        Summary     250
        Suggested Activity     250
        References and Further Readings     251

Index     253

# *Preface*

This book was written by an early childhood specialist and a child psychologist. We have collaborated on many projects, including research, teaching, writing three books, and initiating and administering a campus child care center. In the course of working together, we have discovered that, despite the differences in our training and the differences in our specific approaches at times, we share a basic philosophy and orientation. Our ideas about how to develop and administer an early childhood center are grounded in our mutual and separate experiences as administrators of early childhood centers that have varied in size and nature; that is, our ideas are based on practical experience. The ideas offered here are also based on research (our own and that of others) and on theoretical models concerned with child development and educational goals.

Before we embark on a full-scale presentation of our guidelines for early childhood administration, we shall briefly identify some of the basic assumptions that underlie our approach. First, a fundamental assumption is a *developmental* orientation. This point of view has always had special significance in working with young children but is even more critical now, as we extend our efforts to programs for infants and toddlers. Second, our orientation is *ecological*. We have increasingly recognized that the time children spend with us in the classroom is only one aspect of their total daily experience. Our research efforts have been directed toward tracking children during the hours before and after their daily attendance at our center to help us understand the significance of the experience we provide in the total context of their lives.

Finally, we share a *humanistic* orientation. It is our firm belief that administrative policies and practices must be based on the assumption that all persons—adults and children—have within them the capacity to develop to their fullest potential and that, as administrators, our primary function is to provide a hospitable environment for this process to occur.

Some of the ideas offered here are more obviously humanistic than others. However, all of our suggestions are humanistic in their purpose and in their application. Our goal orientation is a good example. Some of the goals outlined are behavioral. We do not consider this inconsistent with a humanistic philosophy. The specification of goals provides a direction to our work, but the goals are not determined apart from a consideration of the individual child; they further our humanistic purpose in that they allow for individualization in our programming. The specification of individual goals also helps us examine the relationship between our intended objectives and our methods.

Many early childhood programs pay lip service to one or more of these principles, but far too many neglect to include them in their daily planning and in their relationships with staff, parents, and children. We are well aware of how difficult it is at times to keep the child, the child's environment, and the growth of all the center participants in mind, but we have found that this can be done without sacrificing efficiency and organization. We feel it is well worth the effort, and we hope, after reading our book, you will feel the same way, too.

Although this book is written primarily for students of early childhood administration, it will also be useful to directors who are initiating new programs and to those who are responsible for the continuing leadership of existing early childhood centers. It is a practical book, offering tips on selecting staff, purchasing, setting up classrooms, recruiting students, working with parents, and all of the many other tasks that fall within the range of early childhood administration. It stresses the importance of a sound, well-thought-out philosophical and theoretical base, giving serious attention to curriculum design and to evaluation. All in all, we believe we have created a useful balance between theory and practice in our attempt to provide a humanistically oriented guide to early childhood administration.

NOTE: Throughout this book, we use *she* to refer to the director and *he* to refer to a child. To avoid the sexist bias that this usage implies, we had attempted to mix the genders of the pronouns in such references, but, alas, the result proved to be too confusing. We regret the implication but trust you will understand this usage in no way implies that the early childhood director must be a woman nor that every child attending a center must be a boy.

# *Acknowledgments*

We would like to thank the many children, families, and teachers with whom we have worked over the years. This book has evolved from our experiences with them. We are grateful to our own families for their patience during the time we have spent preparing this manuscript. A special debt of thanks is also due our typist, Kay Gottlieb, who continued to plow through our scribbling and return beautiful copy for our further disfigurement and dissection.

B.G.
C.K.

# Introduction

## WHAT IS AN EARLY CHILDHOOD CENTER?

An expanded version of the traditional early childhood center has emerged in response to the changing needs of families in contemporary society. The early childhood center of which we speak may be in a one-room house, serving perhaps fifteen or fewer families, or in a much larger facility. It may provide either part- or full-day sessions, or it may have a flexible schedule whereby the children come and go at varied times.

An early childhood center goes well beyond providing daily custodial care for its children; it even goes beyond offering a high-quality program for children. Rather, it is an educational and service center for *families*, a place where parents can discuss their children with competent, caring professionals, a place where its director and teachers are available to talk about all aspects of child rearing. The early childhood center is a place where parents feel free to ask questions about discipline, about toilet training, or about their children's future schooling. It is also a place that recognizes the alternative forms of modern families and attempts to meet the special needs of each type of family, such as the working mother who may need help with schedules or the single parent who may be concerned about a child's visits with the former spouse. The center often has activities that parents and children may share and discussion groups for parents in which they can exchange ideas with other parents and work out solutions to some of the complex problems involved in child rearing today.

A distinguishing feature of such an expanded early childhood program is its recognition that each child has his own ecological environment. The school experience is significant, but it is only one aspect of the child's total experience. What happens before and after a day at the center has a decided influence on the child's behavior while he is there. Is his mother impatient in the morning because she is late for work? Is the child upset after a weekend visit with his father and a new family? Is he tired or irritable in school because he attends another child care program earlier in the day?

In dealing with these experiences, the center director and teachers work with parents, allowing them to use their own resources and good judgment to find solutions to the complex problems that often beset them in planning for their children. At the same time, the director and teachers, recognizing the additional pressures with which parents are likely to be contending (e.g., economic, psychological, social) that may limit what they are able to do on their children's behalf, attempt to work toward solutions that may require some adjustments for the center as well as for the parents. The ultimate goal, of course, is to provide the most secure, growth-promoting environment for children.

The early childhood center as we define it begins with a philosophical orientation that helps an administrator develop behavioral goals. Its purpose is to facilitate the child's growth directly through the program in school and indirectly through the strengthening of the family's role. The purpose of a center is to be an extension of and a support for the family. In her address to the National Association for the Education of Young Children, Betty Caldwell (1979) suggested that early childhood programs are helping support families and, in that sense, are taking the role of an extended family.

Everything provided by the early childhood program, from information about development to confidence that children can be left with caring people without guilt or worry, is designed to contribute to rather than detract from the family's functioning as a unit of society. All parents can benefit from the resources an early childhood center has to offer, but working parents and single parents especially can profit from the extended family support that such a center provides.

Over 25 percent of mothers of preschool children are working now, and the number of working mothers of children in the primary grades is even greater. Many of these working mothers are single parents who do not have the support of another adult in the home. For them, child care is not only a practical necessity, but also a psychologically valuable form of family support.

## THE HUMANISTIC PHILOSOPHY

Throughout our discussions in this book, we suggest that administrators adopt a humanistic orientation. What do we mean by *humanistic*? As described by Carl Rogers (1977), the humanistic point of view is based on the assumption that "there is in every organism, at whatever level, an underlying flow of movement toward constructive fulfillment of its inherent possibilities" (p. 7). To apply Rogers's (1942) suggestions for psychotherapy, the implications for this point of view are that education "is not a matter of doing something to the individual, or inducing him to do something about himself. It is instead a matter of freeing him for normal growth and development, of removing obstacles so that he can move forward" (p. 29).

The fields of humanistic education and humanistic psychology have developed in response to the increasing danger in modern times that professionals might lose sight of their clients as people and regard them as organisms to be manipulated and controlled. There is a related danger of viewing clients from a single professional perspective, thus not taking into account their wholeness.

Humanistic educators remind us we must take the total child into account, even if we have a particular concern with intellectual or academic growth. Recently, the affective domain (Ringless 1975) has become a legitimate curricular entity, and a child's feelings are considered a significant factor in making educational decisions. Clearly, a child's emotional and social well-being greatly affects his ability to learn. Humanists also regard learning about feelings and acquiring interpersonal skills as essential to a child's total development as learning about science and math.

In the field of psychology, the humanists are opposed to the reductionistic tendencies observed in science and in medicine, which tend to break an individual down into separate components for either investigation or treatment. To understand a child, the humanists consider it essential to take into account not only the individual child but also his family and his social and cultural milieu. They take a phenomenological rather than a behavioristic point of view. This assumes that the child is not a passive creature reacting to environmental stimuli but an active human being who interprets and integrates experience into an existing mental and emotional organization. This makes the humanistic orientation less manipulative than a behavioristic approach. The child is not "done to" but is a dynamic part of what takes place in his growth and learning.

The humanistic approach is based on a faith in the self-actualizing principle within human beings that directs them toward developing and integrating their natural capacities. Humanistic education is an attempt to go beyond the mere adaptation that is the hallmark of much traditional education. This approach encourages the development of human potential that may surpass conventional limitations. To be most meaningful, a humanistic educational experience must be integrated into a child's own needs and aptitudes. Many children seem to lose their zest for learning, and even for living, because they have not been given an opportunity to make choices and to fulfill their own exploratory and investigatory needs when they are younger. This need-fulfilling capacity must be nourished.

The humanistic approach also allows teachers and administrators to develop genuine relationships with the children, with the parents, and with each other. Genuineness, or *authenticity*, is a key concept in the humanistic philosophy. If you are controlling or manipulating people, it is difficult for you to view them as full-fledged human beings. In such a situation, they may come to regard themselves less favorably—a clearly undesirable as well as nonhumanistic situation. For example, a requirement that all teachers do the same thing in the same way has an effect on them similar to its effect on the children. It denies individual differences, and it denies natural needs for autonomy. Teachers need to develop programs and to evaluate results. They also need to be able to use their own initiative and to develop their own unique teaching styles.

Similarly, parental involvement is an important aspect of an early childhood center. This involvement means *being a part* and it means *doing*. An administrator who successfully involves parents not only is contributing to her program by supplementing paid workers but also is enhancing the effectiveness of her center by acknowledging the strengths of parents and allowing them to demonstrate their caring and competency actively. We don't do parents a favor by taking over their responsibilities, thus making them the passive recipients of our professional efforts. In sum, the humanistic philosophy is a respect for the uniqueness and the wholeness of each person as well as an acknowledgment of the individual's inner resources

## THE DIRECTOR'S ROLE: AN OVERVIEW

The director is the linchpin of the early childhood center. She is responsible for all areas of the center's functioning, even though in large centers some of these responsibilities may be delegated.

The director's administrative and educational functions include (1) recruiting, hiring, and orienting personnel; (2) recruiting, enrolling, and orienting children; (3) preparing the budget; (4) preparing reports; (5) overseeing the physical plant; (6) handling publicity and public relations; (7) purchasing start-up equipment and supplies; (8) educational planning for the children; (9) training and supervising staff and student volunteers; (10) educating parents; (11) acting as advocate for children and family; and (12) having the ultimate responsibility for the safety and welfare of the children (Axelrod and Buch 1978; Cherry et al. 1978).

Early childhood administrators often begin their careers as teachers of young children. They may have been excellent classroom teachers, but how do they actually learn the specific tasks required of a good administrator? The skills and attitudes of a caring teacher who is tuned into everyone's needs can be quite useful for a director, but for administrative purposes they must be balanced with a decision-making orientation that may require a degree of impersonality and even an authoritarian stance at times. Are these compatible? We believe so, but the necessary balance is often difficult to maintain (Dombro 1983).

In *Talks with Teachers*, Lillian Katz (1977) describes four developmental stages that directors are likely to experience. The first stage is *survival*: "Can I get through the day in one piece?" "Can I really do this kind of work day after day?" "Can I make it until the end of the week?" The second stage is *consolidation*, whereby the director focuses on one or another aspect of the center that needs modifications to better meet identified goals. In the third stage, *renewal*, the director examines innovations in the field, shares ideas with other directors, and is active in professional associations. The fourth stage, *maturity*, is a time of questioning and searching for answers to more abstract questions about growth, learning, and decision making and, perhaps, the time for considering a return to school for an advanced degree.

The information in this book is designed to help directors of early childhood programs, who may be at any of these stages, to identify their goals, review their program operations, and develop their own schedules. An overriding goal of any administrator is to be able to match one's practices with one's goals. Thus, students of administration need to be encouraged to identify goals even as they learn to meet the daily challenges of administration.

How does an administrator who must be concerned with the operation of the center, including its economic and political survival, maintain the humanistic orientation we discussed earlier? How does the director balance the business aspects and the humanistic qualities? As already mentioned, having a solid theoretical foundation on which to build daily practice is essential. Also, a director can accomplish management and administrative tasks most efficiently by organizing, budgeting her time, and delegating responsibilities. Organizing will leave more time for the director to respond in a humanistic manner to the people participating in the center. It is often very difficult to consider the points of view of all of the center's constituents and to be open to the ideas of staff, parents, and children. However, we believe that such responsiveness is as much the responsibility of the director as paying the lighting bill and ordering supplies.

In the remainder of this book, we devote our attention to the director's roles as philosophical leader and role model of the center as well as handler of the "nitty-gritty" of administration.

Part I deals with starting a center, setting up the classroom, and engaging in public relations activities. Part II discusses the director's relationships and functions in regard to staff, parents, and children—the cornerstone of a humanistic orientation. Finally, Part III covers selected aspects of the actual administrative functions.

### References and Further Readings

Axelrod, Pearl, and Buch, Esther M. *Preschool and Child Care Administration*. Course handout, Mobile Training for Directors of Day Care Centers, 1978.

Caldwell, Betty. Keynote address, Annual Meeting of the National Association for Early Childhood Education, Atlanta, November 1979.

Cherry, Clare; Hunness, Barbara; and Kuzma, Kay. *Nursery School and Day Care Management Guide*. Belmont, Calif.: Fearon-Pitman, 1978.

Dombro, Amy. Personal communications, Bank Street College of Education, New York, 1983.

Katz, Lillian. *Talks with Teachers*. Washington, D.C.: National Association for the Education of Young Children, 1977.

Ringless, Thomas A. *The Affective Domain in Education*. Boston: Little, Brown, 1975.

Rogers, Carl. *Counseling and Psychotherapy.* Boston: Houghton
    Mifflin, 1942.
Rogers, Carl. *Freedom to Learn.* Columbus, Ohio: Merrill, 1969.
Rogers, Carl. *On Personal Power.* New York: Delacorte, 1977.
Weinstein, Gerald, and Fantini, Mario D. *Toward Humanistic Edu-
    cation: A Curriculum of Affect.* Published for the Ford
    Foundation. New York: Praeger, 1970.

*Early Childhood Administration*

# Part I
# Creating
# the Center

*If you are considering opening an early childhood center, the three chapters in this part will assist you with your plans. If you already direct a center and are planning additional locations or expansion of the center, these chapters will help you with such activities as investigating needs. Chapter 1 also discusses generating community support for your center. Chapter 2 focuses on the actual setup of the rooms in the center, while Chapter 3 concentrates on identifying the target population, marketing the center, and fund raising— topics that concern both experienced and new directors.*

# Chapter 1
# Establishing
# an Early
# Childhood
# Center

## NEEDS ASSESSMENT

An effective way to determine the need for an early childhood center is to conduct a needs assessment. Such an assessment involves collecting information on the number of children of pre-school age in the area, the income level of parents, the number of working parents, the availability of transportation, and the nature of existing child care services. Much of this information can be obtained from U.S. Census data, labor and employment service data, annual school district census data, state and county department of social service data, and some child care organizations' data. It is also important to obtain information directly from parents, since you are interested in how many of the parents actually need child care services and would be likely to use them if available.

In a small neighborhood or an apartment complex, a door-to-door canvassing may be conducted; or an article about the proposed program in a local newspaper, with a request for responses, might help you estimate the need in that community. A church-sponsored school might begin by polling the church membership. On a college campus, you might be able to obtain the addresses of married students for a personal mailing, or you might use the campus newspaper to describe your program. In one school district, letters were sent to all parents of eligible 4-year-olds to determine their interest in a cooperative preschool that the district was preparing to initiate.

In any of these cases, you may wish to offer such alternatives as a parent cooperative or a largely tuition-sponsored program. You may offer a choice of a full- or part-time service, with flexible or standard hours, and then assess the hours that parents prefer. Of course, you will need to know the ages of the children. In addition, it is important to ascertain not only whether the families agree that the center would be useful for the community and whether they would offer their support but also how likely they would be to use it for their own children. Full descriptions of various needs assessments are available in the references at the end of this chapter. Figure 1.1 is a sample needs survey for a community where you already have a facility or know the population.

**FIGURE 1.1**  Sample Needs Survey

What are the ages of your children?

_____ Infant/toddler            _____ $2\frac{1}{2}$-6 years old            _____ 6-10 years old

Is your child disabled, or does your child have special needs?_____

_____

Where do you leave your children when you attend classes or work?

          Other nursery school
_____ or day care:            _____ Cost/hr.    _____ Cost/wk.    _____ Cost/mo.

          Name:_____

_____ Babysitter in home:      _____ Cost/hr.    _____ Cost/wk.    _____ Cost/mo.

_____ Family day care home:    _____ Cost/hr.    _____ Cost/wk.    _____ Cost/mo.

_____ Relative's home

_____ Home alone

What kinds of child care services do you need?

*a.* _____ Part-time day care            _____ Part-time day care
          (infant/toddler)                        ($2\frac{1}{2}$-6 years old)

b._____Full-time day care
(infant/toddler)

_____Full-time day care
$(2\frac{1}{2}$-6 years old)

c._____Evening care (4-6 P.M.)
(infant/toddler)

_____Evening care (4-6 P.M.)
$(2\frac{1}{2}$-6 years old)

_____Evening care (4-6 P.M.)
(6-10 years old)

d._____Evening care (6-8 P.M.)
(infant/toddler)

_____Evening care (6-8 P.M.)
$(2\frac{1}{2}$-6 years old)

_____Evening care (6-8 P.M.)
(6-10 years old)

e._____Weekend care
(infant/toddler)

_____Weekend care
$(2\frac{1}{2}$-6 years old)

_____Weekend care
(6-10 years old)

f._____None

If we offer the services you need, would you use the child care center?_____

If you would like some information about the child care center or would like to begin to use the facility, please print your name, address, and telephone number:

Name_____

Address_____

_____

Telephone_____

## SPONSORSHIP AND FUNDING

The possibilities for sponsorship of a center are varied. For an on-campus school, with which we are most familiar, sponsorship might come from an academic department (e.g., education, psychology), the student government, the university administration (as a service to students or as a fund-raiser), women's groups, or an alumni association. In the public area, prekindergarten programs are being sponsored by some local school districts as the impor-

tance of early education becomes more evident and as lowered
enrollment frees classroom space for this purpose. In other cases,
a public school prekindergarten may come about through the
work of the PTA or an ad hoc parent committee. One school
district (School District 14, Hewlett, New York) has been able to
sponsor four different programs for children aged 3 to 5: a state-
funded prekindergarten; a cooperative preschool (which was
initiated after the prekindergarten met with such success); a half-
day program for 3-year-olds, sponsored by the National Council of
Jewish Women; and a parent-and-child program (You and Your
Preschooler), sponsored by the library and developed as a community service for parents and their 3-year-olds. Similar forms of
sponsorship are likely to exist in your area. Figure 1.2 presents a
wide range of schools and sponsorship options.

**FIGURE 1.2**  Types of Schools

| Type | Sponsorship | Source of Income | Characteristics |
|---|---|---|---|
| **Private** | | | |
| Proprietary schools | One or more individuals | Tuition | Profit-making; freedom to initiate program; limited resources for income |
| Educational corporations | Group of people | Tuition | Shared resources for planning, purchasing, maintenance; curriculum planned by originators, implemented by director |
| Franchise | Corporation | Tuition | Expertise supplied by franchisor if franchisor is knowledgeable |
| Company, hospital or apartment | Owner(s) of company, hospital or apartment | Tuition, supplemented by owner(s) | Location close to work or residence |
| Cooperative or playgroup | Member families | Tuition and fund-raising | Intense parent involvement; less costly to operate; opportunities for parent education |
| Private laboratory | Private college or university | Tuition and departmental supplements | Model program design; used for practice teaching placements |

| Parochial | Church | Tuition and church supplements | Policies determined by church; use church facilities; part of the church educational program |
| Community | Community organizations | Fund-raising and contributions; tuition | May be designed for handicapped children; requires knowledge of the community |
| **Public** | | | |
| Child care centers | Local school district | Federal, state, county, city; tuition | Director functions as a manager; often must accommodate large numbers of children; school district resources available |
| Head Start | Public or private nonprofit agencies | Federal funds; minimal tuition | Designed to overcome deficiencies and prepare child for school; community participation and control |
| Student day-care centers (laboratory) | Student body association, public college or university | Student body funds and university or college supplements | Conflicts may arise over content of program, student's ideas, and college administration; must be scheduled to meet student class times |
| Parent observation classes | School district | Adult education funds | Parent is enrolled, child attends; purpose is education of parent |

*Source:* Phyllis Glick, *Administration of Schools for Young Children* (Albany: Delmar, 1975), p. 15.

## Initial Funding

The initial expenses of renting space, renovating, equipping the classroom, hiring and paying staff, advertising, and so forth, usually involve a substantial outlay of funds that may be particularly difficult to manage before any tuition income is realized. If you were beginning a business, you might apply for a loan that you would repay as you began to receive income. However, taking out a loan for a child care center may be difficult because of the relatively high tuition that would be required to repay the loan and provide operating expenses. Another negative aspect of commercial borrowing is that a loan usually requires collateral.

Therefore, you may want to go to your community, which may be eligible for federal funds, to begin and/or support an early childhood program.

Perhaps the most well known federally funded early childhood program is Head Start. This program was initiated in 1965 by the Office of Economic Opportunity as an attempt to combat the negative effects of poverty on the development of young children. In addition to funding, the government also offers participants a great deal of support in terms of curriculum guides, inservice training, parent education, community involvement, and so forth.

Sometimes, initial funding for an early childhood program (particularly a nonprofit one) can be secured in the form of an outright donation for seed money. For example, at one university, $2,000 was donated as an outright gift for equipment; at another, $40,000 was secured from a dean's budget.

### Bureau of the Handicapped

The federal Bureau of the Handicapped is concerned with expanding educational opportunities for handicapped children. In particular, it is responding to research suggesting that early intervention in handicapping conditions can substantially lessen their negative impact. The bureau has an Early Childhood Division that actively seeks proposals for demonstration and research projects concerned with the education of young handicapped children.

### State, County, and Local Town Funding

Other sources of funds for early childhood programs include state, county, and town governments. Again, specialized concerns for the handicapped or economically disadvantaged are likely to be the focus of such programs. State boards of education or offices of the handicapped are good sources of information about these funds. Very often, government funding is offered on a matching basis, in which case you would still be required to find other types of support (usually local) in the form of equipment, space, or operating expenses.

### Private Foundations

Private foundations may not support an early childhood center per se, but you may find that they are interested in a particular aspect of your program, such as equipping an outdoor area or conducting a special music curriculum. In addition, foundations that are dedicated to helping combat particular diseases and disabilities (e.g., Easter Seal Foundation, March of Dimes, Associations for the Blind and the Deaf, United Way) may be interested in a program that would include the children they serve.

### Local Civic Organizations

Local civic organizations, such as Kiwanis, Odd Fellows, Masons, Lions, chambers of commerce, and the like, are usually willing to help with small donations and may be good places to look for seed money for your program. They may even provide continued modest support annually, which may prove helpful for special projects.

### Universities

Although universities are generally facing severe financial restrictions that preclude assumption of the complete costs of an early childhood program, they may be willing to provide initial funding or offer in-kind services, such as space, heat, light, and custodial services. Other campus organizations, such as women's groups, service organizations, and even deans' offices of various professional schools, may be asked to contribute their educational support. In some of these cases, academic departments may be able to allocate a portion of their budgets, since students will be able to use the center to gain direct experience with young children. The departments might contribute to the cost of a campus school—as they would to a laboratory facility in another field of study.

### Cooperative Nursery Schools

In some cases, initial funding is supplied by a group of families who wish to begin a center for their own children. For one cooperative nursery school, initial fund-raising consisted of a square dance and auction, which netted enough to get a program started. The program was then maintained by tuition and further fund-raising.

### Church-Related Schools

Some parents of young children in your church or synagogue might be interested in beginning a preschool program. Again, fund-raising may be the way to begin, but it helps if the church or synagogue can provide the space and possibly some seed money.

### Private Industry

Affiliating a child care center with a private industry that employs mothers of young children is sometimes an excellent way to get started. As we will note later, a factory or business may have space to donate or might be willing to provide the funds to get a center started if the company is convinced that the program will reduce employee absenteeism and improve morale and the company's image. Hospitals sometimes offer funds or space (which is usually harder to come by) to provide a day care center for their nursing, medical, and housekeeping staffs.

## COMMUNITY SUPPORT

A viable early childhood program requires not only initial sponsorship but also the widest possible community support. This support often arises naturally as the program gets under way and provides a meaningful service—for which the recipients often are ready to fight if necessary. However, to ensure continuing success, it is extremely helpful to establish a board made up of community members who have political power, expertise, or fund-raising capacities.

In one community, the ad hoc board included a lawyer, who drew up bylaws, incorporation papers, and a nonprofit statement; community residents who were familiar with federal regulations regarding day care; a pediatrician and a psychiatrist, who helped set up health policies; and a PTA president and an engineer, who were well versed in planning the physical site (Lorton 1972). It is also important for the board to have at least one early childhood professional.

Community support may also be generated through requests for donations. Apart from the usefulness of donated materials and services, community involvement and support are types of participation that may have far-reaching implications for the long-range viability of a program. A useful way to begin is by preparing a list of requirements, including space, equipment, materials, and volunteer services. Churches may be contacted about space, and they may also be willing to offer other kinds of help through their congregations. Civic organizations, such as Kiwanis, chambers of commerce, and Lions, may be contacted for funds and other kinds of donations. Also, many businesses periodically replace office equipment and other furnishings, and they may donate such items for use in an early childhood center. Local merchants, banks, and realtors are often sources for equipment and materials; for example, a file for computer cards may be turned into storage space for curriculum materials.

## LICENSING REQUIREMENTS

In a recent article, Raymond Collins (1983) compares day care licensing requirements throughout the United States. The federal government's regulations were contained in the Federal Interagency Day Care Requirements. These were replaced in 1980 by new regulations, which have not been enforced because of their potential cost to centers and to the government sponsors. Consequently, state and local requirements tend to have the most impact on center operations, and the regulations vary from state to state.

Sadly, Collins points out, the state education requirements often fall short in the areas found to be most critical for successful early childhood programs. For example, according to the National Day Care Study (1979), group size is a very important variable. As measured by the Preschool Inventory (PSI) and the revised Peabody Picture Vocabulary Test (PPVT) the following picture emerges in regard to group size:

> Children's gains on the PSI in groups of 12 children reflect a 19 percent advantage over PSI scores for children in groups of 24. Gains on the PPVT were 23 percent higher in groups of 12 children compared with classrooms containing 24 children. (Collins 1983)

Despite these research findings, however, thirty-three states had no requirements for group size for 4-year-olds in 1981. Among the remaining twenty-one states and the District of Columbia, the most frequently specified group size was twenty, with Texas regulating a group size of forty-five. Most states do regulate child-staff ratios, but only four specify a ratio more favorable than ten to one.

The National Day Care Study (1979) also found that teachers' credentials are highly related to the children's performance on the research tasks, yet most states did not require a bachelor's degree for early childhood teachers in 1981; of the ten states that did, only three specified that the degree had to be in early childhood education or human development. The Child Development Associate (CDA) credential and assurance of preparation and performance were required by twenty-seven states, and many others were in the process of instituting this requirement.

## LOCATING THE CENTER

There are a great many factors to take into account when you are making a decision about where to locate an early childhood center. It is helpful to visit other centers to see where they are located and to note child care options available in the community. Your own choice of location depends on a combination of factors, including your program goals, availability of space, regulations, and local politics.

## Regulations

Besides the licensing requirements discussed in the preceding section, there are state and local building, fire, and health regulations with which an early childhood program and its site must comply. Federally funded programs are regulated by the Department of Health and Human Services. At the state level, most state departments of education provide guidelines and require registration. In addition, many state departments of social services serve as regulatory agencies for licensing, especially for Medicaid recipients. There are specific laws regarding day care licensing, since, for full-day programs, provisions need to be made for preparing and serving hot meals and for appropriate rest facilities. In some states, the departments of social services also regulate day care centers in the areas of health, safety, and quality of care. In addition to the state departments mentioned, many public school districts have requirements that focus on adult-child ratios, space per child, educational qualifications of staff, records, curricular goals, and the like.

One does not always have the opportunity to select an ideal setting in which to develop an early childhood center. Many times the building layout, location, and availability of bathrooms, sinks, and playground areas are less than optimal. However, there are some important considerations to keep in mind in selecting a site, particularly in less-than-optimal locations.

In New York, the State Board of Education requires that 35 square feet of space be provided for each child in a preschool classroom, exclusive of toilets, cloakrooms, and storage. This should be viewed as an absolute minimum. To allow for adequate freedom of movement, building spaces for blocks, separate spaces for painting and carpentry, a quiet corner, and so forth, 40 to 60 square feet per child is preferable.

Generally, a room measuring approximately 24 feet by 24 feet is regarded as appropriate for sixteen nursery-school-age children; for a class of twenty-five kindergarteners, a room measuring approximately 30 feet by 30 feet is suggested. Although room shape, like size, may not be controllable, rectangular rooms seem to be more versatile than those that are square or L-shaped (the latter makes supervision difficult). Creative planning, however, will make the most of any shaped room. As noted earlier, you may be required to operate in small rooms, such as those typically used for church Sunday schools. In such cases, you might want to use one of the rooms as a gym or arts and crafts room that can be shared by children from several classrooms.

The ground floor of a building is generally the best choice for classrooms for young children—for safety reasons, for easier access for children who have difficulty with stairs, and for greater accessibility to the outdoor area. It is especially desirable to have a door in the classroom that leads outside to facilitate indoor-outdoor activity.

A location near toilet facilities is recommended (generally one toilet and sink for every ten children). Having a sink in the classroom itself is a decided advantage; it comes in handy for drinking, washing, cleanup, painting, cooking, and generally providing water for play. If this is not possible, it is important to have a source of water near the classroom and a container of water within the room (a large coffee urn with a spigot works well) from which water may be drawn and which may be refilled periodically. Large windows that allow lots of natural light to enter the room and allow the children to look out are desirable. (Low windows are nice, but we have found that they present security problems in some areas.)

Having an outdoor play area at or near the school is essential. Consider how easily the children are going to be able to get to the area as well as how safe it is. For example, we had to cover the wells around our basement windows to prevent children from falling in. A fenced-in yard is important (preferably a fence that can be looked through but not climbed over) to keep children from wandering off and to keep them out of danger from traffic or from the edges of buildings (in the case of rooftop play areas).

## Some Possible Sites

### PUBLIC SCHOOL ROOMS

Early childhood classrooms are increasingly being located in public school buildings. In Freeport, New York, for example, an early childhood education center has been developed by a school district in a former elementary school. The director of this program has made constructive use of all of the rooms. The gymnasium is spacious by preschool standards and is filled with unique opportunities for climbing and exploring. Its interesting internal environment naturally encourages the child's involvement in a variety of movement activities. The building itself is inviting to parents in many ways. The foyer is decorated as a welcoming point, with current information available in English and Spanish, and there are rooms for parents to meet in small groups. Other community programs are also housed in the building, including homemaking training courses and workshops for teenager parents.

Sometimes, only a single room in a public school is allocated for an early childhood center. If it has been a kindergarten room, it is likely to be quite large and to include water and bathroom facilities.

Although more and more money is being made available for this purpose, school districts are not always able to underwrite early childhood programs. In Merrick, New York, the PTA sponsored the school's first prekindergarten program when space became available. The district provided the room, some materials, and consultation; the PTA paid for the teacher and other costs through fund-raising and tuition.

### CHURCH CLASSROOMS

Church classrooms are frequently used for early childhood programs. Sometimes, the space is donated or is available for a modest rental fee. It may already comply with fire and safety regulations. This kind of location may present a series of problems, however. The space often must be shared with a religious school, which requires that the materials and equipment be put away on weekends or even during the week. Sharing space also imposes restrictions on the materials that may be used and on modifications you may wish to make. Rooms that accommodate religious classes are often very small, with limited storage and playground areas. Although this is not true in every case, it is important to be aware of these potential drawbacks.

### PRIVATE HOUSES

Private houses may be converted to early childhood centers, and the homey atmosphere may be preferred to an institutional environment. Usually, there is a yard for a play area. The advantage here may also be economic, in that a group (e.g., a cooperative) or an individual may be able to purchase a house rather than renting space.

The possible disadvantages to such a site are small rooms, narrow hallways, and stairs. In some cases, the interior spaces may be modified. For example, walls can be taken down to enable arrangement of classrooms in a much more open and versatile way. This type of modification is costly, however, since it may require replacement of supporting beams. Another way of modifying a house is to plan a bilevel space with the help of an architect. In one school, an upper deck was designed for block building and dramatic play, and lower areas were arranged with tunnels for crawling through. Another problem with some older houses is that walls may have been painted with lead-based paint. It is important to check for this possibility and have the lead paint removed if necessary.

### STOREFRONTS
Storefronts have been used for early childhood programs, particularly in low-income areas. The advantages are easy accessibility, high visibility, and sometimes low rent or even donated space in areas where business is on the decline. The disadvantages are the lack of adequate toilet facilities and water and a high potential for security problems. In addition, outdoor play areas are not likely to be available in business areas. These disadvantages can be minimized by outings to parks and other local places, such as zoos and nature preserves.

### PREFABS
Prefabricated modular buildings are often good choices for early childhood centers, since they are relatively inexpensive, portable, expandable, and temporary (as the need may be), and they can be designed with open space inside. A prefab may be placed in an open field or near a park or schoolyard to provide outdoor play space. Being at ground level is another advantage of a prefab center.

### INDUSTRIAL SITES
A factory building or warehouse space can be used for an early childhood center. Such a center may be close to where parents work, allowing convenient visiting. Factory or warehouse space may be selected because it is relatively low in cost. Whatever the reason may be, we have seen some very interesting uses made of wide-open industrial spaces with high ceilings that have

been partitioned into large areas or converted into bilevel designs to allow for climbing, private work areas, and exciting play space. A good paint job and cleaning goes a long way toward making former industrial space into a pleasant day care center. Again, if hazards such as lead paint and asbestos are detected, they must be eliminated.

## EQUIPMENT, MATERIALS, AND SUPPLIES

The nature and goals of your program are the primary considerations in choosing materials, supplies, and equipment. What types of activities do you wish to encourage? What types of activities and materials are developmentally appropriate for the children with whom you plan to work? Budgeting considerations and the size of your center are also major factors. Given these requirements, there are a variety of sources for the items you will need for your center.

### Manufacturers and Distributors of School Supplies

Commercial suppliers of school materials and equipment are a major source for early childhood programs. Buying from such suppliers can save you time that you might spend hunting for separate items or making your own materials. This is especially convenient if you're buying for a large center. Buying from commercial manufacturers and distributors is sometimes the most expensive way to shop; on items that must last a long time, however, it becomes less expensive to buy well-made, more costly items because they don't have to be replaced as often. For example, commercial suppliers offer a wide selection of wooden toys that have well-sanded edges and are naturally finished. These toys usually need less maintenance to look good. In addition, some major suppliers (Childcraft, for example) will help you design your center and offer suggestion lists for equipping classrooms, which you can use as a basis for making your decisions. Large companies often have representatives in the field who will visit your center and help you decide what you need. You can also send for catalogs from a variety of national suppliers.

### Large Discount Stores

Some items can be purchased less expensively in local discount stores than from school supply companies. Some local discount or toy stores sell games (e.g., Lotto) and puzzles that may at least serve as a supplement to those purchased more expensively from commercial suppliers. Household items (e.g., sponges, straws, brooms, measuring cups, egg beaters, etc.) are also available at local discount and grocery stores and serve just as well as more expensive counterparts purchased from local suppliers. Whether you buy from commercial distributors or from discount stores, you must take care that what you buy will withstand considerable use and is developmentally appropriate. For example, a puzzle should not have too many pieces or be too difficult for a 3-year-old to manipulate. Also, outdoor equipment, such as swings and slides, that is made for home use is usually not constructed well enough to withstand the daily activity of a group of children. From the point of view of safety as well as wear, it is advisable to buy equipment made expressly for school use.

### Making Your Own Equipment and Materials

Very often you can imitate and improve upon items represented in commercial catalogs. You can also adapt them for the particular use of the children who attend your center. For example, you may wish to cut out flannelboard figures that coordinate with a discussion or story you want to share with your class. Although commercially available figures might have a more finished appearance than yours, yours will have a more special meaning for the children—and they will be much less expensive. Budget and time are important considerations in deciding whether to make something or purchase it. For example, sound cylinders can be made relatively easily from film canisters filled with such materials as beans that rattle around, but it would be more difficult, though possible, to make a puzzle. If you are administering a large center, you may wish to encourage teachers and parents to make materials for the classroom by having a workshop where the work can be done on a group basis (See Chapter 8 for a discussion of parent involvement.)

Outdoor equipment can be designed and made to specification by teachers and parents if they have the necessary time and talent. This is much less expensive than buying such equipment commercially. We built a very large wooden slide that could be used by several children at once. The top of the slide was built onto a deck, where the children could experience being up high. The area below the deck provided a house (with windows and a door) for make-believe play or for being alone. It worked wonderfully after we discovered that a wooden slide is likely to give splinters and that the sliding part should be covered with metal. Outdoor equipment that uses and conforms to the natural environment around your school, such as hills and trees, is very appealing, both practically and esthetically.

### Donated Materials

Although public requests for donations often result in many nonusable items, it has been our experience that some donated toys, games, and furniture can come in handy. Using donated items is often a good way to begin until you can afford to purchase newer and perhaps more appropriate equipment and materials. You may have to cut a table down to a height usable by young children, or you may want to paint classroom furniture and storage pieces to give them a brighter and complementary appearance. In order of priorities, however, such activities may be secondary to getting your program under way and spending your time and energy in preparing curriculum materials. Selma Greenberg (1978) points out that we should make a special effort to use reclaimed material and equipment to demonstrate to the children that one does not always need to have new things.

### A "Scrounge" List

There are many useful free materials available if you use your imagination and keep your eyes open. You might find a lumber company near your home or school that will save scraps of wood for you to use with a workbench so that the children can do simple carpentry projects. A cooperative lumberman might even put aside for you the best sizes in a soft wood, such as pine. You might find an electric cable company willing to donate some large, empty wooden spools, which make great outdoor tables and climbers. You might get sponge rubber or fabric scraps from a local upholsterer. Once you have begun your program, you can alert the staff and parents to look for certain items for the program.

If you are part of a larger program housed in a public school, company, or university, you can send out a request to other departments for materials that might be useful in an early childhood program. Computer paper, packing foam, art supplies, carpet scraps, and plastic containers are some materials that might be available from businesses. At one university preschool, the drama department donated an unused part of a spaceship set and some steps to be used in the outdoor playground.

Another school sent out a letter to parents at the start of a program, requesting materials (Figure 1.3). Such a list may be sent to parents periodically (modified as needed) to replenish supplies.

## Homemade Curriculum Materials

Many games and curriculum activities can be made from "found" materials. These activities may be constructed by the teachers, by other staff members, by parent volunteers, or by teachers and children working together. For example, lockboxes or latch boards can be constructed from scrap wood and a variety of purchased items, from hook-and-eye latches to door bolts. Also, old game boards can be covered with contact paper and prepared with different game formats that are appropriate for young children. *Workjobs* (Lorton 1972) and *Primerrily* (McGinn and Rudnick 1978) are useful sourcebooks for ideas.

## Government Resources

The federal government is a good source of publications on nutrition, health, safety, and development. Many of these publications are offered in quantity at nominal cost and may be dis-

**FIGURE 1.3** Materials Request Letter

Dear Parents:

The following is a list of materials that you would ordinarily discard. Please save them for our use at the child care center.

| | |
|---|---|
| styrofoam | egg cartons |
| foam rubber | shells |
| clothes pins | rocks |
| cake box string | shoe boxes |
| feathers | |

We use these materials for crafts, sorting and classifying projects, and woodwork—to name but a few.

We are also collecting materials to outfit some prop boxes for dramatic play. Please save for us any leftover items that would be suitable props for the following:

| | |
|---|---|
| florist | auto mechanic |
| electrician | forest ranger |
| camper | beautician |
| plumber | |

These items could be plastic flowers, vases, old spark plugs, switches, worn-out windshield wipers, old fuses, canteens, flashlights, curlers, hairnets, hair rollers, or paint rollers.

Other handy items we are seeking are lunch boxes (not new ones necessarily) to house our prop supplies, old clocks without their glass, and

| | |
|---|---|
| bells | cookie cutter |
| old steering wheel | buzzers |
| magnets | prisms |
| hoses | |

Thanks for your help!

tributed to parents. You can also get instructions for planting, scientific experiments, and animal care that you may be able to use directly with the children. Local governments may also offer materials and services. For example, Nassau County, New York, has a mobile puppet show. Many areas have mobile libraries. Others offer agricultural demonstrations. You may also get representatives of uniformed services, such as firefighters and police officers, to come in for discussions.

### Telephone Companies

The telephone companies in many areas will provide you with actual telephones and mini-communication systems for at least some portion of the school year. This service is designed to acquaint the children with the use of the telephone. It also offers a wonderful opportunity for promoting and developing language skills. The telephone companies may also provide you with books for children that describe the telephone and how to use it.

### Local Professional Societies

Local professional societies, such as dental and optometric associations, may be able to send representatives to talk to the children about dental care or eye care. If you are going to use such experts, we suggest that you have a briefing with them in advance—much as you might when a parent is going to speak to your class.

Keep in mind that, although many resources may be available to your center for programs and for materials, the first priority should be not their availability but their appropriateness for the children's development and the goals of your program. This does not mean that spontaneous happenings or availability of materials may not be integrated into your program successfully. For example, one of us (Grossman 1970) used material from a nearby construction project for classroom activities. If you keep your mind open to the possibilities, you may well discover some events taking place near your school that would be of interest to the children and would fit with your curriculum plans.

### Suggested Activities

1. Analyze the needs assessments described in this chapter and prepare a needs assessment instrument. Add questions that may be pertinent for your community.
2. Conduct a needs assessment for an early childhood center in your neighborhood, in your classroom, or in a particu-

lar area where you think there may be a need for a program.

3. If you were to begin a center, what children would you intend to serve in terms of age, special needs, socioeconomic status, and so forth? Why?

4. Prepare a list of free materials that would be useful in your center. If you are running a center, delegate a staff person or parent volunteers to locate sources for free materials; then write letters requesting donations of these materials.

### References and Further Readings

Abramson, Paul. *Schools for Early Education.* New York: Educational Facilities Laboratory, 1979.

Auerbach, Stevanne, ed. *Model Programs and Their Components*, Vol. II of *Childcare: A Comprehensive Guide.* New York: Human Sciences Press, 1976.

Auerbach, Stevanne, ed. *Creative Centers and Homes*, Vol. III of *Childcare: A Comprehensive Guide.* New York: Human Sciences Press, 1978.

Bureau of Child Development and Parent Education. *Children's Spaces.* Albany: New York State Educational Department, 1970.

Collins, Raymond C. "Child Care and the States: The Comparative Licensing Study." *Young Children* 38(5), July 1983, 3–11.

Glick, Phyllis. *Administration of Schools for Young Children.* Albany: Delmar, 1975.

Goldmier, Harold. *Needs Assessment Instructional Kit.* Boston: Massachusetts Committee for Children and Youth, 1976.

Greenberg, Selma. *Right from the Start: A Guide to Non-Sexist Child Rearing.* Boston: Houghton Mifflin, 1978.

Grossman, Bruce. "Building for Experience." In *Curriculum Is What Happens.* Washington, D.C.: National Association for the Education of Young Children, 1970.

Lorton, Mary Jane. *Workjobs.* Menlo Park, Calif.: Addison-Wesley, 1972.

McGinn, Joyce, and Rudnick, Fredda. *Primerrily: A Collection of Multisensory Materials and Games for Young Children.* Hewlett, N.Y.: Hewlett-Woodmere School District, 1978.

National Day Care Study, Final Report. *Children at the Center: Executive Summary.* Cambridge, Mass.: Abt Associates, 1979.

Skutch, Margaret, and Hamlin, Wilfred G. *To Start a School.* Boston: Little, Brown, 1971.

Superintendent of Documents, U.S. Government Printing Office, Washington, D.C. 20402. Send for list of government publications.

Taylor, Katherine Whiteside. *Parents and Children Learn Together.* New York: Teachers College Press, 1967.

U.S. Department of Health, Education and Welfare. *Project Head Start Series.* Washington, D.C.: U.S. Government Printing Office, 1973.

U.S. Department of Health, Education and Welfare, Office of Child Development, Bureau of Child Development Services. *Guides for Day Care Licensing.* Washington, D.C.: U.S. Government Printing Office, 1974.

Zanoff, Richard. *Guide to the Assessment of Day Care Service Needs at the Community Level.* Washington, D.C.: Urban Institute, July 1971.

# Chapter 2
# Setting Up
# a Classroom

## GENERAL PRINCIPLES

A well-designed classroom environment is safe, healthy, organized, aesthetic, and stimulating, and it provides opportunities for children to make sense of their experiences. It sets the stage for learning and gives a sense of security as well as a place to play, to enjoy, to discover, and to learn.

Both the design of the classroom and the materials available for the children are important curricular as well as practical decisions to be made by a director and her staff. They are curricular decisions in that the way in which the classroom is arranged has a great deal to do with the movement of the children and the accessibility of the materials. An incorrect design—one that looks pleasing but doesn't work—can be a source of frustration for the children and thus can impede the learning process. In the same sense, the classroom design and the materials should be stimulating and, perhaps, even more important, inviting to the children. The appropriate choice of materials is as significant as any educational decision the director and teachers are apt to make.

An early childhood center is furnished with child-sized equipment and is organized into interest areas that are equipped with a wide variety of instructional materials and supplies appropriate for the developmental level of the children. These interest areas should be arranged for a balance between activities that are quiet and noisy, active and sedentary, and wet and dry—all appropriately situated to allow learning activities to proceed in each area without disturbing the others. The room arrangement must take into account traffic patterns of activities that will be mutually exclusive (e.g., woodworking and reading).

Traditionally, early childhood interest areas include spaces for block building, art, and manipulatives or table toys, a family center or housekeeping area, an area for dramatic play, a language arts or library corner, a science and pets area, and places for woodworking and sand and water play. These centers may be changed, eliminated, or added as time and interest motivate.

The noisiest areas are likely to be the block construction center, the woodworking area, and the family center. Playing with manipulatives or table toys is a sedentary activity, whereas an open space is needed for active rhythmic and dramatic activities. The noisy and active areas should be separated from the language arts center, which is considered a quiet area. The expressive centers of art and sand/water play may be distinguished as those that consist of wet activities, such as easel painting and water play, and those that offer dry activities, such as drawing, cutting, and the like.

Interest areas should be clearly defined and readily identifiable by the children through their arrangement, materials, and appropriate pictures. Learning materials should be stored and arranged in an orderly manner, with pictures or symbols to identify them, and they should be within the children's reach so that the children can use them independently. It is important to keep in mind that the child's physical learning environment is an integral part of the program and, to a large extent, influences the learning that occurs. We have observed many situations in which changes in the placement of interest areas and the availability of materials have had a very positive effect on the emotional climate as well as on the activity in a center.

## INTEREST AREAS

### Block Area

Block building provides a variety of opportunities for the child to problem-solve, create and integrate concepts and skills. It becomes a representation of a child's world in three dimensions, helping him to develop perceptual skills, spatial concepts, motor coordination, dexterity and a sense of balance.

## LOCATION

The center for block building should be the largest space, out of the way of traffic to protect the "buildings" and deter conflict. If located adjacent to the family center, it facilitates enriched play that often extends into both areas. Since block play is defined as a noisy, active area, it should be situated away from a quieter area such as the language arts center.

## FLOORING

A flat carpet in the area will help cut down on extraneous noise.

## MATERIALS

| *Basic Materials* | *Modifications and Comments* |
|---|---|
| One nursery set of hardwood unit blocks | Empty milk cartons |
| One hardwood storage unit | Shelves or boards placed on cinder blocks (whether commercial or homemade, shelves should be labeled for the easy recognition, organization, and clean-up by the children) |
| Block accessories, such as miniature cars, trucks, trains, planes, boats, gas pumps, traffic signs, rubber or wooden people and animals | |

*For outdoor or gym play:*

One set of large wooden blocks — Wooden crates can be substituted
One storage cart to facilitate moving blocks
Walking boards of varying widths
Sawhorses for climbing and support.

## Family Center (Dramatic Play Area)

Dramatic play stimulates fantasy and creativity. Children can practice a variety of adult roles and, at the same time, develop social and interpersonal skills. A family or housekeeping center also affords opportunities to expand expressive language and facilitate speech production. It should be set up in a variety of ways to reflect different family styles. This area may be changed and modified as the interests and motivations of the children change. Alternative settings might be a supermarket, hospital, post office, fix-it shop, or beauty shop, in addition to diverse home arrangements (e.g., apartment or a trailer).

## LOCATION

Although the family center is an active and noisy area of the preschool classroom, it should be situated away from the main traffic flow. The area should be defined by the use of room dividers and the furniture to create a homelike, private atmosphere.

## FLOORING

A few scatter rugs can add warmth to the family center.

## MATERIALS

| *Basic Materials* | *Modifications and Comments* |
|---|---|
| Housekeeping furniture, including a refrigerator, stove, sink, cupboard, child-sized table and chairs, bed, and so forth, and a storage unit for props; props should include dolls, doll clothes, a doll carriage, miniature dishes, plastic food, pots and pans, empty food boxes and cans, mops and brooms, a cash register, play or real telephones, dress-up clothing for male and female roles in the family and community, stethoscope, suitcases, and the like | Some furniture can be made from large cardboard appliance cartons

Dolls should include both sexes and all races

All dress-up clothing should be altered for young children; it should include shoes, hats, jackets, and so forth |

## Creative Arts Area

The creative arts center enables exploration and construction with a variety of materials and media that meet diverse social and educational goals. For example, painting provides an opportunity for creativity, expressing individuality, and developing motor coordination and spatial concepts.

## LOCATION

The art center should be near water and light, preferably natural.

## FLOORING

Linoleum or washable floors are easier to maintain. Some centers cover a portion of the floor with transparent, heavy plastic, especially under easels.

## MATERIALS

| *Basic Materials* | *Modifications and Comments* |
|---|---|
| Commercial double or triple easels | Single easels may be built into walls or constructed from plasterboard and moved to tables (as an A-frame); newspapers placed under easels provide protection for the floor; coverings on easels prolong their life |
| Assorted brushes (3/4″ and 1/2″ brushes with 6″ to 8″ handles) | |
| Liquid tempera paint | For easel or table use, paint can be poured into juice cans or baby food or jelly jars |
| Fingerpaint and fingerpainting paper | Shelf paper may be substituted |
| Newsprint (18″ X 24″) | Local newspapers may provide free newsprint in rolls |
| Manila paper (12″ X 18″) | Paper should be stored near tables and easels for children to use independently |
| Construction paper in assorted colors | |
| Collage collection: scraps of colored paper, wallpaper, aluminum foil, ribbon, yarn, styrofoam packing, straws, and the like | Should be stored neatly adjacent to tables |
| Drying rack for art work | A standard laundry or lingerie rack is a perfect substitute; a clothesline suspended across the room also suffices |
| Smocks or protective aprons | Should be hung near easels, can be cut from old shirts or rolls of vinyl or oilcloth. |

| Basic Materials | Modifications and Comments |
|---|---|
| Sponges and pails | |
| Scissors, both blunt and pointed, right- and left-handed for small hands; one or two pairs of training scissors | |
| School paste | Useful for paper pasting; essential for |
| Elmer's glue | three-dimensional collages and leather/wood gluing |
| Clay | Must be stored in an airtight |
| Clayboards | container |
| Play dough | Homemade |
| Jumbo nonroll crayons | Organized on shelf according to color |
| Chalk | |

## Language Arts Area

Looking at books and listening to stories are pleasurable pastimes. Activities in this area also develop readiness skills and attitudes, such as concentration, sequencing, recall, and vocabulary. In addition, they enhance creativity and fantasy.

### LOCATION

Arrange the books in a quiet area of the room. The area should allow comfortable seating on the floor and/or on furniture and space for storage of the language materials, such as audiovisual equipment and a flannelboard.

### MATERIALS

| Basic Materials | Modifications and Comments |
|---|---|
| At least 24 to 30 books should be available at all times | Teacher-made and child-dictated books are appropriate, in addition to commercially published picture books, a children's dictionary, poetry, and so on. |
| Display unit | Units can be handmade |
| Storage unit | |
| Lotto games, materials for matching/ copying letters, flannelboard for for telling stories | Optional language materials may include a primary typewriter, a record player, and a tape recorder |

## Music and Listening Area

Music is vital in the early childhood classroom. Musical activities should include singing, playing records, using instruments, body movement, and dancing. Through these activities, the child has an opportunity for self-expression and also can develop aesthetic appreciation, gross motor skills, body coordination, auditory perception, and positive social skills.

### LOCATION

Because many music activities involve body movement, a large, open space is required. Musical instruments should also be displayed attractively within the children's reach.

### FLOORING

Standard linoleum is best suited for this area.

### MATERIALS

| *Basic Materials* | *Modifications and Comments* |
|---|---|
| One set of nursery rhythm instruments, including triangles, bells, sand blocks, tambourines, drums, cymbals, rhythm sticks | Instruments can also be constructed from everyday objects, such as coffee cans (drums), film canisters with dried beans inside (shakers), and smooth sticks (for hitting together) |
| A sturdy record player; earphones are optional | |
| Records | The assortment of records should reflect various kinds of music, including the children's cultures |
| Storage unit | |
| Optional instruments, depending on the teachers' skills: piano, autoharp, guitar | |
| Scarves, hoops, streamers | Useful for dancing, rhythms, and creative expression |

## Manipulative Materials Interest Area

Manipulative materials, or table toys, develop eye–hand coordination, fine motor skills, figure–ground perception, and increased attention span. They are also an important base for many cognitive tasks, such as classification, patterning, number concepts, and the like. The math area is generally a part of the manipulative materials center. Most significantly, manipulative materials afford young children a feeling of success and enjoyment as they repeat successful tasks. In the beginning of the year, a few of the most simple and concrete materials should be set out for use. As the children gain mastery, the materials should be changed and more difficult tasks should be introduced.

### LOCATION
Tables, chairs, and shelving are crucial for this area. Since it is a relatively quiet area, it can be situated adjacent to the language area.

### FLOORING
Standard linoleum is best suited to this area.

### MATERIALS

| *Basic Materials* | *Modifications and Comments* |
|---|---|
| Storage unit | Can be constructed of wood or plasterboard |
| Individual storage units for each game | Boxes, shoeboxes, and coffee cans can be substituted for commercial storage units |
| Puzzle rack | |
| Puzzles, pegs and peg boards, Lego blocks, beads and string, small colored cubes, Tinkertoys, and the like; math materials, such as Cuisenaire rods, number sorters, and so forth | Collections of identical objects can also be used for counting experiences: chips, stones, shells, spools, and the like |

## Science and Pet Area

The science area must not be static but must grow and change as the curriculum develops. The biological and physical sciences should be represented. Water/sand play, woodworking, and cooking activities might also be considered part of the science area.

### LOCATION

It is desirable to have the science area adjacent to water and light sources. It should be away from the traffic pattern (e.g., not near doors).

### FLOORING

Standard linoleum is most suitable for this area. It is also a good idea to place plastic or absorbent paper under the water/ sand table.

### MATERIALS

| *Basic Materials* | *Modifications and Comments* |
|---|---|
| Environmental objects, such as leaves, shells, rocks, and so forth | |
| Plants | |
| Aquarium | |
| Animals and cages | Hamsters, mice, gerbils, and guinea pigs make good classroom pets |
| Terrarium | Can also house lizards, newts, and the like |
| Lock boards | Can easily be constructed on a board with hardware items |
| Magnets, prisms, pulleys, scales, electrical equipment | |

## Water/Sand Play Area

Water and sand play provides sensory experiences and opportunities for cooperative play and refinement of fine motor skills. It also contributes to the development of science concepts involving properties of materials (e.g., weight, fullness, emptiness).

### LOCATION

Sand and water play is essential to an early childhood classroom, but it must be situated in a space that is convenient for clean-up. Sand and water play can also be an outdoor activity. Laundry tubs or basins can be used on the playground to contain the materials. Large buckets, shovels, spoons, and assorted trucks should be available outdoors on a regular basis.

**FLOORING**
Be sure to have protective covering in this area.

**MATERIALS**

| *Basic Materials* | *Modifications and Comments* |
|---|---|
| Water or sand table | Contents of table can be changed regularly, from water to sand and vice versa; plastic tubs or trays can be used to hold these materials when an actual water tub is unavailable |
| Storage containers for sand | Large, plastic-lined ice cream or clay containers can be used |
| Accessories, such as plastic bottles of various sizes, funnels, eye droppers, basters, clear tubing, scoops, cups, shovels, spoons | Many of these items can be brought from home or can be made from recycled everyday objects |

## Woodworking Area

Woodworking is a high-interest area for all children, both girls and boys. It provides practice for gross and fine motor skills, spatial perception and balance, measurement, creativity, and, most important, a sense of accomplishment.

**LOCATION**
Since a woodworking table is portable, it may be moved to an out-of-the-way corner when this activity is ended for the day. When in use, it must be easily and closely supervised. It should be located away from traffic patterns and quiet areas.

**FLOORING**
Standard linoleum is suitable for this area.

**MATERIALS**

| *Basic Materials* | *Modifications and Comments* |
|---|---|
| Workbench or woodworking table | Can be homemade from a cut-down wooden table |
| Hammers | Medium weight (11–13 oz.), with balls, not prongs, opposite hammer end |

| | |
|---|---|
| Wire or box nails | Should have good-sized heads (3/4″ to 1-1/2″) |
| Saws | Crosscut (10-point saw, of 12″ to 16″ long) |
| Wood | Should be soft wood; generally available in scrap boxes at lumber yards |
| Vise or C clamps | |

## Cooking Activities Area

Cooking provides opportunities for sensory experiences and for the acquisition of important concepts in science and nutrition. Cooking activities are compatible with the family center and other classroom spaces. Some schools have kitchen facilities available on a temporary basis for cooking.

### LOCATION
Like woodworking, cooking can be a portable activity; that is, it can be moved to an accessible location.

### FLOORING
Standard vinyl tile is suitable for this area (and easy to mop).

### MATERIALS

| *Basic Materials* | *Modifications and Comments* |
|---|---|
| Hot plate | This equipment is necessary if there |
| Electric frypan | is no access to a kitchen |
| Portable oven | |
| Tools, such as peelers, spatulas, bowls, wooden spoons, measuring cups and spoons, strainer | |
| Clean-up materials: sponges, paper towels, and so forth | |

## ARRANGING THE ROOM

Before arranging the interest areas, there are some questions to ask yourself: What behaviors are you trying to encourage? What goals (long-range and short-range) do you have?

A useful way to plan a room arrangement is to draw a room design as if you were furnishing a house. Draw a scale outline of the room. Then draw the pieces that you expect to use, cut them out, and move them around your room outline. Consider variations in design to see possible alternatives.

In addition to arranging your room on paper, it is useful to visit other early childhood centers to see how their rooms look, both when children are there and when they are not. Consider how these centers arrange their equipment, furniture, and supplies and how the flow of activities works.

The following are some specific principles to consider as you arrange the room:

1.  Safety is important. While providing a challenging experience, you should minimize the potential for accidents. Analyze the arrangement of the room and be sure it incorporates certain safety features, including adequate free space for movement and a layout that allows a teacher to supervise all areas of the room, including entrances and exits.

2.  Labeling the toys at child's-eye level helps the children see what is available as well as where it belongs.

3.  Toys should be arranged in an orderly manner to develop the children's independence and their ability to control their environment as well as to translate the message of organization and structure.

4.  Materials arranged in a thoughtful way serve as an invitation to the child to participate or explore. For example, a magnifying glass can be placed on a table next to some interesting shells or near an open book with some interesting pictures.

5.  A special corner for a child's privacy is as important as open areas for group activity.

6.  The physical arrangement of the classroom should be reassessed regularly and altered when necessary to assure a live, productive environment wherein children and teachers can grow.

Keep in mind that a classroom grows and changes. In the beginning of the year, it is helpful to have only a few interest areas, arranged with a minimum amount of materials. As the children become more familiar with classroom management and limits, more and different materials may be brought out.

The materials and equipment should be arranged in a way that is easily understood by the children as well as by adults. This facilitates the children's positive interaction and their productive use of what is available and eliminates the need for extensive instructions. The child's sense of organization develops as adults consistently model productive uses of materials, demonstrating and verbalizing the rules for taking them out and putting them away.

You can control the number of children participating in an area by limiting the amount of materials available or by having the furniture arrangement define the number of children that can work in an area.

Some additional areas to consider if space is available are an observation area, a parent room, a staff lounge, and an indoor gym.

Some schools have a nurse and a special first-aid center. If your early childhood center is just one room, however, it's important that you have a first-aid kit as well as a place to isolate a sick child.

## BASIC EQUIPMENT AND SUPPLIES

Equipment needs vary according to the size of the room, the number of children, the type of program, and the goals of the program. It is best not to clutter a room, of course, since children need space in which to move around.

Ask yourself the following questions when you are selecting materials and/or equipment for the classroom:

*Construction*
- Will it last with constant use?
- Is little maintenance necessary?
- Is it nonflammable?
- Is the paint nontoxic (no lead)?
- Are edges rounded, rather than pointed or sharp?
- Is it easily cleaned?

*Use*
- Is it developmentally appropriate for the children in your program?
- For which ages is it most suitable?

- Does it develop eye–hand coordination and manual skills?
- Does it stimulate problem-solving ability, creativity, and curiosity?
- Does it promote language and social relationships?
- Can it be shared?

### Suggested Basic Hardware

The permanent equipment and furniture in an early childhood classroom is considered "hardware" in your budget. Generally, these items, constructed of wood, sturdy plastic, or metal, constitute your largest single unit expense. It is important to have hardware that is versatile, easy to clean, child-sized, and portable.

#### CHAIRS
There is generally one chair for each child, particularly in programs that serve meals. Plastic chairs are less expensive and lighter than wood; they are also easier to clean and can be stacked where space is a problem.

Larger chairs, for the adults in the classroom, can be rocking chairs, benches, couches, pillows, stools, or folding chairs.

#### TABLES
It is recommended that tables be 15 to 22 inches high and large enough to serve four to six children. The preferred table shapes are rectangular and round. If necessary, small tables can be combined to make a larger table area. If your budget is limited, you can make do with cut-down kitchen tables.

#### STORAGE UNITS
Commercial cabinets or homemade shelves should be accessible to children.

#### CUBBIES
Commercial units are desirable, but hooks or boxes for individual children can be substituted.

#### INDOOR EQUIPMENT
#### FOR LARGE-MOTOR DEVELOPMENT
If you are not fortunate enough to live in an area where children can get outdoor exercise almost every day, it is useful to

have some equipment to allow children to work with their large muscles and to develop balance. Again, space and budget concerns may limit what you can provide in this area. We have found that rocking boats (which can be purchased commercially), an indoor climber, sawhorses, balance boards, tumbling mats (or old mattresses), and a cloth tunnel are all useful as incentives for indoor large-motor play. You may also have enough space to use some riding toys indoors. Usually this equipment is limited to use at particular times of the day, but you may wish to include some of it in free-play time.

### OUTDOOR PLAY AREA

You do not need to create a typical playground outside of your center. Usually, swings, slides, and climbing apparatus are very expensive and do not inspire very creative outdoor play. Instead, the children and you can have many interesting adventures on outside walks, for example, which provide opportunities for running, climbing, and even rolling down hills. For the yard, you can bring some of the inside large-motor equipment outdoors; it can then be brought inside again, especially if you are concerned about vandalism. You may get an old boat or even an old car to play in, tires, a large sandbox made from railroad ties (which will accommodate many children), large wire spools, such as those used by the telephone company, and other "found" objects, which can turn your center's yard into a special place to play. You may add some riding vehicles (bikes, wagons, scooters) and some plants and wooden boxes, which may be used by the children in a number of ways. If there is a school of landscape architecture in your area, you might be able to get one of the students to help you design an outdoor play area. If some of the children attending your center have creative parents, this is a good area for them to contribute their talent. You are likely to get something very special if you consult with them about what you want to accomplish with your outdoor space.

### SUMMARY

Although the cost of the basic hardware may be high, these purchases are made only once. Authorities suggest that the initial purchases be only those items that absolutely cannot be handmade or donated. Figure 2.1 suggests the hardware appropriate for equipping a sample class of sixteen children. Adequate (minimum)

**FIGURE 2.1** Suggested Basic Equipment for an Early Childhood Center

| | Adequate (Minimum) | Optimum | Alternatives (Limited Budget) |
|---|---|---|---|
| Tables | (3) 24" X 48" or 30" X 48" tables, with adjustable legs and plastic tops | Same, plus (2) round and (2) of another shape | Several cut-down kitchen tables |
| Chairs | (16) plastic stacking chairs | Same, plus extra for family center and (3) larger for adults | |
| Cubbies | (2) five-section cubbie units, with two hooks per space. | (3) of same | Nail hooks in wall, with bench underneath, or boxes |
| Library units | (1) library unit | (2) of same | Bookshelf of plasterboard or bricks and boards |
| Toy shelves | (3) storage shelves | (4) of same | Boards and cinder blocks |
| | (2) block shelves | (3) of same | |
| Wheel toys | (2) institutional tricycles | (3) of same, plus (2) of other wheel toys | Donated tricycles |
| Balls | (3) wonder balls | (1) 10" ball and (1) 7" ball plus assorted sizes | |
| Indoor toys | Rocking boat | Rocking and rowing boat | |
| | Wooden sawhorses | Aluminum sawhorses | |
| | Wooden board with cleats | Cleated boards, plus various ladders, punching bag, hollow blocks | Walk boards |
| | Bean bags | Same | |
| | Hardwood blocks | Same, plus animal sets (farm and zoo), jump rope, block, family and community worker figures | |
| | Traffic signs | Same | Homemade traffic signs |
| | Steering wheel | Same | Donated steering wheel |

40

| Category | Items | Additional | Alternative |
|---|---|---|---|
| Woodworking equipment | Commercial workbench | Same | Cut-down table |
| | (2) ball hammers | (3) of same | |
| | (1) child-sized saw | (2) of same | |
| | C clamp | | |
| | Sandpaper | | |
| Sand/water play equipment | (1) commercial sand or water table | (1) of each | Plastic laundry tub |
| Manipulatives | Lego blocks | Same, plus Tinkertoys, Megabric, Pipe put-together | |
| | Beads and string | | |
| | Sorting box | | |
| | Pounding bench | | |
| | Parquetry | | |
| | Bristle blocks | | |
| | Colored cub | | |
| | Lotto games | Same | Homemade games from magazine cut-outs |
| | Staking rings | Same | |
| | Pegs and pegboard | | |
| | Hammer-and-nail sets | | |
| | Puzzles with a range from simple to more difficult | Same plus Seequees | Homemade puzzles from magazine cut-outs |
| | (a) puzzle rack | (2) of same | |
| Math materials | Large dominoes | Same, plus Cusenaire rods, scale geo-shape board, number match-ups, Unifix cubes and frames | A variety of teacher-made games |
| | Number learner | | |
| | Counting games | | |
| Science materials | Easy-view magnifier | Same, plus metric materials | Many science concepts can be reinforced through raw materials, such as rocks, shells, etc. |
| | Prism, magnets, iron filings | | |
| | Stethoscope | | |
| | Animal cages | | |
| | Aquarium and accessories | | |

**FIGURE 2.1** (continued)

| | Adequate (Minimum) | Optimum | Alternatives (Limited Budget) |
|---|---|---|---|
| Art materials | (1) double easel | (1) triple easel | Tri-wall easel |
| | (10) 1-1/2" brushes | Same, plus (6) 3/4" brushes | |
| | (4) easel clips | (6) of same | |
| | (6) plastic smocks | (10) of same | Cut-down old shirts |
| | (4) clay boards | (6) of same | Old puzzle frames |
| | | | Lingerie rack or clothesline |
| Music materials | (1) commercial rhythm band set | Same, plus cymbals, maracas, 8-tone bell, autoharp, piano, or guitar | |
| | (1) phonograph and assorted records | Same, plus cassette tape recorder and tapes | |
| Language materials (Library) | (24) assorted picture books | (36) of same, plus dictionary, poetry, etc. | Library books |
| | (1) flannelboard and cut-outs | Same, plus magnetic alphabet board, cassette tape recorder, earphones, camera | |
| | (1) set of animal puppets and puppet stage | Same, plus (2) sets of family puppets, black and white | Puppets can be made from various materials |

42

| Family center | (1) refrigerator | Same, plus bureau for clothes, |
| materials | (1) stove | clothes rack, ironing board and |
| (dramatic play) | (1) sink | iron, doll carriage, and high chair |
| | (1) small table | |
| | (1) chair | |
| | (1) doll bed | |
| | (1) full mirror | Same, plus three-way mirror, |
| | (1) aluminum lunch set | cash register, plastic fruit and |
| | (1) aluminum cooking set | vegetables |
| | (1) set flatware | |
| | Assorted dolls of various races | |
| | and both sexes | |

equipment and optimum equipment are listed, and—for those with limited budgets—alternative suggestions are given for some items.

### Supplies

The following is a list of suggested expendable supplies to outfit one early childhood classroom initially (the quantity depends on the size of the class):

Clay
Tempera paint (gallon jugs)
Fingerpaint
Paste
Marking pens (assorted colors)
Elmer's glue
Newsprint (18″ × 24″)
Manila paper (12″ × 18″)
White paper (12″ × 18″)
Fingerpaint paper
Construction paper (12″ × 18″, assorted colors)
Oak tag (12″ × 18″ or 18″ × 24″)
Tissue paper (assorted colors)
Crayons
Payons
Kindergarten pencils
Ice cream sticks
Beads
Lanyard cord
Masking tape
Paper clips
Rubber bands
Fasteners
Thumb tacks
Staples
Macaroni—for stringing
Doilies
String
Paper cups
Paper towels
Napkins
Tissues
Detergents—for cleaning and for making bubbles
Buckets
Brooms

Orange juice squeezers
Assorted funnels—for water and sand play
Measuring cups—for water and sand play and cooking
Flour and salt—for making play dough
Food coloring—for coloring play dough and for other projects
Pitchers—for pouring juice
Sponges
Strainers—for sand play
Bowls—for mixing during cooking, for water play, and for
    making play dough
Cotton
Lunch bags—for creating puppets and for other projects
Small plastic bags
Wax paper
Aluminum foil

## TIMETABLE OF ACTIVITIES

As we've noted in these first two chapters, developing an early childhood program involves many activities. In the following list, we have arranged these activities in an order that reflects one possible time sequence. The sequence may vary, of course, and the specific activities depend on who initiates the plan.

1. Survey the need
2. Form a committee for
    a. Organizing
    b. Fact-finding
    c. Fund-raising
    d. Establishing initial direction
3. Formally create a board for
    a. Formulating policy and description
    b. Selecting a site
    c. Creating a budget
    d. Initiating publicity
    e. Hiring a director
    f. Recruiting staff
    g. Seeking donations
    h. Ordering equipment
    i. Ordering supplies
4. Hire staff (mutual responsibility of director and board)
5. Enroll the children
6. Set up the room(s)
7. Hold an orientation session for parents and children
8. Begin the program

## Suggested Activities

1. Plan room designs for a one-room early childhood center and a two-room early childhood center, observing the guidelines for location of interest areas.
2. Create two teacher-made learning materials for your center.
3. Locate community sources for materials that you may be able to get as donations for your center. Use your imagination; see if you can identify materials whose original purpose was not for early childhood education use— preferably "recycled" materials.
4. Identify local community members for an early childhood center board of directors. Then prepare a presentation for the initial meeting of your board.

## References and Further Readings

Cohen, Monroe, ed. *Selecting Educational Equipment and Materials for School and Home.* Washington, D.C.: Association for Childhood Education International, 1976.

Dean, Joan. *Room to Learn.* New York: Citation Press, 1973.

Evans, E. Belle; Saia, George; and Evans, Elmer A. *Designing a Day Care Center.* Boston: Beacon Press, 1974.

Greenberg, Selma. *Right from the Start: A Guide to Non-Sexist Child Rearing.* Boston: Houghton Mifflin, 1978.

Lorton, Mary Jane. *Workjobs.* Menlo Park, Calif.: Addison-Wesley, 1972.

McGinn, Joyce, and Rudnick, Fredda. *Primerrily: A Collection of Multisensory Materials and Games for Young Children.* Hewlett, N.Y.: Hewlett-Woodmere School District, 1978.

Moffit, Mary. *Woodworking for Children.* New York: Early Childhood Educational Council, 1969.

Osmon, Fred. *Patterns for Designing Children's Centers.* New York: Educational Facilities Laboratory, 1975.

Parents Nursery School of Cambridge. *Kids Are Natural Cooks.* Cambridge, Mass.: Parents Nursery School, 1972.

Southwest Educational Development Laboratory. *How to Fill Your Toy Shelves Without Emptying Your Pocketbook.* Reston, Va.: Council for Exceptional Children, 1976.

# Chapter 3
# Public Relations

Public relations is an administrative activity that must be maintained on an ongoing basis. The first step in public relations is letting the community know that you exist, particularly when your center is just starting out. However, public relations goes beyond initial publicity for the facility. From our humanistic standpoint, we are concerned that the public knows what we are like—our philosophy and our services—so that parents can make the most appropriate choice for their children and for themselves. A public relations and marketing program for an early childhood center might include some direct advertising, but it basically involves techniques that cost little and yet get the word out. The intent is to provide a service to the community as it learns about your program. This chapter discusses some public relations and other marketing techniques.

## IDENTIFYING YOUR TARGET POPULATION

What families do you want to inform about your service? First, identify their characteristics:

> *Parent characteristics*—working parents, single parents, teenage parents, income level, home and job locations, hours of need, and transportation requirements.
> *Child characteristics*—infants, preschoolers, school-age children, children with special needs.

Then identify the needs of these families—whether they are seeking caretaking, developmental activities, socializing experiences, readiness activities, health services, or other specific services.

Finally, identify the agencies and other referral sources from which parents seek information about child care, including city health departments, welfare agencies, private social and family service organizations, libraries, churches, women's organizations, unions, licensing agencies, pediatricians, college early childhood departments, elementary schools, parenting classes, childbearing classes, United Way agencies, local chapters of the National Association for the Education of Young Children, and other child care associations.

It is important to inform these organizations about the kinds of parents and children you are able to serve. This can be done by sending them brochures about your center and by calling or visiting them and discussing your center. It is also useful to invite their representatives to visit your center so that they can see the kind of program you are providing.

## REACHING YOUR TARGET POPULATION

### Low-Cost Advertising

A good place to advertise your program is in your community's local newspaper. This advertising is usually relatively inexpensive and, in larger communities, allows you to target your message to an area close to your school.

### Public Service Announcements
### in Newspapers and on Radio

Newspapers and local radio stations often allow you to make free public service announcements. You can use this service to announce special events, such as an arts and crafts open house for preschoolers or a meeting of single parents, that are open to the public. This lets the public know that your center sponsors a variety of activities. You can also use public service announcements to let everyone know about the initiation of a new program at your center, such as a class for toddlers or a cooperative project with a local high school child development class. You may use such an opportunity to announce the schedule for your fall registration or to let the public know that there are some openings left in a particular age group.

### News Stories

Some of the aforementioned announcements are easily turned into news stories. In fact, any change that you are making may be newsworthy. For example, if you are planning to extend your program to infants or toddlers, you can send this story to the local paper. This not only tells the public about a specific news feature, but it also reminds them about your program in general.

### Feature Stories

Your staff, children, parents, or program may be of special interest to the public and thus worthy of a feature story on TV or in a magazine or newspaper. Feature stories may include pictures and may occupy more space than a news story or an announcement. It is useful to find out who on your local newspaper writes articles about children and education and invite that person to your center to get a first-hand view of what is taking place. The reporter may want to get some pictures of the children for a particular story or for future reference. If so, it is necessary to get releases from the parents, but the free publicity is invaluable.

As you review activities at your center, you will probably find that you have several human interest stories at your center. For example, one center had a story about preschool children visiting an art gallery. In addition to pictures of the children at the exhibit and interviews with them about their reactions, the writer commented on how the children's own art work was influenced by what they had seen at the gallery.

Another school had a feature story done about an assistant teacher who was visually disabled. The article described the assistant and her guide dog in their activities with the children. It was very worthwhile for the newspaper's readers to realize that a person who was visually disabled could work effectively in an early childhood program. It also brought the center a great deal of attention. Another worthwhile project that interested a commentator on a TV broadcast concerned parents of the children at a center who were returning to school while their children were in the preschool program. This appeared as a feature story on a TV program that focused on new opportunities for women.

## A Center Newsletter

A center newsletter serves many functions, not the least of which is public relations. It is a good way to get parents involved, since parents with a particular talent for writing, photography, or art usually enjoy contributing their talents and skills to such an effort. They may write about special events at school, about the teachers, and about things that the children have done at home and at school. The newsletter can also contain helpful hints on parenting, crafts projects for children, ideas for science projects at home, book reviews, and news about coming events. The parents and the children who attend the center enjoy this kind of publication, and it is also good publicity if you distribute it to other members of the community who may be interested in your program, including public school personnel, pediatricians, and clergy. If your circulation becomes widespread, you may be able to sell some ads to local merchants to advertise services and products that would be useful to young children and their families. You might also publish some announcements about babysitters and clothing or service exchanges that apply to your population.

At our campus child care center, the newsletter, which comes out at least once a term, provides sketches of our staff members, a brief review of our aims, and some special reminders for our often-changing population of parents.

## An Annual Report

An annual report is a useful document for public relations and serves several other functions as well. In a university setting or in an industrial or business situation, the annual report provides information to the administrative hierarchy that usually makes decisions regarding the continuance of your program about your costs, your income, and your contribution to the setting that sponsors your center and to the community. If you are in charge of a parent cooperative program, a report for the board reminds them about the activities and services you have provided during the course of the year. This report, or a portion of it, may be distributed to the parents and to the parents of alumni. You can use it as an opportunity to get them involved in meeting your needs for services, materials, and funds as well as lending general support to your program.

The annual report also serves as one form of yearly evaluation for you. The account that you prepare of the center's previous year's activities provides information to help you examine your own efforts. It is particularly useful in terms of matching practice to goals and forecasting your needs for funding, staff development, materials, space, and other resources.

Your report should include statistical data, such as the center's income, the number of children served, the number of credit hours taken by parents who use your center if you are affiliated with a college, or the reduction in absenteeism if you are industry-supported. It should also include educational items, such as your curriculum innovations, functions for parents, and other contributions to the community that you serve. At our campus school, we include such items as training and observations for students and service to the community at large, such as speakers and events we may have sponsored or visits from high school classes. You may wish to send portions of your report to individuals or agencies that might lend support to your efforts. It is appropriate to include parent testimony or even questionnaires documenting the aspects of your program that have been the most useful to parents.

### Community Programs

Sponsoring an educational and/or entertainment program for the community in which your center is located can serve a variety of purposes, including public relations. If you hold a workshop for children and their parents, it can serve as an open house for your center as well as a very worthwhile community activity. We have had great success with science workshops for children and parents and with arts and crafts open houses. You might wish to offer a children's concert, where preschool children would be entertained but would also be able to participate in songs and, possibly, dance. This could also serve as a fund-raiser if you charge a small admission fee. You might put on a play at the end of the school year or have each class do a performance. You would want to invite the parents, of course, but you can also invite other relatives and friends in the community, giving them an opportunity to view your facility and your program. You might also sponsor programs for parents, on topics related to children and families, that are open to anyone in the community as a public relations and community service function. In addition, professional workshops for teachers and administrators at other centers increase the quality of your program, contribute to professional development, and, of course, call attention to your staff's expertise.


## FUND-RAISING

Fund-raising helps keep the cost of tuition down, provides some extras at your center, and serves as a community service activity. As you plan your fund-raising activities, try to plan events that are consistent with your center's philosophy and contribute to positive public relations. The following are some examples of fund-raising projects you might wish to try.


### A Bake Sale

A bake sale does not usually raise a great deal of money, but it is good as a small fund-raising activity. Children can be involved in both the preparation of the food and the sale itself. The bake sale can take place at a busy spot on a college campus or in front of a store in the community (with the cooperation of the store owner, of course—point out that the bake sale will draw attention.)

The baking of the cakes and cookies can be done at home, which is a nice family activity. It can also be done as a school project, with a somewhat more educational emphasis. Cooking allows children to see the transformation of materials and combinations and to practice measuring and the like. The children can also participate by handing the baked goods to the customers or by taking the money or returning the change. This gives them an opportunity to be part of an exciting process, and many questions may arise about the exchange of goods for money, the cost of the preparation relative to the cost of the product, and other aspects of selling for profit. This is a very meaningful way to teach economics, even to preschoolers.

### A Carnival

Many schools use a carnival or fair as a fund-raising activity because it is fun for families and children and is usually a good source of revenue. For a carnival to be successful financially requires extensive effort on the part of the committee responsible for organizing and directing the efforts of the families that volunteer to run games of skill and chance. You may need to help in designing the games to see that they are developmentally appropriate for young children. There may be some more difficult games to challenge the older children, but the preschoolers will need games that are appropriate for their age. We have found that if each family prepares its own game, with some consultation and coordination from the committee, you are off to a good start. You will also need prizes, which may be donated by local merchants. A system of selling tickets to play the games and other tickets that can be redeemed for prizes usually proves to be effective. Or each booth can give out its own prizes. You may also want to sell food and drinks at the carnival. A "white elephant" table or a children's clothing exchange or sale is also a nice auxiliary function; again, you will need to provide for staffing by volunteers. If you hold your carnival outdoors, you can have relay races and other athletic events or a pet show.

### A Children's Concert or Theatrical Production

A children's concert or a theatrical production for children is a fund-raiser that provides a nice experience for children and their families to share. In that sense, it serves a very worthwhile community service while helping to raise funds for your center. We have discovered that when you are planning a musical or dramatic production for young children, it is essential that you provide for high audience involvement. Such involvement is more important than artistic excellence. A folk guitarist who sings children's songs and invites the children to join in is a good choice. A high school or college drama group could be invited to construct a production from a children's story, also allowing for audience participation. The children like to see their favorite stories enacted. This theatrical event may also include the sale of cookies and punch at intermission.

### A Dinner-Dance

A dinner-dance is clearly a more adult-oriented fund-raising activity. Besides being a potentially good source of revenue, it also helps to bring parents and staff together in a social activity—a desirable event. This type of function does involve considerable prior arrangements. The music source and the dinner hall or restaurant must be selected and reserved. Invitations or tickets must be written, printed, and mailed. You may wish to have a menu printed to commemorate the event. You may also wish to have a guest of honor. Inviting someone who is well known, such as a local radio, newspaper, or TV personality, might increase the interest and attendance at your dance. You can also heighten interest by including a raffle or door prize. Remind people that all of the contributions, including admission to the dance, are tax-deductible.

### A Potluck Supper

A potluck supper could be a family function or it could be just for adults. If it is just an opportunity for parents to get together, each family would bring a dish and share with the others. To use it for fund-raising, too, each family would make an extra amount of a covered dish or some other meal that would serve others who buy tickets of admission. Usually, these guests would be friends of the school and friends of the parents, so it could be a great deal of fun. However, you probably wouldn't raise a large amount of money this way.

### An Ad Journal

An ad journal is an excellent fund-raiser. A committee of parents and friends of the school, including families of alumni, might be called upon to purchase space to express their good wishes (grandparents are great for this) or to solicit advertisements from local businesses. The journal can be mailed (a large mailing is impressive to commercial advertisers), or it can be distributed at a dinner-dance.

## PUBLIC RELATIONS ASSESSMENT

The following are some questions a director might ask in reviewing her public relations activity. Remember that your early childhood program is a *business* that provides child care services and an early childhood program.

1. *Understanding our services*: Does the staff know the features of the program we want to emphasize—its goals and its unique aspects?
2. *Quality of the product*
   a. Are we producing a quality early childhood program?
   b. How do we know?
   c. Are parents bringing their children?
   d. Are parents referring others to us?
3. *Packaging*
   a. Is the center clean? What kind of first impression does a person get?
   b. Are the people working in the center properly dressed?
   c. Is there a sign that identifies the center?
   d. Is there a sign that tells what hours we are available?
   e. Is there a sign that describes our services?
   f. Are there attractively arranged posters describing our various services?
   g. Do the customers have a pleasant experience at our center?
   h. Do staff members speak courteously to parents and children?
   i. What kinds of messages are given to our customers?
   j. Is the telephone being answered courteously?
   k. When parents come to visit, are they greeted promptly and pleasantly?
   l. Are potential users of the center offered a tour of the facility?
   m. Are visitors introduced to the staff and the children?
   n. Do we stress the strengths of the center in our descriptions to potential customers?
4. *Use of the media*: Which of these are we using?
   a. Low-cost advertising
   b. Public service announcements
   c. Newsletters
   d. Annual report
   e. Newspaper articles

    f.   Fund-raising activities
       (1)  Bake sale
       (2)  Carnival
       (3)  Children's concert or theatrical production
       (4)  Dinner-dance
       (5)  Potluck supper
       (6)  Ad journal

## Suggested Activities

1. Design a brochure for your center or for a prospective center.
2. Plan an advertisement for your school.
3. Plan an activity for your center that will serve a public relations function as well as being a possible fund-raiser.

## References and Further Readings

Axelrod, Pearl, and Buch, Esther M. *Preschool and Child Care Administration.* Course handout, Mobile Training for Directors of Day Care Centers, 1978.

Cherry, Clare; Hunness, Barbara; and Kuzma, Kay. *Nursery School and Day Care Management Guide.* Belmont, Calif.: Fearon-Pitman, 1978.

Glick, Phyllis. *Administration of Schools for Young Children.* Albany: Delmar, 1975.

Hewes, Dorothy W., ed. *Administration: Making Programs Work for Children and Families.* Washington, D.C.: National Association for the Education of Young Children, 1979.

Neugebauer, Roger, ed. *Child Care Information Exchange.* Belmont, Mass.: Bimonthly publication.

Schon, Bruce, and Neugebauer, Roger. "Marketing Strategies that Work in Child Care." *Child Care Information Exchange,* September 1978, 23–31.

U.S. Department of Health, Education and Welfare, Bureau of Child Development Services. *Project Head Start Series.* Washington, D.C.: U.S. Government Printing Office, 1973.

U.S. Department of Health, Education and Welfare, Office of Child Development. *Day Care Series.* Washington, D.C.: U.S. Government Printing Office, 1971.

# Part II
# Working
# with People

*The chapters in Part II address the people concerns of an early childhood center. Our humanistic approach begins with the first contacts we have with prospective staff members. Chapter 4 describes the application and employment process. Since many directors express a desire for more concrete information about staff development, Chapter 5 discusses many forms of staff development that focus on helping the teacher grow in a supportive environment. Chapter 6 focuses on designing an environment that will help children grow, and Chapter 7 offers ideas for working with children and families with special needs. Finally, Chapters 8 and 9 describe the planning necessary to provide a supportive environment for parents and volunteers.*

# Chapter 4
# Staff Selection

## CONCERNS IN STAFF SELECTION

### Teacher as Person

We have discovered, from our own experience and from the observations of others, that, from the administrator's point of view, the cornerstone of a humanistic service to children and parents is a humanistic treatment of the staff. It is pointless to expect teachers and other support staff to view the persons for whom they provide service as "people" if these staff members are themselves viewed only as workers, not as people. No matter how good the program is in theory and no matter how devoted it is to developing individual human potential, if the people who are offering the service do not sense that their talents, interests, and concern for others are recognized and encouraged, the program will take on a mechanical quality that contradicts its purpose.

It is important for teachers to have the opportunity to help in developing programs and evaluating results. It is also important for them to be able to use their own initiative in fulfilling their functions and to develop and present their own unique styles. Requiring all teachers to do the same thing in the same way affects them just as it would the children—it denies individuality. It also counteracts natural needs for autonomy and suppresses the special qualities that each human being has to offer.

Aside from the humanistic commitment a center director has to her staff, it simply makes good sense that a staff whose needs are met will be better able to meet the needs of the children. In July 1983 the National Association for the Education of Young Children (NAEYC) published guidelines for staff development in early childhood centers (Center Accreditation Project 1983). This report points out that an essential administrative function is helping to meet the needs of the adults in the center. Clearly, a center director cannot be expected to solve the teachers' psychological

and family problems. However, a healthy, well-protected, and professionally supported staff is a good investment as well as an
administrative responsibility.

The NAEYC report makes the very practical suggestion that
health insurance and sick leave are included in the staff's needs.
Staff members also require time, space, and support for planning.
This may involve released time from teaching, additional paid time
as needed, or planning time built-in to the job. The administration
can provide help in setting goals and in the evaluation process. The
staff members should be encouraged to do long-range planning,
and they are more likely to do so if administrative support is available for these efforts. An important finding of the National Day
Care Study (1979) was that programs are more successful when
planning is emphasized. By focusing on careful planning, an administrator can assure the quality of her program. (Chapter 5
offers a more detailed account of how a center director contributes to staff development.)

This point of view may sound idealistic, since it assumes that
teachers care about children and want to do their best. We do not
think this is idealistic; rather, we regard it as natural. Good teaching requires considerable emotional and intellectual commitment.
Obviously, teachers can be more effective in a humanistic classroom environment, which is created to a large extent by the administrative climate. Certainly, good teaching of the kind we
mean cannot be merely prescribed. Administrative support and
encouragement are as essential as direction to good teaching. This
administrative approach requires that the staff be involved in
decision making and that the initiative of individual staff members
be supported. In that sense, the teachers are seen and treated as
people rather than as role players. Such administration helps the
staff members feel good about what they are doing, thus encouraging them to make the extra effort that is required for a
superior early childhood program. This process should start from
the time persons are interviewed for positions at the center.

### Choosing the Staff
### for an Early Childhood Program

Staff selection may be the most important task a director
has. The director sets the tone of the center; her philosophy and
goals are reflected in its design and operation. She will exert influ-

ence through her policies and example. Ultimately, however, it is the teachers who determine the classroom atmosphere and have the responsibility for implementing the program in the classroom.

It is important to keep in mind that the staff persons in the center work together and that each person's strength enhances the classroom system and the center as a whole. Potential staff members' skills and their ability to communicate with one another are essential considerations in the hiring process. (We will discuss these factors again in Chapter 5.) Although job descriptions are separate and itemized, it is important when hiring staff for a director to review her own perceptions and expectations of how the staff persons are expected to act as an integrated group and what they are to do to fulfill their roles in the classroom. One administrator's goal is that each staff member should learn to function as head teacher in the classroom, even if that person is an assistant or a volunteer. Staff members come in contact with children both as individuals and as members of a group, and they are expected to learn management skills for both kinds of situations. They also come in contact with parents at one time or another, and they are expected to learn to interact well with the parents. Staff members are also expected to communicate with each other before, during, and after classes on a variety of issues. In many centers, it is customary for the head teacher to do the planning, but programs are usually more successful and more exciting when all staff members are able to contribute to planning.

When staff members are selected, specific requirements for their primary responsibilities must receive the utmost consideration. However, consistent with our humanistic orientation and the goals for staff we have just outlined, we recommend that a director should keep the following general criteria in mind when hiring teaching staff and even support staff: How well is the prospective staff member likely to relate to children? What goals does she have for the young children? What are her views about the materials and the methods used at the center? How effectively does she relate to parents and to other staff members?

## Staffing Needs for Various Types of Centers

For a parent-cooperative nursery school, where parents participate in the classroom, you may need fewer paid staff members. Keep in mind, however, that a higher ratio of adults to children is often necessary when working with nonprofessional personnel. The same principle applies if you plan to use volunteers, such as in a center on a university campus, or paraprofessionals, as in a day care center. You may be able to reduce the number of paid staff, but in that case you need to allow for a somewhat larger combined staff of professionals, students, and volunteers than would be necessary if the entire staff were paid professionals. If your center is small, a head teacher may also serve as director, but in that case it is essential to have a strong assistant.

How do you determine the staff size you will need? Clearly, a major factor is the size of your student population, but many other considerations are also involved. Your state or local licensing agency may have very specific guidelines for staffing. For example, the younger the children are, the more staff is required. The Department of Health and Human Services offers the following guidelines: for children from birth to 2 years, a one-to-three adult–child ratio; for 2-year-old children, a one-to-four ratio; for 3- to 6-year-olds, a one-to-nine ratio; and for 6- to 10-year-olds, a one-to six ratio.

## THE EMPLOYMENT PROCESS

The staff employment process consists of recruitment, interviewing, selection, notification, and orientation and training.

### Recruitment

If your program is just beginning, announcements of staff openings may be sent to professional organizations, such as the Day Care Council and the Early Childhood Council, and to placement bureaus at colleges and universities with undergraduate and graduate programs in early childhood education. Some centers also place ads in community newspapers and local school newspapers.

These announcements should include brief descriptions of your program, the available positions, and the application process; the starting date of the position; necessary qualifications; and salary. The name, address, and telephone number of the center and the person to whom applications should be sent should also be included. If your school is already established, you may want to

announce a new opening to current staff first, to provide opportunities for career advancement within the organization.


### The Application Form

Initial screening of applicants can often be accomplished by a
telephone call or by a review of their letters and resumes. Then
application forms can be mailed to those who qualify. The application form should ask for the following information:

Applicant's name, address, and telephone number
Social security number
Marital status
Position sought
Previous work experience
Hobbies
Plans for continuing education
Educational background
Credentials
Membership in professional associations
Published works
References
Applicant's statement of why she wants the position
Applicant's statement of her qualifications for the position

The form should also include instructions regarding where to
return the form and a description of subsequent procedures in the
employment process, such as interviews, notification, and so on.


### The Interview Process

The interview process takes place after a preliminary review
of the applications. Although it is not always possible, the interview process should consist of three parts: an interview, some time
working with the children, and a tour of the facility.

In some centers, the director alone is responsible for interviewing and hiring; in other centers, board members and teachers
participate in the interview and/or the selection process. The interview should give some insight into the candidate's teaching philosophy and personality. Some interview questions about dealing

with classroom situations should also give you an idea of the candidate's competence. It is advisable to ask all prospective applicants the same questions so that you can make effective comparisons. Preparing an interview schedule in advance helps reduce the possibility that you will omit questions that you consider important. The following are some suggested questions for an interview:

1. What are your goals for the children you work with?
2. Can you describe a typical daily plan that you have used?
3. How does this plan implement curriculum goals?
4. What do you regard as your strong and weak points?
5. How would you handle the following management situations that might come up in the classroom?
   a. You have gathered the children for singing, but only one of them is interested.
   b. A child who does not speak your language bites another child.
6. What are your plans for personal growth?
7. Do you have any health problems that should be taken into account?
8. Do you have children? If so, what would be the procedure if your own child were sick?

Then, by briefly observing the applicant working with the children in the classroom, you can get some additional information on her teaching ability and on how she would interact with the children and with other staff members. Even on an initial visit, a person's attitude toward children is usually evident. Does she bend down to a child's eye level? Does she listen? Does she talk in a normal tone of voice?

### Making the Final Decision

After the interview, and before making the final selection, credentials and licenses must be verified and references should be checked. It is helpful to get verbal references immediately and ask for written ones for your files. It is important to verify the relationship between the reference source and the applicant—whether the applicant actually worked for that person? You should also ask why the applicant left. Finally, ask for information about the applicant's understanding of children, management and instructional techniques, professional conduct with staff and parents, and continued education.

In choosing between two final candidates, it is sometimes better to select the one who has less experience and whom you would have to train. Such a decision would be made if the alternative candidate had a style and point of view that was incompatible with your center's philosophy. This is not to say that all teachers are expected to behave in the same way. It is possible and even desirable for a teacher to develop her own style, so long as it is consistent with your basic philosophy and meets the needs of the children and parents.

In making the final selection, you might want to balance the staff, so that they represent different ages, cultures, sexes, styles, and strengths. However, keeping those factors in mind, an overriding consideration is whether the applicant who fulfills most of your criteria has a philosophy that coincides with the basic philosophy of the center.

## Notification of Employment

Each person who has applied for a position deserves to be notified in writing about the results of the employment process. The person who is accepted should be sent a contract or letter to sign and should be informed in writing of the starting date of employment. A note of thanks is appropriate for those who are not hired. Their records would then be kept on file for a certain period of time; with notations regarding why they were not hired, in case they make further inquiry or another opening comes up.

## Notifying the Parents

Informing the parents of any changes or additions to the staff is part of a commitment to positive parent–center relations. A note informing parents that a teacher is leaving and who her replacement will be or giving some information about a new teacher who is joining the staff is reassuring to parents and helps them in preparing their children for changes.

## Notifying the Children

If a change in staff occurs during the year and the children will be coming upon a new teacher in the classroom, it is important to inform them in advance and to help them adjust to the change. It is very important that the children be given an explanation whenever staff members, even volunteers, leave the center.

# POSTEMPLOYMENT PROCEDURES

## Orientation of a New Staff Member

Orientation of a new staff person should include a conversation with the director about the philosophy and goals of the center. The new person should also read literature about the center, staff manuals, parent handbooks, and statements of center policies, procedures, and employee policies, asking questions about any details that need clarification. The new staff member should be given a detailed tour of the facility by someone who can point out the locations of materials and essential resource persons. After the guided tour, she may want time to wander around herself to become more familiar with the center.

## Personnel Contracts

Even for small schools, personnel policies should be clearly stated in writing. The following are some topics to include in personnel contracts:

*Sick leave*: How many sessions are allowed for sickness or personal leave for each teacher? Is this leave cumulative? Some schools allow teachers ten days' leave per year if they are working five mornings or afternoons per week. Some schools have cumulative leave for up to two years.

*Released time*: Describe the paid time (if any) allowed for professional purposes, such as conferences, workshops, or visits to other schools.

*Provision for termination of the contract by either party*: Many schools have a provision for termination of the contract by either party on 30 days' notice.

*Professional growth*: Some schools pay staff members' professional dues, conference fees, and/or tuition for in-service training.

*Contract renewal*: In cooperative schools that have a set calendar year, the contracts are usually offered for renewal for the ensuing year on March 1, to be signed by April 1.

*Teachers' working conditions*: A full job description should be given, including the hours of work, the evening meetings the teacher is expected to attend, and the personnel available to assist the teacher.

## Job Description

A detailed job description for each staff position should include the following information:

*Minimum qualifications*: personal, health, educational, certification, and any others.

*Working conditions*: working hours, break time, and planning time.

*Benefits*: vacation, sick leave, and other leave.

*Relationships*: relationship with other center positions.

*Responsibilities and duties*: all areas in which the person has responsibility—who does what.

*Evaluation procedures.*

## Employee Files

A file folder should be kept for each employee. The folder generally contains the following:

1. The employee's original application, including name, address, social security number, and person to contact in case of emergency
2. Records of education and relevant experience
3. References
4. Credentials
5. Transcripts
6. Notices of employment, dismissal, or resignation
7. Health forms and TB test results
8. Evaluations

9. Records of absences and leaves
10. A checklist, including dates of hire, separation, last TB test, and physical examination; salary records; the contract; and the class assignment

## Personnel Policy Manual

A personnel policy manual should include the following information:

1. An organizational chart of the school, mapping the various positions
2. Job descriptions, listing the duties and responsibilities of each position, the qualifications for each job, and the categories of employees and including
   a. Salaried or hourly status
   b. Full-time or part-time status, stating number of working hours per day
   c. Tenure and seniority (if they are part of your school's policy)
   d. Daily work schedule, including arrival time, breaks, lunch, and end of day
   e. Initial probationary period
   f. Contract stipulations
   g. Titles
3. Compensation policies
   a. How and when personnel are paid
   b. Compensation for meetings
   c. Reimbursement for education expenses
   d. Overtime pay
   e. Salary scales
4. Benefits
   a. FICA (social security)
   b. Workers compensation
   c. Health insurance
   d. Retirement and unemployment compensation
   e. Other benefits
5. Leave policies
   a. School calendar and holidays
   b. Vacation
   c. Sick leave
   d. Personal leave

     e.  Maternity leave
     f.  Emergency leave
     g.  Educational leave
     h.  Procedures for taking leave time
     i.  Documentation
     j.  Substitute policy

6. Hiring practices (including affirmative action)
7. Evaluation procedures
8. Termination policies
    a. Firing or resignation
    b. Rights of personnel
    c. Grievance procedures
9. Training policies
    a. Center requirements
    b. In-service and center-sponsored training
    c. Conferences
    d. Workshops
10. Housekeeping details
    a. Where to park
    b. How to get keys
    c. How to maintain room and equipment
    d. How to get supplies
11. Other center policies
    a. Health and safety regulations
    b. Classroom procedures
    c. Purchasing procedures
    d. Student and volunteer supervision
    e. Management information
    f. Budget
    g. Bylaws

## Suggested Activities

1. Prepare a series of questions that you might wish to ask a prospective employee. Then analyze the questions, determining what you hope to learn from each one. Did you leave out some questions that you might now include? Explain.
2. Conduct a simulated interview with a classmate, using your prepared list of questions.
3. Write a detailed job description for a prospective classroom teacher. Share it with actual classroom teachers to

see if they believe the description accurately describes their work. How does your description differ from their experience?

### References and Further Readings

Axelrod, Pearl, and Buch, Esther M. *Preschool and Child Care Administration.* Course handout, Mobile Training for Directors of Day Care Centers, 1978.

Center Accreditation Project (CAP). "Three Components of High Quality Early Education Programs," *Young Children 38*(5), July 1983, 53–58.

Cherry, Clare; Hunness, Barbara; and Kuzma, Kay. *Nursery School and Day Care Management Guide.* Belmont, Calif.: Fearon-Pitman, 1978.

National Day Care Study, Final Report. *Children at the Center: Executive Summary.* Cambridge, Mass.: Abt Associates, 1979.

Sciarra, Dorothy J., and Dorsey, Anne B. *Developing and Administering a Child Care Center.* Boston: Houghton Mifflin, 1979.

# Chapter 5
# Staff
# Development

Lillian Katz (1977) has described how staff members' needs and behaviors change as they gain experience. In the first stage, a question asked by many teachers is "Can I get through the day?" Ongoing supervision by the director is the best way to relieve this feeling of frustration in this initial stage. End-of-the-day conferences for reviewing the day's experience with the children are also very useful in the beginning. By this process, the teachers accumulate baseline data on what the children are like and acquire a beginning grasp of curriculum development and programming.

The second stage described by Katz occurs after the teacher has been able to consolidate her learning somewhat. During this second stage, the teacher may be able to use specialists and on-site support to meet the children's needs. She may also gain a greater understanding of curriculum planning. Understanding increases in the third stage (which Katz calls "renewal"), during which attendance at seminars and conferences and the pursuit of advanced degrees take place.

The director should take notice of the developing needs of her staff and can encourage the teachers' growth from stages one to two to three by a variety of methods, including orientation, meetings, in-service training, conferences, supervision, and evaluation.

The types of meetings a center requires will vary. Meeting formats and times will largely depend on the hours of operation of your center, the staff schedules, and your goals. Some schools hold breakfast meetings, while others prefer lunch-hour or end-of-the-day meetings. Meetings that take place in the late afternoon or evening, or on a weekend, may have fewer time constraints.

Such meetings may be partially social, so that the staff can exchange ideas and share problems on an informal basis.


## IN-SERVICE STAFF DEVELOPMENT

Staff meetings provide a form of in-service staff development in that the director and staff share ideas about the program, teaching methods, and child development. This may be augmented by inviting an outside consultant to present particular techniques or experiences at a staff meeting, such as addressing a specific problem the staff is facing or a particular interest they have shown (e.g., helping the single parent or dealing with developmental disabilities). A more extensive version of in-service staff development would involve inviting a consultant to give a series of presentations. Local universities and professional organizations, such as the local or national associations for young children or the county mental health or psychological associations are good resources for in-service education consultants.

These local organizations and universities may also provide in-service courses for early childhood professionals; your staff might be encouraged to attend individually or as a group. If possible, you can help to defray the costs of such workshops by offering training through your center. National, state, or regional conferences held in your area would be another source of in-service education. Many schools post a current list of courses on the staff bulletin board.

In-service staff development courses cover a wide range of topics. Some may be aimed specifically at a problem in your center, such as dealing with a certain type of behavior or staff relations. Many successful staff development series are focused on topics teachers have suggested.


### Working as a Team

Teachers in training are taught how to work with children, how to plan curriculum, and sometimes even how to talk to parents, but college courses rarely focus on how to work with more than one adult in the classroom: What should the division of tasks be with more than one adult in the room? What kinds of communications are necessary between staff members working in the same room? How can you best develop the eye contact and anticipation that helps the room run smoothly? In some centers, one person is designated supervisor and is in charge of overall functioning, management, and transitions; another person may work with groups of children; and a third person works with individual children. At role-play sessions, teachers can take the various parts of the leader, group worker, and person working with an individual child. As we said earlier, it is essential that all staff persons develop the ability to assume all functions.

### Interpersonal Relations Between Staff Members

In centers where new and more experienced staff members are working in the same class, in-service seminars in interpersonal relations can help establish a climate in which staff members are open to exchanging assistance, especially if one member is trained and one is a paraprofessional. Sometimes, staff persons are unaware of their differences in perceptions, and a discussion helps to clarify and resolve these differences. For example, an assistant teacher may declare, "I could have done that if she [the teacher] didn't come flying over." The teacher may then be able to explain her policy: "It is the well being of the children that determines when I will intervene." Honest, open communication between adults helps clarify timing, individual roles, attitudes, and teamwork.

### Techniques of Program Management

Program management consists of procedures related to routines, to how activities begin and end, and to social behavior regarding taking turns, cooperation, and fair play when it is reactive, not instructional. Many teachers have not developed expertise in classroom design and other management procedures. For example, they may need help in developing classroom rules. When children understand the rules and what to do next in the schedule, there is less need for external discipline. Topics such as preparing schedules for the day, establishing rules with the children, moving from one activity to another indoors and outdoors, providing choices for children, anticipating and informing the children, and performing the adult role in transitions are appropriate for in-service training in this area.

### Basics of Curriculum

Some staff members need courses that review or present information on how to display materials, how to make the classroom effective, and ways to interact with the children. Specific early childhood curriculum areas, such as music, science, math, health, and nutrition, could be covered weekly by knowledgeable staff persons and specialists.

### Child Development

An essential ingredient in the successful preparation and continued effectiveness of a teacher, especially a teacher of young children, is a knowledge and understanding of child development. A finding of the National Day Care Study (1979) was that teachers who had studied child development and early childhood education were generally more effective than those who had not. We have found that many of the personnel in child care centers are not knowledgeable about child development. They do not always know the capabilities of children of particular ages, which adversely affects their planning and their expectations. The director can play a very positive role in helping her staff become aware of some basic principles of child development.

## PROFESSIONAL GROWTH AND DEVELOPMENT

It is vital that staff members be encouraged and supported in their efforts to acquire advanced training through degree programs, in-service courses, attendance at conferences and professional meetings, and subscriptions to professional journals. Membership in national and local professional societies not only provides opportunities for additional training but also provides a peer support group and access to publications. If all of the teachers at the school cannot afford to join all of the pertinent groups, perhaps each of them could join one or two groups and share the resources. Some schools provide in their budgets for staff attendance at one or two conferences per year or for membership in particular associations.

Professional conferences—local, regional, or national—offer a wide variety of workshops and seminars, ranging from practical to theoretical. National conferences are held by the National Association for the Education of Young Children, the National Head Start Association, the Association for Childhood Education International, the National Coalition of Campus Child Care, the Council for Exceptional Children, the National Black Child Development Institute, and several other associations. These conferences—usually annual—are located in different parts of the country. State-level organizations, such as the New York State Council for Children and the Southern Association for the Education of Young Children, also hold yearly conferences, moving about a particular state or region. These conferences are announced in periodicals focused on early childhood, such as *Young Children*.

Most national organizations also publish a journal, and other organizations related to early childhood often publish magazines or journals as well. For example, *Young Children* is published by the National Association for the Education of Young Children, *Day Care and Early Education* by the Day Care Council, and *Child Development* by the Society for Research and Child Development.

In addition to full degree programs at universities and colleges, there are also week-long courses, or short series, particularly in the summer. For example, the Center for Parent Education offers three-day series in parent education in different parts of the country and a summer series in Cambridge, Massachusetts. Each summer, Wheelock College offers several week-long seminars on various topics in day care management. Figure 5.1 provides a sample list of organizations that focus on young children.

**FIGURE 5.1**  Possible Professional Groups for Early Childhood Staff

Association for Childhood Education International: Holds annual conferences; publishes *Childhood Education*

American Educational Research Association: Holds annual conferences; publishes *Reviews of Research*

Day Care Council of America: Holds annual conferences; publishes *Day Care* and *Early Education*

National Association for the Education of Young Children: Holds annual conferences; publishes *Young Children*

National Coalition for Campus Child Care: Holds annual conferences

National Head Start Association: Holds annual conferences

Society for Research in Child Development: Holds biannual conferences; publishes *Child Development, Child Development Abstracts,* and monographs

## WORKING WITH PARENTS

In recent years, increasing numbers of early childhood centers have added parent programs. With the increase of parent programs has come an increase in resources to help administrators and teachers work with parents. There are parent education newsletters for professionals. For example, the Center for Parent Education, a public service organization dedicated to assisting professionals concerned with the education of children in the first three years, publishes a newsletter that includes Dr. Burton White's discussions of the latest research, book reviews, critiques of films, and information from other parent newsletters. The Working Mothers Institute, organized by a group of working mothers, supports the principle that all mothers are working mothers and that mothers who are employed outside the home have two jobs. The institute publishes a newsletter that is geared to such topics as dual careers and after-school alternatives. The Family Resource Coalition is a network of family support programs in the United States and Canada. Such programs as community-based drop-in centers, parent cooperatives, and family life education programs have been organized to promote an exchange of information and resources, to sponsor conferences, and to publish newsletters. For example, Education for Parenthood Exchange publishes a newsletter that contains information about parenting programs and a brief exchange of resources and ideas for professionals engaged in parenting and early childhood. The addresses of these organizations are as follows:

> Center for Parent Education
> 55 Chapel Street
> Newton, MA 02168
>
> Education for Parenthood Exchange
> Education Development Center
> School and Society Programs
> 55 Chapel Street
> Newton, MA 02168
>
> Family Resource Coalition
> 230 North Michigan Avenue, Suite 1625
> Chicago, IL
>
> Working Mothers Institute
> P.O. Box 1053
> Bellmore, NY 11710

## CURRICULUM PLANNING
## AND IMPLEMENTATION

What is the director's role in curriculum planning for the classroom? The director has the responsibility of making sure that all staff members know and understand the philosophy, goals, and objectives of the program. Although some centers have both an administrative and an educational director, most centers have only one director. She is responsible for training and guiding teachers, consulting with parents, and approving and providing the space, equipment, and materials needed by the teachers to implement the curriculum (Stengel 1982). Her role is to provide guidance and information about child development theory, curriculum models, and teaching strategies. She may also assist the classroom teachers in the actual design of their programs. In some cases, she acts as the clinical supervisor in supervising and evaluating programs; in other cases, she may actually do some of the planning and implementation in the classroom for a teacher. Sometimes, the director is also the teacher and has the direct responsibility for planning and implementing the curriculum of the center as well as running the school. In addition, she has the responsibility of observing classroom operations and raising questions about the activities and procedures taking place. Therefore, a director must become familiar with different curriculum models and resources and compare them with those in the literature and with the functioning of her own center. Some sources for curriculum models are included in the references at the end of this chapter.

Curriculum planning begins with identifying the philosophy, goals, and objectives of the programs. It is most important to define the program's goals and objectives. As one administrator noted, if you don't know where you are going, you won't know when you get there. Goals and objectives evolve from the professional and personal beliefs of the administrators, the funding source, the advisory board, the staff, and the families.

*Goals* are general statements of what the children are expected to accomplish. The goals provide the framework for making long-term decisions and achieving short-term objectives.

*Objectives* are more specific statements of the behaviors that will be expected as evidence that the goals have been achieved (Stengel 1982). For example, a long-term goal of the Kammi and Devries (1978) program is for the children to feel secure with adults. How would such feelings show in a child? What behaviors would a teacher encourage? Some of the objectives for reaching such a goal might be (1) that the children ask for help when necessary for personal reasons or for learning; (2) that the children be able to express both negative and positive feelings to the staff; and (3) that the children be able to maintain their own point of view, even when challenged by teachers (Schwartz and Robison 1982).

There is a consensus in the literature about what children should be learning. In "The Fundamental Learning Needs of Today's Young Children," the NAEYC Committee for Early Childhood (1975) suggests that we think about "how a child can be helped to learn to become a capable, self-confident, sensitive, independent inventive person with strength and courage to meet the problems of the future and enjoy life at the same time" (p. 25). The article notes that it is not necessary to start from scratch, because there is now a solid body of knowledge about how young children learn and grow and over a half-century of teaching experience related to the care and education of young children in day care centers, nursery schools, and early childhood programs. The committee suggests that good early childhood programs have three basic characteristics: (1) rich and varied learning experiences; (2) a caring, informed, and trained staff; and (3) a physical environment that is safe as well as attractive, which promotes learning and healthy development.

Programs for children aged 3 to 5 should include the following opportunities:

> To develop language skills through conversation, stories, word games, records, tape recorders, visual aids, etc., as well as through experiences with seeing written words, labels, numbers, charts, books;
> —develop a mathematical understanding through counting, measuring, comparing size, weight, shape, grouping, estimating;
> —learn at first hand about the world through visits and trips, and vicariously through stories, books, films;
> —develop large and small muscle coordination and physical skills through using games, puzzles, tools, paints, crayons, clay, sand, water and other manipulative material equipment; through building, carrying, climbing, lifting, pushing, pulling, balancing, swinging, running, jumping, pedaling;
> —discover how things work—floating, sinking, balancing, friction, wheels, inclined planes, pulleys, magnets, electrical circuits, evaporation, boiling, melting, freezing, weighing, condensation;

—learn about living things through observing, caring for and talking about plants and animals;
—develop a relationship to a variety of art experiences including rhythms and music, color and pictures, dramatic play;
—learn about appropriate, safe and healthy modes of group life;
—develop a zest for learning and activity. (Committee for Early Childhood, 1975, p. 27)

Sometimes, a center uses a theoretical model as the basis for its curriculum plan or chooses to replicate a model program completely. Other times, a center may develop model program characteristics and responses according to its own unique needs.

When a new director first comes to a center, there may already be a curriculum in use, in which case it is important that she learn about it and then analyze it in relation to the goals and objectives of the school.

If a curriculum has not been developed in a formal way, then it is up to the director to lead the center in curriculum development. In planning curriculum, the center's goals and the needs of individual children are taken into account. A director might plan some staff development sessions or individual conferences to help teachers develop appropriate curriculum goals and the activities necessary to meet those goals. *Designing Curriculum for Early Childhood*, by Schwartz and Robison (1982), is a useful text for curriculum development. It provides a conceptual framework, including a discussion of curriculum form, purpose, views of content, views of knowledge, views of development and learning, long-range goals and short-term objectives, and curriculum sequences that will enable a director to design a curriculum to meet the needs of the children in her center. In *Teaching Practices: Reexamining Assumptions* Bernard Spodek points out that a curriculum must be based on sound theoretical principles and current research in child development to guarantee its relevance to the needs of the children, and he presents some questions to use in determining the worth of the activities being planned: Is what is taught to the child developmentally appropriate? Is what is taught to the child worth knowing? Is what is taught to the child testable by the child? What is developmentally appropriate can be answered from our understanding of child development. What is worth knowing is related to the cultural context; that is, in this cultural context—classroom, school, and community—it is important for the child to know this. The question of testability is answered according to theories of knowledge—whether the child can validate his findings on his own.

## Curriculum Goals Based on the Needs of Children

A significant consideration in curriculum design is the children's basic needs: a sense of security, a need for independence, the opportunity to explore, a sense of self-confidence, a sense of accomplishment, and a sense of others. Keeping these needs in mind, we have developed a list of curriculum goals that takes into account the child in relation to society. These goals begin with the question of what kinds of skills and values children need to develop to their fullest potential in the context of society. Some specific curriculum goals related to the needs of children are as follows:

*Skills*
The ability to work cooperatively
The ability to analyze critically
The ability to solve problems
The ability to communicate effectively
The ability to make choices
The ability to utilize all the senses
The ability to enjoy solitude

*Self-Understanding and Acceptance*
Understanding oneself
Valuing oneself
Trusting oneself
Being self-directed
Being self-actualizing
Being self-confident

*Feelings Toward Others*
Having concern for others
Being open-minded
Feeling a connection with mankind and nature

## Goals Based on Values for Survival

It is rather awesome at times to think about preparing children for the future when society is changing so rapidly. What adaptive skills might children require to survive in the future? A number of psychologists, sociologists, and educators have considered this question. Urie Bronfenbrenner (1977), Kenneth Kenniston (1977), and Edward Ziegler (1976) have identified several aspects of contemporary society that pose adaptive problems for children growing up now:

The uncertainty of the future
The complexity of modern life
Overcrowding
Technology
The influence of television
Reduced confidence in established institutions (church, government, etc.)
Isolation of families
The increased divorce rate
The breaking down of traditional barriers (religion, racial stereotypes, etc.)
Changing roles for women and men

Figure 5.2 provides some solutions to these problems that combine goals based on children's needs with those based on the skills and abilities that are essential for developing children's fullest potential in the context of society.

A director might work with teachers to help them design activities in the classroom to achieve the solutions given in Figure 5.2. For example, if a teacher wanted to promote caring and awareness of others, she might look at how she greets the children. Young children usually do not verbally acknowledge the comings and goings of others as a formal practice. However, parents may insist that their children say hello or goodbye routinely. In one child care center where children come and go at different times, the adults make a particular point to greet each child as he enters the room and say goodbye as he leaves. The other children begin to say hello and goodbye spontaneously, which suggests that, rather than just being mannerly or doing an adult's bidding, they have a genuine interest in one another.

Similarly, if a teacher wanted to encourage independence, she might help the children develop a variety of self-help skills, such as buttoning or zippering, dressing, wiping spills, and putting away puzzles or games. If her expectations are reasonable and if she supports the children's efforts by arranging storage space (e.g., providing a place for the blocks to go) and reminding them (e.g., saying "Why don't you get the sponge on the sink" if they've

**FIGURE 5.2** Problems for Children in Contemporary Society and Suggested Solutions

| Problem | Solution |
|---|---|
| Reduced confidence in established institutions (church, government, etc.) | Help children develop a sense of autonomy, self-control |
| Increasing technology | Promote humanistic concerns and a feeling of relatedness to others; encourage creative activity; help develop a general connection to mankind and to nature |
| Influence of television | Encourage active play, play and fantasy, critical thinking and a questioning mind |
| Breakdown of the family<br>  Diminished influence<br>  Isolation<br>  Increased divorce rate | Help children learn to communicate effectively, develop a concern for others, develop the ability to share and help each other, promote a feeling of self-acceptance |
| Changing roles for men and women | Help children to overcome sexism and stereotypical sex roles in the classroom, discover themselves as they experiment with a variety of materials and roles |

spilled something), she will find that they enjoy the experience of being helpful and independent.

The children in our center love to bring out the playground toys, which we store in a large closet; some of these items are quite large, but they are light. A visitor was amazed one day when she saw a group of children trying to figure out how to move an aluminum climber around a hedge to get it back into the building. After much discussion and trial and error, and with the teacher serving as a facilitator, the children figured out that the only way to move the climber through the hedge opening was by turning it on its end. This was a great lesson in problem solving as well as independence. The major requirement is that the adults don't move in too quickly to take over but stand back a bit to observe and to assist when necessary.

As our world becomes increasingly complex, it is especially important that we learn to work together. That is true in science, government, and industry and in the relationships between schools and parents, between old and young people, and so forth. How do we promote this cooperative spirit and develop a sense of community within the school and in relationship to the society outside? We talk about the workers upon whom we depend. We demonstrate the value of cooperative efforts in the classroom. Teachers don't direct children; they participate with them. By the same token, children help in the clean-up. Teachers talk about the satisfaction of working together and point out that this gets the job done faster (e.g., "We really worked nicely together at clean-up today. It was a big job, but we got it done by working together"). Children are expected to participate, but their help and cooperative efforts are not taken for granted; they are acknowledged and appreciated.

The same holds true in problem solving. The teachers help the children share ideas with one another in building, in dramatic play, and in just about every aspect of classroom life. The teachers also provide a model by working cooperatively with the other adults in the classroom. That is why good interpersonal relations in the classroom are so important.

Critical analysis is an important first step in problem solving that even young children can begin to acquire. They can be taught to observe, to describe the nature of a problem, and to make note of some of the possible ways to deal with it. It may be just a matter of reviewing alternatives—for example, how can we prevent blocks from falling? We may have to begin with a wider base or build another row of blocks alongside. The teacher doesn't solve the problem for the children, but she may make a suggestion or help them create some solutions. She helps them look over the situation and select the best alternative.

Once the observations have been made, as we've noted, solutions need to be proposed. How does a young child acquire the skills of problem solving? It may come about naturally, in what Piaget refers to as an "intuitive step." Teachers can help by encouraging experimentation and then by helping the children examine what has happened. For example, in our classroom, one of the children's favorite records broke. A child brought it to the teacher, wondering what to do about it. Rather than simply discarding it, the teacher invited the child to think about some solutions. He suggested that it might be glued. She wasn't sure if it could work, but since it was the child's suggestion, she felt it would be worth a try. Together they glued it, let it dry, and tested it out. It worked for a while, but it didn't last. The solution wasn't entirely successful in terms of saving the record, but it was a very successful learning experience for the child, for the other children who participated, and for the teachers who were involved.

Although the examples provided here have not been primarily in the affective range, the same process would be utilized to develop criteria and activities related to skill development and cognition. Before we conclude our discussion of choosing curriculum let us consider some general guidelines.

### Choosing a Program for Your Center

There is no one "right" program for a center. The important task is to match the program to the children and the community and to ascertain the best combination of individualization, small group work, direct teaching, and freedom for the children. A review of the program should clarify the specific goals; the emphasis on cognitive areas, academic skills, and/or the whole child; the relationship between cognition and affect; the emphasis on either a structured or an open environment; the emphasis on teacher-initiated or child-initiated activities; the emphasis on prescribed or open-ended material; and the level of the parents' involvement.

The following questions are useful as a guide in making decisions about a curriculum:

1. What are your own long- and short-range goals for the children? What is your district kindergarten's philosophy? What are the parents' goals?
2. Are your goals consistent or compatible with any of the described models?
3. What are the demographic characteristics of the population you intend to serve?
4. What curriculum model meets the needs for your particular group of children?
5. Are there parts of one or another model program that you would like to use in developing your own unique model?
6. Are prepackaged materials and plans important to you?
7. Which program would be most realistic in terms of implementation, considering your staff and its background?
8. How much time do you have available for training? What degree of training do you seek?

9. How much time do you have available for supervision and guidance to ensure successful implementation?

## Facilitating Curriculum Innovations

Although curriculum innovation is highly desirable, one often confronts a resistance to change among teachers. A significant aspect of an administrator's role is to help her staff overcome any reluctance to experiment and grow. We all have a tendency to continue to do the familiar—the "tried and true"—rather than making the extra effort and accepting the risk that is a natural by-product of innovation.

Judith Stalmack (1981) has described a very interesting and relatively inexpensive method of encouraging curriculum innovation. S.W.A.P., as it is called, involves a collaboration in study and practice among teachers. Briefly, a group of teachers (all or part of a staff at a child care center) agrees to read on a topic together and to decide on some curriculum material or a piece of equipment that they would like to try in their classrooms. If the item is expensive, the cost may be shared. When it is used, the teachers observe and then share the results of the experience with the other teachers in the group. Meetings may be held at which ideas and materials are "swapped." Teachers in the group are also encouraged to observe the use of the materials in other classrooms. This system gives the teachers the benefit of one another's experiences and is an impetus for them to experiment with new ideas.

In Stalmack's district, the technique helped in implementing a new curriculum and in allowing purchases to be made that one teacher alone could not justify. It also led to a newsletter describing these experiences that gave other teachers the benefit of a group's experiment. Formal workshops evolved on theory as well as practice, and parent education materials and programs were also developed. This idea could certainly be adapted for use at a center or for a consortium of early childhood programs.

Once the philosophy, goals, and objectives of a program are clearly established, it is necessary to plan actual curriculum activities. In some prepackaged or model curriculums, there are daily plans that seem to meet the goals of some centers. These models may be particularly useful to teachers who are in the first stage of development (which we discussed at the beginning of this chapter) and who may have to conquer both program management and early childhood curriculum. Other centers may choose a more eclectic approach, based on the needs of children, as described earlier, or on the unique aspects of the particular center.

Whichever choice you make, once the philosophical framework is established, long- and short-range plans should be developed, by the year, month, week, and day. In the daily plans, attention should be given to each activity area, to groups of children, to individual children, to alternative possibilities and strategies, and to staff roles. This means planning for independent activities, enriched activity, and special needs of the children. Careful attention should also be given to program management features, such as how activities are initiated and ended, how transitions are managed, what the cleanup procedures are, and how many children are in an area. How the materials are used and how successful the activities are often depend on the classroom management techniques that have been developed. Good classroom management encourages a productive, live classroom.

We believe in a well-structured program with carefully planned activities and experiences for the children and carefully designed management procedures, because we believe that teachers with plans and planned activities are more productive. However, this does not deny that spontaneous activities are an integral part of a center's program. When children or adults have new ideas, it is certainly important to act on them, particularly when some of your goals involve developing inventive, creative people.

In actual classroom planning, several questions are useful as guides:

1. What can we plan that the children can do alone? This might include painting, water play, and play with clay, blocks, and table toys.
2. What can we do to enrich the 2½- to 6-year-old? Whether you have multiage grouping or not, your children do have varying developmental levels and abilities. You might plan to make play dough, which would satisfy the sensory mixing need of a 2½-year-old and would teach a 4- to 6-year-old about transforming materials.
3. What does a particular child need? Perhaps one child needs large motor activity and another needs to be encouraged to socialize.

In making specific plans for the activities, the following questions often clarify the plans:

1. What is the nature of the area?
2. What can and cannot be done in the area?
3. Is the material or activity real?
4. Does it offer a range of possible working levels?
5. Does it require close adult supervision?
6. Can we live with it?
7. Will it help develop concepts of lasting values?
8. What is the teacher's role to be?
9. What special ideas might you use?
10. What problems do you foresee?

## PERSONAL NEEDS OF STAFF MEMBERS

It is important that staff members leave their personal problems at home when they enter the classroom. A director can be helpful, as well as demanding, in this regard. When personal problems do arise, a director's sympathetic ear is likely to be helpful to the teacher and will also enable the teacher to function effectively in the classroom. With the director's support, a teacher undergoing a personal crisis may be able to put her problems aside temporarily and work with her class. If she cannot, some arrangement should be made so that she does not return to the classroom until she is able to behave professionally.

In some situations, a problem may arise from the teacher's experience in the classroom. For example, we had a teacher in our center who was experiencing problems in her second year. During the first year, she was functioning at the "survival" level. In the second year, she was ready to grow personally. At that point, she was given the responsibility of helping other beginners come up to her level of proficiency. In some respects, this was helpful to her own teaching, but it also interfered with her efforts to increase her own skills. This developed into a frustrating position for her until the problem was identified in a personal conference with the director, and the teacher was relieved of some of her management and supervisory responsibilities so that she could have more time to work with the children and further refine her own teaching ability.

Sometimes, personality problems arise, causing friction between staff members in the same classroom. A director can be helpful in resolving these differences by easing tensions between co-workers that threaten the quality of classroom life. In this regard, a director has a professional obligation to set a good example by not allowing her personal problems to interfere with her work and by being as fair-minded as possible in her relations with her staff. Although she might have a personal favorite or might find some teachers' styles more appealing than others, it is important that she not give in to these personal preferences. When differences arise between staff members, it is particularly important to defer judgment, to help the staff members examine their problems as objectively as possible, and to work with them to find an amiable solution—both for the center's welfare and for their personal satisfaction. A director who plays favorites is not likely to be considered objective by her staff, especially during a crisis, and is therefore likely to be less effective at resolving differences than a director who maintains some degree of professional neutrality.

We noted earlier that a staff bulletin board can be used to post notices about conferences and workshops that would facilitate staff development. The director can also use a bulletin board for short articles from the literature or for hints that would be helpful in the classroom. Messages such as the following might be displayed:

1. *Early morning*: You do not have to take everything out before the children come. Sometimes the early morning children want to talk and help.
2. *Start slowly*: Show the children how to use the material— how to paint, build, paste, put away; how to go to the bathroom, pour, eat, clean up.
3. Encourage the older children to help the younger ones.
4. Try to have each child experience all activities.

Suggestions on a staff bulletin board might have to do with a particular activity of interest, or they might be related to a holiday or seasonal crafts project or to a program that can be duplicated or adapted. We also use bulletin boards in the classroom to remind staff members, especially volunteers, about the day's curriculum or about some of the ways in which they can keep track of their own performance in the classroom.

## STAFF DEVELOPMENT THROUGH
## OBSERVATION AND SUPERVISION

Our assumption is that staff members have both the drive and the ability to grow professionally, with any necessary aid and encouragement coming from the director. A trusting, open relationship between a director and her staff is essential to effective supervision. A director's regular, frequent visits to the classroom (at least daily) help the teacher and the children more than occasional visits or visits by appointment only.

The director and the teachers may decide, in conference together, that some areas need work. These might be curricular matters, or they might have to do with child management or even staff relations. The teacher should keep track of her own activities, and the director will also make observations.

### A Category System

A category system has proved useful in helping adults keep track of their behavior in the classroom (Keyes 1980). The system was originally developed (in the Queens College Title XX Day Care Project, 1981) in response to the need of supervisors to have a nonjudgmental way of providing feedback to teachers in the classroom. It has now been used by teachers, paraprofessionals, and parents.

The systematic observation system described in Figure 5.3 is

**FIGURE 5.3**  A Category System for Describing Adult Responses
to Children's Behavior

**Definitions**

*Early childhood curriculum*—a curriculum broadly defined to include content that promotes physical, social, cognitive, lingual, and affective development.

*Physical development*—relates to a child's development of the ability to master and control the use of his large and small muscles. Curriculum activities to promote large muscle competence might include opportunities for exercise, dancing, outdoor games, jumping, and throwing a ball. Activities to enhance small muscle development might include drawing, cutting, use of table toys, use of rhythm instruments, fingerpainting, or cooking. Teacher behaviors include such actions as providing equipment, modeling, inviting to use, or playing.

*Social development*—refers to the child's development of the use of social skills in group settings with both adults and other children. Social skills are often developed through opportunities to cooperate, participate, and take turns, in both routines and activities. Teacher behaviors may include modeling, directing, leading discussions about social expectations, and participating.

**FIGURE 5.3** *(continued)*

*Language development*—refers to the child's development of the ability to use and understand language. Activities that promote language development might include talking to adults and other children, following directions, listening to others, reading, listening to stories, and dramatic play. Teacher behaviors may include modeling, questioning, listening, labeling, reading, and giving directions.

*Affective development*—refers to a child's development of attitudes, values, interests, and appreciations in regard to himself and others. Learning to appreciate oneself and one's achievement, expressing one's feelings, expressing one's ideas, and accepting differences in people are areas that enhance affective development. Teacher behaviors may include modeling, verbal and nonverbal reinforcement, discussion of feelings, or reacting to children's feelings.

*Cognitive development*—refers to the child's development of thinking processes. Activities related to cognitive development include opportunities for experimentation and problem-solving activities that provide opportunities to classify and pattern as well as activities that provide experiences working with concepts of space, time, and number. Teacher behaviors may include clarifying concepts, defining, questioning, giving information, providing materials, or modeling.

*Program management*—refers to activities and procedures related to routines, how activities begin and end, and social behavior related to taking turns, cooperation, and fair play, where it is reactive, not proactive.

*Teacher behaviors*—refers to all behaviors when the teacher has contact with a child or children. Teachers can produce new behaviors by responding to a new child or children, changing a topic, asking a new question. Each new behavior represents a new behavior to be coded. The behaviors are to be interpreted within the context of an activity, which consists of a set of behaviors that cluster around one purpose. Playing dominoes or moving from outside to inside are examples of activities. Some activities may have more than one part. For example, a flag-making activity may incorporate looking at flags, picking one, getting a smock, and painting.

**Categories of Behaviors**

*Instructional behaviors*—behaviors that adults use in response to a child's actions in the context of the early childhood curriculum.

*Management behaviors*—adult responses to a child's actions that appear in the context of the program management. Within the instructional and management mode, teacher behaviors are further categorized as follows:

*Stop*: The adult halts or limits a child's actions, verbally or nonverbally.

*Change*: The adult redirects the child, through verbal means, directions, or materials, to a new activity or behavior.

*Sustain*: The adult makes a neutral comment or a brief response or participates without influence.

*Extend*: The adult extends or expands a child's activities through such actions as giving information, challenging, adding new materials.

*Procedure*: The focus of the observation is interactive behavior, including the child's initiation and the adult's response. The adult's response to the child's behavior is coded. A teacher's behavior is coded as instructional or managerial. Within that mode, the behaviors are identified as stops, changes, sustains, or extends.

*Source:* Carol Keyes, *A Descriptive Study of Campus Child Care Centers in the New York Metropolitan Area.* Ph.D. dissertation, Union Graduate School, 1980.

**FIGURE 5.4**  Sample Summary Form

Date:_____        **Person Observed:**

Time:_____        _____

Recorder:_____

|            | Sustain | | Extend | | Change | | Stop | | Total | | % |
|------------|---|---|---|---|---|---|---|---|---|---|---|
| Instruct   |   |   |   |   |   |   |   |   |   |   |   |
| Manage     |   |   |   |   |   |   |   |   |   |   |   |
| Totals     |   |   |   |   |   |   |   |   |   |   |   |
| Percentage |   |   |   |   |   |   |   |   |   |   |   |

based on the assumptions that teaching involves behaviors and that these behaviors can be understood and controlled by the teacher. Instructional improvement can then be achieved by teachers' controlling and modifying some of their own behaviors. One procedure for collecting observation data is to take 5-minute samples of teacher behavior over a period of time and then summarize the data on a form such as that shown in Figure 5.4.

### Clinical Supervision

A director can observe teachers' behaviors and determine the match between these behaviors and the center's theoretical orientation. For example, in a classroom oriented toward child development, a teacher would be expected to demonstrate considerable sustaining behavior toward a child's activities and actions. There might be some change or stop behaviors when one child interferes with another. There would be little extension of activities.

In a classroom based on behaviorist theory, a teacher would be expected to demonstrate considerable sustaining behaviors in regard to approved behavior by the child. A teacher may also use stops and changes to shape a child to a certain target behavior and then sustain closer approximations. Extending behaviors on the part of the teacher in this type of class would take the form of didactic instruction.

In a classroom based on cognitive theory, the teacher is committed to sustaining a child's curiosity and inventiveness and extending his interest into other challenging areas.

In a classroom with a psychosocial orientation, a teacher would exhibit a variety of behaviors, including many sustaining behaviors, stops and changes in response to conflicts, and some extending behaviors.

As a director collects data, she might find a teacher in a classroom with a cognitive orientation continually stopping and changing children and using no sustaining or extending behaviors. In that case, a director–teacher meeting would be appropriate to discuss modifying the teacher's behaviors to make a better match between orientation and behavior.

In the same way, the category system can be used to keep track of a match between stated goals and actual practices. If a teacher wants to encourage positive self-concept but her behavior in response to the children includes 50 percent changing and stopping behaviors and no extending behaviors, she might question whether her behaviors are supportive of developing a positive self-concept. A teacher whose goal is to encourage independent and creative children and whose behavior includes 80 percent instructional extending and sustaining behaviors would have reason to believe that her practices are matching her goals.

Systematic observation by the category system can also help in evaluating which activities in a center promote the most instructional behavior and the least management on the part of the teachers. It is also useful for assessing how well a teacher is meeting the goals for individual children.

If a teacher finds that she is continually stopping a child, she should try to discover what the child has actually been trying to do. Next, she should try to find ways to be supportive of the child's efforts where appropriate and possible. The basic question for a teacher in such a situation is, "What can I do to enable the children to do what they want in an acceptable way?"

In our day care center, for example, a teacher was continually stopping the children from dumping sand out of the sandbox. They would fill up a pail and empty it outside the sandbox. In consultation, we hypothesized that the children would like to empty the sand somewhere other than in the sandbox. What could the teacher do? We decided to provide a barrel; the children then poured the sand into the pail and emptied it into the barrel.

There is no right or wrong amount of one kind of behavior in our system. All adult behaviors may be appropriate within a system, depending on the stated goals and objectives. However, in a center where teachers exhibit many stopping and changing behaviors at the end of the year, it seems appropriate to question the management design of the center. For example, if a center is aiming at optimum development of children, then rules and management policies should be set up early in the year in ways that both children and adults understand. If the policies are successful, the management behaviors at the end of the year would reflect more sustaining or extending behaviors than stopping and changing behaviors.

The category system described in Figure 5.3 was used during a day care training project. The system was introduced to the teachers, assistant teachers, and aides in the classroom. In exploring the use of the system with the staff, we found that using only the four terms *stop, change, sustain,* and *extend* to keep track of their own behavior worked out well. The teachers had a set of common terms to use that were familiar and easy to keep in mind. At first, the consultants observed, tallied their responses, and raised questions based on collected samples of similar behavior, without singling out any one individual. As the center became more interested in using the system two sets of guidelines were developed (Figures 5.5 and 5.6). The guidelines help in organizing the systematic observations and using the results in the planning process.

**FIGURE 5.5** Guidelines for Decisions Needed in Planning Activities

*Management*
How does the activity begin?
How many children can engage in the activity at one time?
What are the guidelines for behavior for this activity?
How long can someone perform this activity?
How does the activity end?
What does the child do next?

*Curriculum*
What is the goal of the activity?
Is that goal appropriate for the age of the children with whom you are working?

**FIGURE 5.5** *(continued)*

What kinds of questions will you ask while the children are playing to sustain and extend their involvement?

What kinds of responses will you give to their questions to sustain and extend their activity?

How will you participate in the activity?

*Evaluation*

Were the children involved in the activity?

How long did they perform the activity?

Did they perform the activity *after* you left?

Did you think of new ideas for their play at that activity?

**Guidelines for Monitoring Your Own Behavior in Response to the Children**

During the activity, how did you behave in response to the children's behavior? Did you stop, change, extend, or sustain the children's behavior and/or actions?

*Stop*: The adult stops, halts, or limits a child's actions, verbally or nonverbally.

*Change*: The adult redirects a child's behavior to a new activity or behavior, through verbal means, directions, or materials.

*Extend*: The adult extends or expands a child's activities through such actions as giving information, challenging, adding new materials.

*Sustain*: The adult sustains a child's involvement by making a neutral comment or a brief response or participates without influence.

*Source*: Originally created in the Queens College Title XX Day Care Project, 1981.

**FIGURE 5.6**  Analyzing Adult Responses to Children's Behavior

| **Stopping and Changing Behaviors** | | **Sustaining and Extending Behaviors** | |
|---|---|---|---|
| *Describe* | Keep track of your behavior with the children so that you can analyze it at the first free moment. | *Describe* | Keep track of your behaviors in response to the children. |
| *Analyze* | Identify the areas and/or children with whom you are exhibiting a great deal of stopping and changing behavior. | *Analyze* | Identify the areas in which you are exhibiting sustaining and extending behaviors. |
| *Reflect* | Think about how else you could plan that time or that interaction with the children in terms of the developmental level of the children and and the values in the center. | *Reflect* | Consider those areas as the times and/or children with whom you are accomplishing your stated aims. |
| | | *Project* | Plan to increase your sustaining and extending responses to other areas. |
| *Act* | Make a change. | *Act* | Make a change. |
| *Describe* | Keep track of your behavior in response to the children to see if there are now fewer stops and changes. | *Describe* | Keep track of your responses to the children to see there are now more sustaining and extending behaviors. |

The teachers in the day care project were comfortable with the category system. Once they had practiced with the system for a while, the directors and consultants went around to the classrooms to try out the system as a method of on-site staff development. The directors had some useful questions regarding criteria; they wondered if there was a right or wrong amount for a category. The responses to such questions are contextual. For example, there might be more management stop and change behaviors in a center early in the year, as the teachers encounter new children. If the goal is to have children develop independence in movement and choice in the room, the teachers should inform the children about ways of doing things and design procedures whereby the children can manage for themselves. In this way, the stops and changes will be reduced. The guidelines shown in Figure 5.7 were prepared for use by directors.

**FIGURE 5.7** How to Use Systematic Observation and Categories for Describing Adults' Responses to Children's Behavior (for Staff Development)

1. *Uses*
   a. To assess the degree to which teachers support children's involvement.
   b. To examine the effectiveness of a management design.
   c. To assess the degree to which children meet teachers' expectations.
   d. To analyze the quality of interaction according to developmental principles and the values of the center.
2. *Initial Staff Development Session*
   Before beginning data collection, discuss the reasons for the observation and data collection with your staff.
   a. Review the goals of the center.
   b. Review the training sessions and the goals of the teachers in relation to the described system. (In the centers, the teachers agreed that they were working toward increasing their ability to sustain the children's involvement and extend the children's behavior or change their activities.)
   c. Review the definitions of the categories.
   d. Review how the teachers can monitor their own responses.
   e. Invite the teachers to use the system to see where they are succeeding and where they have problems.
   f. Discuss the plan to collect general data randomly and then to proceed to chosen times and areas with specific teachers.
3. *Observation Procedures*
   a. Observe each adult for five minutes in the classroom.
   b. Tally the adults' responses to the children's behavior, using the described categories and prepared forms.
      (1) *Stop:* The adult stops, halts, or limits a child's actions, verbally or nonverbally.

**FIGURE 5.7** *(continued)*

    (2) *Change*: The adult redirects a child's activity or behavior to a new activity, through verbal means, directions, or materials.

    (3) *Extend*: The adult extends or expands a child's activities through such actions as giving information, challenging, and adding new materials.

    (4) *Sustain*: The adult sustains a child's involvement by making a neutral comment or a brief response or participates without influence.

  c. The rhythm of the system is as follows:

    (1) Child behaves, adult responds

    (2) Child behaves, adult responds

    (3) Each time the child behaves and the adult responds, it is a new teacher behavior.

4. *Observation*

  a. Begin with brief contextual notes that reflect the time, day, setting, and activity.

  b. Collect baseline data on all the adults in the center.

  c. Count the number of scores in each category and the total number of interactions for each adult.

  d. Find what percentage each category is of the total number of interactions for each adult.

  e. Do a summary of the center as a whole. Total the number of interactions of each kind in the center and find its percentage of the whole.

  f. Summarize the data for numbers and kinds of interactions (how many sustains, stops, extends, and changes) and find what percentage of the whole each category is.

5. *Staff Development Session*

  a. Report to the staff your general findings on the numbers and kinds of interactions, the average number of interactions, the low and high numbers of interactions, and the percentage of each category.

  b. Relate the discussion to the following:

    (1) Is an activity appropriate for the developmental level of the children in the room?

    (2) Is an activity appropriate for the goals and objectives of the class and the center?

  c. Emphasize the need for a match between adult responses, the developmental level of the children in the room, and the goals of the center.

  d. With the staff members, plan the areas of the program that they would like to assess.

6. *Observation*

  a. Observe the same area/program or kinds of children in all of the rooms to promote common staff development through interaction on related topics.

  b. Observe the numbers and kinds of interactions specific to the activity and/or routine.

  c. Summarize the data in terms of numbers of each category and percentage of the whole, as well as numbers of interactions.

  d. Examine the distribution in terms of questions to raise with the staff.

7. *Staff Development Session*

  a. Report to the staff the areas and/or times in which there are many more sustaining and extending responses to children's behavior.

    b. Report to the staff the times and activities in which there are many stopping and changing responses to children's behavior.

    c. Report to the staff the times when there are minimum or maximum numbers of interactions and the average number of interactions.

    d. Raise questions regarding adult responses to children's behavior: whether they are appropriate for the developmental level of the children in the room, whether they are appropriate for the goals and objectives of the class and the center?

    e. Plan alternative strategies for the time, for the curriculum, and for the children.

8. *Follow-up to Staff Development Sessions*

    a. Teachers implement new strategies or changes.

    b. Director observes again to see the results of the alternative strategies.

    c. Procedure is repeated for each new topic.

*Source:* Originally created in the Queens College Title XX Day Care Project, 1981.

## STAFF MANUAL

Another means of staff development is a staff manual, which serves as a written reminder of activities that need to be accomplished by the staff in the center. The manual states the responsibilities of each staff member in very explicit terms. The most useful kind of manual is organic—a document in process. Our center has already revised its manual twice, as we grow in goals, objectives, and design. A staff manual should cover the following activities, which are both informational and attitudinal:

Director's perceptions of how staff members should function

Perceptions of an assistant at the center

First days with the children

Quick references regarding bills, messages, curriculum, organization, children, cleaning, conversations

Description of functions—early morning, midday, entering, midday leaving, end of day

Important items related to children, curriculum approach, outside activities, bathroom, transitions, routines, emergencies, releasing children, reminders for adults

Job descriptions

Job tasks

Description of special task assignments, registration packet form, curriculum forms, attendance forms, emergency clothes, storeroom shopping and inventory, condition of toys, replacement of forms, bulletin boards, newsletter, bills

Daily check-out duties
Hiring and salary information
Staff evaluation of center

### Preparation of a Bilingual Handbook

Sometimes staff development needs emerge during the school year. For example, during the past year, two new children entered one of our classes—one who spoke only Spanish and another who spoke only Japanese. The staff was not having much success with verbal communication with these children. Bilingual dictionaries were available, but they did not have the phrases the staff needed. To remedy the situation, the staff members began to write down phrases they used often but did not know in Spanish or in Japanese. A bilingual parent of another child in the class began to translate the phrases that would become part of the staff manual into Spanish; and a professor and his son who were participants in the center and who had just returned from Japan translated phrases into Japanese. The translated phrases included the following:

1. He is taking his turn right row.
2. You will have a turn when he is finished.
3. It's time for the children who are outside to go inside.
4. He would like to do it himself.
5. Tell me in English.

## MONITORING AND EVALUATING
## TEACHER EFFECTIVENESS

Since teachers are central to any effort in the classroom, several approaches have been developed to assess teacher competency. We have found that the Child Development Associate (CDA) criteria are very useful. The CDA credential was established to help improve the quality of care of young children in early childhood centers. The credential is a professional certification that a person is competent to work with children aged 3 to 5 years in a group setting. The formal definition of a Child Development Associate "is a person able to meet the specific needs of a group of children in a child development setting by nurturing children's physical, social, emotional and intellectual growth, by establishing and maintaining a proper child care environment, and by promoting good relations between parents and the child development center" (Grossman and Keyes 1978, p. 182).

The CDA criteria can be the basis for a formal external evaluation or for a self-assessment procedure that a center can develop. To be awarded the CDA credential, a teacher must be found competent in six different competencies with thirteen functional areas. The six competency areas are defined as follows: "establishes and maintains a safe and healthy learning environment, advances physical and intellectual competence, builds positive self-concept and individual strength, promotes positive functioning of children and adults in a group, brings about optimal coordination of home and center child rearing practices and expectations and carries out supplementary responsibilities related to the children's program."

The CDA system is useful as a self-assessment procedure. Staff members in a center can develop a list of indicators and can assess themselves on their competency in meeting the criteria. Are hazardous items stored out of reach of children? Are toys all in good repair? Are the safety rules in the classroom aimed at having children move about without interfering with each other?

Goldman and Anglin (1979) describe a teacher-evaluating system that is based on anthropological methods. In visiting a classroom, if the director saw on the bulletin boards children's artwork that included a few string paintings, a collage with styrofoam, some eyedrop paintings, tie-dyed paper towels, and daisy chains, she could infer that the teacher was giving the children a variety of experiences. A different interpretation might follow if the bulletin boards displayed fifteen Christmas trees, all cut out alike and with the same stickers, even if they were done by different children. Perhaps this second teacher needs some instruction on allowing children to produce their own artwork.

### Staff Self-Evaluation

As noted in our discussion of the CDA criteria, self-evaluation is a very important part of teacher development. Teachers should be encouraged to engage in self-monitoring and in evaluation of the center's functioning in relation to their own performance, rather than relying exclusively on the director's perceptions and initiative. Figure 5.8 is a sample teacher self-evaluation form that can be used to encourage and record this evaluation process.

The staff member begins by assessing her personal growth. Then the staff member is expected to consider her part in the center's operation. For example, in one center, a staff member

**FIGURE 5.8**  Sample Staff Self-Evaluation Form

What did you hope to gain from your experience at the child care center?

Were your goals met? How?

Please list any suggestions you have for improving the child care center:

1. *Staff*

2. *Children*

3. *Parents*

4. *Other* (administrative, custodial, etc.)

concluded that the assistants in the center seemed to need additional orientation to administrative details to be able to answer parents' questions properly. This teacher also suggested that the assistants could benefit from an outline of all activities available to the children, especially during transitional and free-choice periods.


## Suggested Activities

1.  Prepare a survey to investigate topics a center staff would be interested in for in-service training.
2.  Ask teachers and directors to tell you their philosophy of the center. Use a tape recorder or take very accurate notes.
3.  Learn the terms in the systematic observation described in this chapter and analyze your own behavior at a particular point in the school day.


## References and Further Readings

Biber, Barbara; Shapiro, Edna; and Wickins, David; in collaboration with Elizabeth Gilkeson. *Promoting Cognitive Growth and Developmental Interaction, Point of View.* Washington, D.C.: National Association for the Education of Young Children, 1971.

Bronfenbrenner, U. "The Changing American Family." In Barry Persky and Leonard Golubuchick, eds., *Early Childhood.* Wayne, N.J.: Avery, 1977.

Brown, Janet, ed. *Curriculum Planning for Young Children.* Washington, D.C.: National Association for the Education of Young Children, 1982.

Child Development Association Consortium. *Local Assessment Team Guidelines.* Washington, D.C.: Child Development Association, 1975.

Cogan, Morris. *Clinical Supervision.* Boston: Houghton Mifflin, 1973.

Collins, Raymond C. "Child Care and the States: The Comparative Licensing Study." *Young Children* 38(5), July 1983, 3–11.

Committee for Early Childhood. "The Fundamental Learning Needs of Today's Young Children." In Dorothy Hewes, ed.,

*Administration: Making Programs Work for Children and Families.* Washington, D.C.: National Association for the Education of Young Children, 1975.

Day, Mary Carol, and Parker, Ronald K., eds. *The Preschool in Action: Exploring Early Childhood Programs,* 2nd ed. Boston: Allyn and Bacon, 1977.

Evans, Ellis. *Contemporary Influences in Early Childhood Education.* New York: Holt, Rinehart and Winston, 1975.

Forman, George, and Kuschner, Davis S. *The Child's Construction of Knowledge: Piaget for Teaching Children.* Monterey, Calif.: Brooks/Cole, 1977.

Fromberg, Doris. *Early Childhood Education: Perceptual Models of Curriculum.* New York: Wiley, 1977.

Goldman, Richard, and Anglin, Leo. "Evaluating Your Caregivers: Four Observation Systems." *Day Care and Early Education,* Fall 1979, 40–41.

Grossman, Bruce D., and Keyes, Carol. *Helping Children Grow: The Adult's Role.* Wayne, N.J.: Avery, 1978.

Kammi, Constance, and Devries, Rheta. *Physical Knowledge in Preschool Education: Implications of Piaget's Theory.* Englewood Cliffs, N.J.: Prentice-Hall, 1978.

Katz, Lillian. *Talks with Teachers.* Washington, D.C.: National Association for the Education of Young Children, 1977.

Kenniston, Kenneth. *All Our Children: The American Family Under Pressure.* New York: Carnegie Corporation, 1977.

Keyes, Carol. *A Descriptive Study of Campus Child Care Centers in the New York Metropolitan Area,* Ph.D. dissertation, Union Graduate School, 1980.

Kostelnik, Majorie. "Practical Approach to Resolving Inter-Staff Conflict. *Child Care Information Exchange,* July/August 1982, 7.

National Day Care Study, Final Report, *Children at the Center: Executive Summary.* Cambridge, Mass.: Abt Associates, 1979.

Ruopp, R.; Tavers, J.; Glantz, F.; and Coelen, C. *Children at the Center: Summary Findings and Implications.* Final report of the National Day Care Study. Cambridge, Mass.: Abt Associates, 1979.

Schwartz, Sydney L., and Mott, Johanna K. *Some Guidelines for On-Site Staff Development Activities.* Queens College Title XX Day Care Project, September 1981.

Schwartz, Sydney L., and Robison, Helen R. *Designing Curriculum for Early Childhood.* Boston: Allyn and Bacon, 1982.

Seefeldt, Carol. *Curriculum for the Preschool Primary Child: A Review of the Research.* Columbus, Ohio: Merrill, 1976.

Spodek, Bernard, ed. *Teaching Practices: Reexamining Assumptions.* Washington, D.C.: National Association for the Education of Young Children, 1977.

Stalmack, Judith E. "S.W.A.P. Strategies Which Affect Programs: A Framework for Staff Development." *Young Children 36* (6), September 1981, 16–24.

Steinmetz, Lawrence J. "Managing the Marginal Performer." *Child Care Information Exchange,* May 1981, 35.

Stengel, Susan. "The Preschool Curriculum: Integrating Process and Content." In Donald T. Streets, ed., *Administering Day Care and Preschool Programs.* Boston: Allyn and Bacon, 1982.

Streets, Donald T. *Administering Day Care and Preschool Programs.* Boston: Allyn and Bacon, 1982.

Wekart, Davis; Rogers, Linda; Adcock, Carolyn; and McClelland, Donna. *Cognitively Oriented Curriculum.* Washington, D.C.: National Association for the Education of Young Children, 1974.

Wilhelms, Fred. *Supervision in a New Key.* Washington, D.C.: Association for Supervision and Child Development, 1973.

Ziegler, Edward. "The Unmet Needs of America's Children." *Children Today,* May/June 1976, 39–43.

# Chapter 6
# The Humanistic
# Administrator
# and the Children

As we noted earlier, it is possible, in your zeal to operate your center efficiently, to temporarily lose sight of the focal point of its purpose: the children and their families. As a director, your humanism should be apparent from your very first contacts with the child—the application and enrollment process and the child's preparation for introduction into the classroom. Of course, this same child-oriented attitude should be evident in every aspect of your administrative work, from ordering supplies to balancing the budget. It is not just the curriculum that determines a quality program. The setting, the implementation, the overall philosophy, and the emotional and intellectual climate of a school all should reflect your commitment to children.

You might ask how an early childhood program can have a commitment *other* than to children? Some programs find that the needs of parents (including scheduling), the children's projects, and even the program goals may have priority over what might be most beneficial for the children themselves. Similarly, the needs of the staff—how they feel in the classroom and the kinds of activities they pursue with the children—may sometimes take precedence over the children's needs. For example, to accommodate staff needs, there may be too many changes of personnel during the school day. In some cases, certain classroom activities are not allowed because they are too messy or require too much storage space or too much effort on the part of the staff or administration, even though it would be more worthwhile to deal with the clean-up or other problems in some way to provide a more academically sound program for the children.

## ENROLLING THE CHILDREN

Most early childhood programs have some form of periodic public notice about the nature and availability of their program. In some small communities, word of mouth—particularly by parents whose children are already in attendance—may be sufficient to fully enroll the center. You may have to use more elaborate recruiting devices (see Chapter 1).

The time for recruitment and enrollment varies with the kind of early childhood program. Some school schedules allow for enrollment of children only in September. In that case, recruitment is a spring project so that classes can be formed for the fall. Other schools have both fall and spring terms. If you have a flexibly scheduled early childhood program, such as that on a college campus or in a day care situation, you may have continuous enrollment based on space available throughout the year, in addition to renewed enrollment at the beginning of each school year.

### Children's Visits to the School

Schools have varying policies regarding visits by children. In some cases, parents bring their children along when they are first choosing a center. Other times, the parents choose a center alone and then bring the children to see the school. Schools that enroll children once a year often have a June visiting time for groups of new children. Then, in September, they may again arrange short visits to help new children get oriented to school. Some centers invite parents and children, a few at a time, to visit during regular sessions, particularly when a program has continuous enrollment. At our campus program, all parents and children have to visit at least once, and often more, before the children can attend without their parents. We believe that the children should have time before they begin, with their parents present, to become acquainted with the children, the adults, and the place where they will be left.

Sometimes, parents object to the preliminary visits because they think you are examining their child. They need reassurance that the visits are for the child's benefit and that they usually facilitate his later adjustment. Parents who are concerned about their children being judged or evaluated are often parents who will need help later on. Other parents object to the preliminary visits because their children have had prior experience in other schools or staying with different people, and the parents believe the children will have no problems adjusting. We have found that children's visits are helpful whether or not the children have had prior experience, since each new place represents a whole new set of experiences.

The child's visit to the school during the enrollment process serves several purposes. Most important, it gives the child an opportunity to explore and get acquainted before his actual admission. It also gives you an idea about any separation problems that might be forthcoming. It gives the staff members an opportunity to observe the child in a classroom setting, reacting to the materials and interacting with the children and adults. It might also give you some ideas about the level of class or type of teacher to assign to the child. In some cases, it will provide you with a more realistic picture of the child than a parent's description would give.

For the child, getting acquainted may involve several stages:

He sits on his parent's lap and watches.
He leaves his coat on while he plays.
He takes his parent around.
He leaves the adults and begins to play.

Parents often need help at these visiting sessions. They have expectations or concerns about how their children will act. A director or teacher can be helpful to the parent by describing the range of behavior that a child may display when looking over a school, explaining that some children watch from their mother's lap; some hang onto their mother's skirt; some move away but turn around every minute to be sure the parent is still there; some take their mothers around the room with them; and some push and shove other children. Only the last behavior is cause for concern, because it has to be controlled. The others are ways a child gets to know a new setting. We have found that if we describe these potential behaviors to parents beforehand, they are much more able to accept whatever behavior their child displays.

Some parents may need help in getting their children to leave the center after a visit. Sometimes a director or teacher will have to gently steer the parent and child outside to help them end their visit and go home. Timing a visit toward the end of a session, when all the children will be leaving, could be helpful in terminating the visit.

### Placing a Child in a Class

It is best to place a child in a class where there are some other children at the same developmental level and where the curriculum is geared to that level. Realistically, however, other factors often need to be taken into account. Sometimes you may place a child in a particular class because you think the teacher might meet that child's special needs. For example, you might place a child with no father with a male teacher or a Spanish child with a bilingual teacher. A child may also be put into one class or another because of the hours of a session. If your classes are arranged heterogeneously, scheduling by hours becomes easier. We have had great success with multiage grouping, which, aside from allowing for more flexible scheduling, provides a range of experiences and interactions that are challenging and stimulating to the children.

### Parent-Child Separation

Despite having had a few visits, some children or parents may still hesitate about the parent's leaving. We have found that, more often than not, it is the parent, not the child, who has these anxieties. The problem becomes apparent in a variety of ways; a parent might say, "I'll stay five more minutes" or "Just one more story" or "Aren't you going to give me a kiss?" Parents often have ambivalent feelings about leaving their children, especially if it's the first time or if there has been a great deal of negative pressure from home. An unspoken concern seems to be that their children won't miss them, which means to them that they haven't been good parents. Some parents will even resort to saying, "Didn't you miss me?" or "I won't be gone too long." It's up to the staff to help parents come in, spend a few minutes, and then leave, reassuring them by saying, "We will call you if there is really a problem."

Some children make the initial separation adjustment very easily but experience a problem several weeks later. An incident at home may trigger the problem: a fire, a loss, a change in the family schedule, a divorce, or a parent getting a new job. It may be that they suddenly realize more clearly that even though they like this place, mother leaves when they come here. A brief series of shared visits and short separations often helps a child readjust fairly quickly.

## IDENTIFYING THE NEEDS OF THE CHILDREN

The task of integrating each child's needs into an educational plan, implementing that plan, and evaluating its effectiveness is a serious undertaking that the director shares with the child. We have outlined here some of the needs of young children that we consider must be satisfied in our program design. There may be others that you would add to the list.

### Psychological Safety

Young children are naturally dependent. They begin life in a totally helpless condition but become more secure as they develop. They learn that other people will help them (dependence), and they gradually develop their ability to help themselves (independence). If children are going to develop a sense of independence, they need to feel secure that if something happens (e.g., they fall down, get lost, or get hurt), someone will help them. Throughout a child's development there is a balance between independence and dependence.

In an early childhood classroom, it is likely that you will observe many signs of insecurity, such as the fear of separating from the parents. Even as you provide a safe environment for that child, he may be wondering whether he still has the support of the adults at home. This may be especially true if the mother is now off to a job, if the parents have recently separated, or if there is a new baby in the family. There are many other examples of insecurity, of course. Children may be wondering about the safety of this new environment and about their own competence if they show an initial reluctance to participate. Some children need much more reassurance than others.

Such insecurity in a child may be a frustrating experience for a teacher who has been trying her best. This is a situation in which help from a supportive director is especially useful.

### Feelings of Self-Esteem

A child's feelings of self-esteem are intimately connected to his feelings of security. It has been demonstrated in young animals (Harlow 1973) and in humans that the more secure toddlers, and even infants, tend to be most open and willing to explore. At first, self-esteem comes from being loved and cared for. Very soon, positive feedback comes to the child as he begins to acquire language, to crawl, to acknowledge others, and to complete small tasks. The child may be critized during this developmental process, too—perhaps for being too noisy or too demanding or for "getting into things." Which behaviors families encourage or discourage are often based on their culture or values. It is hoped, of course, that the positive feedback outweighs the negative and that the child develops feelings of self-worth. Although preschoolers are very dependent on the reactions of others to measure their self-worth, they also begin to evaluate for themselves how self-sufficient and competent they are becoming. As Virginia Satir (1972) points out in *People-Making*, helping children develop as high a level of self-esteem as possible is an important goal for parents and teachers. We do this by our praise, of course, and also by providing experiences that allow children to enlarge their competencies and to acquire feelings of personal satisfaction and success. It has generally been noted by psychologists (Rogers 1961) that an attitude of acceptance goes a long way toward enhancing a person's self-esteem, no matter what his age. By allowing children to be themselves and by helping parents to be more accepting, early childhood programs make a very valuable contribution to the child's developing personality.

## Experiencing Life as Worth Living

This attitude is not separate from the feelings just discussed. Security and self-esteem certainly go a long way toward building a zest for life, but the early group experience contributes to the child's positive outlook in other ways, too. In particular, a good early childhood program offers a child an opportunity to get involved. Being able to explore in a nonthreatening, stimulating atmosphere leads to a sense of excitement. Children in this situation develop a sense of adventure and an eagerness to encounter new experiences, which is essential to learning and creativity.

## Making Sense of the Environment

Young children are curious; they want to know. They naturally tend to explore their surroundings. Unfortunately, older children often seem to lose the urge to make sense of their environment. Perhaps we put too much pressure on them to accept things and not to ask too many questions.

We can encourage and facilitate the child's early urge to know about things. In fact, one of the major contributions an early childhood program can make to children's development is to help them in their natural quest to find order and meaning in the world around them. This support begins with taking their questions seriously. It also includes helping children sharpen their powers of observation, develop their ability to formulate questions, and pursue their exploration of the world and their relationship to it. The questions that children have about how things are made, what people do, what happens next, how things work, how things feel, and so forth, place them in the category of scientists and philosophers, as well as artists and artisans. It can be very exciting for you and your staff to share in their "construction of the world" (Piaget 1969).

## Being Surrounded by Adults Who Care

Adults who care contribute in a number of important ways to children's development. They not only support and accept, as noted earlier, but they also set limits, share feelings and experiences, and, perhaps most important, provide a model to imitate. Caring adults demonstrate a connection with the world, as opposed to isolation or alienation. We cannot expect our future generations to have a sense of community or a sense of concern for those who are older or younger than they are if we do not demonstrate this caring attitude ourselves.

### Being Surrounded by Adults Who Enjoy Learning

This is another important modeling process that teachers at any level should demonstrate but too often do not. Staff members should be selected on this basis and should be encouraged in every way possible to keep their excitement for learning alive. This means that they should not go through experiences in a routine way with children and that they should participate themselves in as many activities as are appropriate. This participation may mean singing, running, and block building at times. It should include sharing the excitement of exploring on a walk or seeing baby gerbils born. This type of excitement is infectious.

## DEVELOPMENTAL CONSIDERATIONS

The developmental needs of children are a central concern of the early childhood administrator. This may seem obvious, but we found that although most programs for young children emphasize this objective, many do not implement it in actual practice.

A developmentally oriented program is based on the notion that children go through several stages in their lives. It assumes the influence of maturation and of experience. This means that the classroom design, the curriculum materials, the staff, and the programs are all chosen with the developmental level of the children in mind.

Figure 6.1 presents an outline of some of the developmental needs of young children. We offer here some examples to demonstrate how these developmental principles relate to administrative decisions.

**FIGURE 6.1**  Some Developmental Needs of Young Children

*Physical needs*
  Activity
  Need to explore
  Fine motor coordination (generally lags behind large muscle development)
*Learning and thinking needs*
  Learning from their own activities
  Learning from experiences with concrete material
  Learning a great deal from imitation
  Dealing with short attention spans
*Emotional characteristics*
  Impatience
  Egocentricity
  Need for autonomy
  Need for dependence
  Easily frustrated
  Often fearful

## Young Children Are Generally Active

An administrative policy to support this developmental need would be to plan a well-designed outdoor period for each classroom, incorporating development of large motor skills and opportunities to be active. A related policy would be one that allows for planned substitute activities on rainy days.

It is important that the activities planned for the children allow some freedom of movement. Requiring children to sit still for more than 10 minutes at a time often frustrates young children and can create disciplinary problems.

Even the development of listening skills can be facilitated by accompanying movement. Classroom programs can be balanced so that activities that require some physical restraint, such as discussions or stories, are followed by activities that provide opportunities for large motor development for those children who require it. Dramatic play and woodworking would fall in the active category.

Sometimes centers, by their physical design, have areas that create a need for restriction. One center had a long hallway that seemed to invite children to run. Even in such circumstances, however, creative planning for the space allows children to be active in a way that is appropriate for center management.

In one center, the director and the teacher decided to encourage alternative kinds of movement at specific times. A creative
use of the space and a clear definition of the times to skip, jump,
run, and slide and the times to walk eliminated the previously
constant repetition of "No, don't run" by the staff.


### Young Children Like to Explore

Infants and toddlers exhibit exploratory needs, but the preschool period seems to be a particularly active exploratory time in
children's lives. Erikson (1950) refers to this period as the time of
autonomy and initiative. Increased mobility and a preliminary
sense of autonomy allow the young child to move forward by
taking a closer look at things. Children at this age like to experiment with such materials as paint, water, and clay. They are also
curious about how things work. This need is demonstrated in
physical activity, but it clearly contributes to intellectual growth.
It also affects children's emotional development, since they
acquire a sense of their competence and security as they learn
more about their environment and how to control it.

The combination of high activity and the tendency to touch
everything, to take things apart, and to play with things that may
be unsafe can present a dilemma for the administrator and for the
teacher. How do you strike a balance between a child's needs in
this regard, considerations of safety and discipline, a general
preservation of equipment and materials, and the rights of others?
This is not easy. We have found that the most positive solution is
to provide acceptable materials and opportunities for active
exploration. This makes whatever restrictions have to be imposed
more acceptable. It also helps the children learn to discriminate
between appropriate circumstances in which to do something and
inappropriate ones—for example, when running is all right, or
which things may be taken apart so that they can be reassembled.

Ideally, the children in your center will not need to stay
away from very many things in that setting. Be alert yourself and
remind others to note unnecessary restrictions. If "Don't touch"
or "Keep away" is heard very often, you should examine the situation to see whether your center needs some redesigning to make it
more accessible to children.

### Young Children Are Generally Impatient

Another physical fact that must be taken into account when planning for young children is that most children of this age find it difficult to wait. There are many reasons for this, including their preference for activity. A major reason for their apparent impatience is intellectual. A young child's subjective sense of time is different from an adult's; this is a cognitive difference, which makes a 5-minute wait seem more like a 30-minute delay to a child.

Still another reason why young children often have a hard time waiting is that their emotional capacity for delaying gratification is less well developed than it is in adults. This may make them appear demanding, but it is a natural characteristic for children at this age to find it difficult to wait for something without becoming impatient, especially when they want it very much. In designing schedules, these factors should be considered in planning for outdoor play, in multiclass settings, and in transition times. In some centers, the policy is for the teachers to have the children sit and wait for their lunches or snacks. Often, the snacks or lunches do not appear when they are scheduled. The result is a classroom full of children sitting at tables, hitting, kicking, and fighting, with the teachers continually saying, "No." and "Stop." The solution if possible, is to have the children sit down after the food has arrived.

There are times, of course, when children have to wait. How can you help them adjust to waiting and learn to extend their capacity to wait? If a delay is unavoidable, such as when the bus doesn't come or when they must wait in line, be prepared to introduce some songs or fingerplays. This makes the waiting time more bearable and it passes more quickly. In such situations, you could also recommend such games as "Simon Says" or even "Telephone" with older children.

### Young Children Learn a Great Deal from Imitation

This is a basic learning principle. It is well to keep in mind that your behavior and that of your staff is likely to have more impact on the children's learning than what any of you say to the children. Your behavior serves as a concrete representation for the children, and their imitative behavior is a form of active learning. In that sense, you serve as a model. Showing enthusiasm, concern, and courtesy is the best way to encourage similar behavior in children. As we point out in Chapter 5, this humanistic approach applies to administrator–staff relations as well. If, as an administrator, you treat your staff with respect, they are more likely to convey the same positive attitude to the children and the parents.

## MATCHING THE NEEDS OF CHILDREN WITH POLICY AND PROGRAM

What is unique about your center that demands special policies to meet children's needs? In designing your program, how can these policies be built into the program design? How does your schedule affect the children? Do children arrive at different times? Do the adults in your center change throughout the day, as in most day care centers? Do you have many volunteers or students who are not there regularly? How do you provide continuity across changes such as these? How do children fare when they enter and leave while activities are going on? How do they cope with different adults and their expectations in the center and then at home? In a campus center, for example, where children come in and out at different times and there is always a class full of children, it is very important that children are greeted when they arrive and said goodbye to when they leave. Consider how it would feel to walk into a room bustling with activity and have no one acknowledge your presence or orient you to what is going on.

Children are often uncomfortable about leaving when others are still playing, as in campus centers. This can be a disrupting experience for them, so procedures have been designed to help them cope with the situation. A procedure of "warning time" involves telling a child a few minutes before his parent is to come that he will be leaving soon and asking him if there is anything he needs to do before his parent comes. This helps him disengage and make a transition from play to the new activity of leaving the center. We discuss this policy with parents, so that if they come before warning time, they will stay a few minutes to give their child the separation time necessary to disengage from the activities.

As we develop such policies in response to programmatic needs, we post a statement of the policy on the bulletin board for parents and teachers. Reminders may also be offered in parents' meetings and by letters or phone calls, if necessary.

The need for special policies is often discovered in the process of developing as a center. For example, a child came to our campus child care center one summer after having attended the previous fall and spring semesters. On the first day of the session, he almost refused to come in. He knew the room, but all the adults and children were different. He had not been told that a new registration occurs each semester and that the adults and children might change.

Where there is a high attrition rate, the problem of a changing teacher population or a changing population of children needs to be addressed. A teacher in one center questioned how she could deal with what she called the "disappearing children." Children can accept such changes, but they need preparation. We have developed a formal goodbye ritual to help children cope with the loss of adults and children to whom they have become attached. We tell everybody that the period has ended and that when they come back, there will be the same room but some of the children and adults might be different.

A unique feature of day care centers is the length of time the children stay. In such centers, it is important to vary the children's activities, to allow them to go on errands, and to hold several sessions outside. It is also necessary to be alert to their eating patterns and to remind them to go to the bathroom.

### Multiage Centers and the Developmental Needs of Children

Multiage grouping allows children to move back and forth on a growth continuum in terms of behavior. Children can watch and play with others who are just a little ahead of them in learning skills. The older children often serve as models for the younger children and provide an impetus to try the higher-level skills.

Children also like the opportunity to play with children who are a little younger, allowing them to act a little younger and repeat some earlier levels of behavior and action. As peers, they can teach and learn from each other. At our center, for example, we often ask a child who can open and close his Thermos bottle to help another child who is having trouble with his. During outdoor play, we showed one child how to use a wagon and then had that child show others. Instead of having adults pull children in the wagon, we encourage the children to pull each other. This does not mean that the adults should not interact with the children. We are referring to policies in response to multiage grouping, which can enhance the value of the interactions between children of varied ages and varied skills.

### Identifying the Characteristics of the Children Who Come to Your Program

What is the enrollment pattern of the children who come to your center? In some centers, the population may be relatively stable; in others, some children come for a few days and some for many days. Also, the ages and lengths of experience at the center may vary considerably. Children who are new need to learn the rules, learn about materials, and learn the other children's names. Children who also go to another school may simply need unstructured opportunities to play and relax.

In our center, we have developed a chart describing each child's enrollment pattern that the adults in the room can see at a glance when they are working with that child. On the sample chart shown in Figure 6.2, you can see that Charles A. comes to the center 5 days a week, attends 3 hours or less, attends another school, is 5 years old, has attended school before, and has a special need. The totals at the bottom of the chart tell us how many children are in each category. The special need column may refer to a physical disability, a language problem, or a family situation, such as a death in the family.

Other characteristics that have a bearing on a child's behavior include family composition (single parent or two parents), whether both parents work, siblings, other relatives in the house, and so forth.

**FIGURE 6.2  Sample Enrollment Pattern Chart**

| | 2 Days/Wk. | 3 Days/Wk. | 4 Days/Wk. | 5 Days/Wk. | Attends 3 Hrs. or Less | Attends 4 Hrs. or More | Attends Another School | Short-Term | 2½ Yrs. Old. | 3 Yrs. Old | 3½ Yrs. Old | 4 Yrs. Old | 5 Yrs. Old | 6 Yrs. Old | New Child | Attended Before | Special Need |
|---|---|---|---|---|---|---|---|---|---|---|---|---|---|---|---|---|---|
| Charles A. | | | | × | × | | × | | | | | | × | | | × | × |
| Joseph A. | | × | | | × | | | | | × | | | | | | × | |
| Shawn B. | | | × | | | × | | | | | | × | | | | × | |
| Jessica B. | × | | | | | | | | | × | | | | | × | | |
| David B. | | × | | | × | | × | | | | | | | × | × | | × |
| Emily C. | | | | × | | × | | | | | | | × | | | × | |
| Vanessa D. | | | | × | | | | | | × | | | | | × | | × |
| Brett D. | × | | | | × | | | | | × | | | | | × | | |
| Kelly G. | × | | | | × | | | | | × | | | | | × | | |
| Joey H. | | | × | | | × | | | | × | | | | | | × | |
| Lenore H. | × | | | | | × | | | × | | | | | | × | | |
| Emily K. | × | | | | × | | | | | × | | | | | × | | |
| *Totals* | 5 | 2 | 2 | 3 | 6 | 4 | 2 | 0 | 1 | 7 | 0 | 1 | 2 | 1 | 7 | 5 | 3 |

## Supporting Children's Individual Requests

A humanistic center is one where children's individual requests are supported, even if there must be a delay in implementation. Sometimes, teachers have to be guided toward this policy. For example, if a child decides he wants to use the record player but it is impossible to honor the request at that time, our policy has been to write on the plans for the next day that this child is coming and that he wants to use the record player. Sometimes a child might want to have some food that another child has brought for lunch. Although the policy of our child care center prohibits sharing of food (because we don't always know the children's allergies or cultural or dietary considerations), we would write a note to the parent, such as "James likes potato chips and would like to bring some for lunch."

## Monitoring Responses to Children's Needs

Sometimes, through its policy or through the behavior of one of the adults, a center inadvertently interferes with the natural pursuits of children. Children often undergo experiences that might be interpreted as disruptive or as interfering with the natural pursuits of their own desires. Jackson and Wolfons (1968) studied the constraints that exist in nursery schools. The following are the categories that were coded in their study:

*Desire versus desire*—Two children are struggling over the ownership of a toy.

*Desire versus inability*—The child cannot lift an object because it is heavy.

*Desire versus clutter*—The child is jostled by others.

*Desire versus environmental limitations*—The child wants more juice but there is no more.

*Desire versus instructional restrictions*—The child has to stop an activity because his bus is ready to go.

*Desire versus teacher expectations*—The child leaves the block area after coaxing the teacher to come and sing.

*Desire versus teacher overlook*—The teacher does not respond to a call for help.

One example from the study described a child who was in-volved in coloring at a table. The teacher came by and said, "Look at all the crayons under your chair. Clean up the crayons under your chair." By her actions, the teacher intruded on the child's involvement. What else could the teacher have done? She could have waited until he was finished, picked up the crayons herself, or asked the child to pick up the crayons when he was finished.

The results of this study indicate that children suffer con-straints about every five minutes. Even in nursery school, which is supposed to be a place where children enjoy going, people inter-fere with one another's activities most of the time.

Are we suggesting that life should be interference-free? No, but we are saying that some of these interferences to exploration, learning, and growth are within our control and that some of the constraints children suffer (e.g., unnecessary waiting and restric-tions on movement) may be imposed at an earlier point develop-mentally than is useful.

We particularly feel that desire versus teacher expectations and desire versus teacher overlook are interferences that teachers should control. In the chapter on staff development (Chapter 5), we described a technique for monitoring teacher response to a child's behavior that might be useful in helping teachers reduce some of their unnecessary interferences.

### Identifying Needs According to a Child's Daily Experiences

An important part of identifying children's needs is knowing something about the part of the day they are not with us. How many adults take care of the children over the course of the day? In how many places do they stay? Do they have friends? Do they spend the majority of their time in front of the television set? What happens before they get to the center? What happens when they return home from school? Is there a pleasant transition from home to school and from school to home?

We did an exploratory pilot study of how children spend their time before and after school (Keyes and Grossman 1979). We wanted to look at the experiences children encountered as they moved between the two settings—their own family setting and the center. How did the experiences at home and center flow into one another? What were the transitions like in terms of what happened before and after a child's attendance at school? To what extent were the values, expectations, and behavioral styles of the parents and caregivers congruent or incongruent?

With answers to these questions, we believed we would be better able to identify and meet children's needs in our center. We would become more alert to promoting consistency among adults and more attentive to teaching children about differences in adult expectations. In our study, each child's family was observed for at least 1 hour before the child was regularly scheduled to attend school. One of us then accompanied the child and parent to the school and noted the entrance to school. When the child was due to leave the center, the observer accompanied the parent and child on the usual after-school routine (e.g., supermarket, cafeteria, home) for an hour.

The flow between home and school was generally smooth. The period before coming to the center was characterized, in most cases, by management tasks in preparation for coming to school. This was somewhat affected by the time the child was scheduled to begin school. When school was scheduled for early in the morning, the period preceding was largely devoted to breakfast, dressing, and watching television. The children scheduled to go to school later had a little more time to become involved in household activities and play. The before-school time was relatively low in interaction and enrichment play and in affective exchange between parents and child.

There were extreme variations in level and style of interaction. At one extreme was a mother who spent the hour before school reminding the child to eat breakfast and get dressed while she was getting dressed. She periodically cautioned, "There is no time." Ignoring the mother's requests, the child stood mesmerized in front of the TV, his fork down by his side and his pancakes lying uneaten before him. Eventually, he did join his mother and they finished dressing together. At the other extreme was a girl who spent most of the hour before school with her father, working on a project. She did not enjoy being interrupted for brushing her teeth or putting on her shoes. Her mother was most effective in helping her accept the interruption and anticipate school. In another instance, a mother whose child had been playing independently in his room, with occasional conversations with her, had a very difficult time getting him to clean up and get dressed for school.

There are also patterns of dealing with separation from the parents at the center that are important for teachers to recognize. Some children rush into an activity or join particular friends immediately. Others hang onto their mothers for "just one more minute" or "one more kiss." Still others look around before getting involved or wait for the teacher to tell them about the activities.

In our study, despite what generally seemed to be a smooth transition, a close look revealed some degree of disruption in the children's activities before and after school. Consistent with the observations of Jackson and Wolfons (1968)—that nursery school children experience a variety of constraints and disruptions in a classroom setting—the disruptions we noted at home tended to be relatively minor but cumulative. Sometimes the disruptions noted did not have to do with preparing for school, but to the degree that these disruptions were distressing to the child, they were likely to contribute to his behavior at school.

As directors and teachers, we may not always sufficiently take into account the variability with which our students enter the class. However, this should be considered another way of responding to children's individual needs.

## EVALUATING THE CHILDREN'S PROGRESS

Evaluating the children is primarily the responsibility of the classroom teacher. The director may contribute directly, through observation and testing, or by advising staff about the available evaluation techniques. These techniques include anecdotal records, clinical observations, standardized tests, criterion reference tests, and naturalistic observations. Although all of these are useful ways to assess the changes in children's behavior that might be evidence of growth, program effectiveness, or a problem needing special attention, they all have their limitations, too. For that reason, it is good to be aware of and use a variety of evaluation approaches. Several books listed in the references at the end of this chapter are good resources for this topic. We outline here in some detail the evaluative method referred to as *systematic observation*.

### Principles of Systematic Observation

Keeping records of the children's behavior provides documentation of their functioning. It helps us understand each child by identifying areas of strength and weakness, learning styles, personality characteristics, and preferences. Detailed observations may be used to describe and record changes in children's behavior in response to changes in teachers' behavior or simply as a function of the children's participation in a program over a period of time.

As several studies have shown (e.g., Rosenthal and Jacobson 1968), teachers are subject to bias. Another use of systematic observation is as a means of improving objectivity. For example, we may be especially impressed by a child's verbal precociousness and may need to take a more careful look at other behavioral evidence of intelligence. In another case, we may be so impressed by a child's disruptive behavior that we fail to note periods of time when that child is engaged in constructive behavior.

Realistically, a classroom teacher cannot be expected to stand back and record the behavior of the children on a regular basis. Therefore, the observational techniques that will prove most useful are those that require the least interruption of direct work with the children. Still, in specific cases or when the teacher-observer can be freed for a brief period from her teaching obligations, more detailed systematic observation may be possible.

### What Observation Techniques
### Are Most Useful to Teachers?

There are many ways of recording children's behavior. Perhaps the most frequent and applicable method in a busy classroom is an anecdotal record. Anecdotal recording does not require that a teacher interrupt her teaching activity for a specified length of time or at specified intervals. To record anecdotes, a teacher may carry a small notebook to record episodes that seem significant about a child or even about a group of children. The behavior may be typical or unusual. The length of recording usually is as long as is necessary to detail the complete behavioral episode. The teacher collecting anecdotal material may do so on a somewhat periodic, random basis, or she may be systematic about recording a certain number of episodes regarding specific children each day. The anecdotal method may also be used when the teacher wants to learn more about a particular child. Anecdotes are likely to be most accurate when they are recorded on the spot; when necessary, however, recording may be done at a later, more convenient time.

Some teachers also keep a log or a diary about their class. The log may be a daily or weekly account, usually from memory, about what has transpired. This is an especially useful way to learn more about group interaction. It is also helpful in determining how the children are using the materials or responding to other aspects of the program. A log or diary represents a continuous chronological account of the progress of a class or of individual children, which helps document changes.

Some other handy devices for recording children's behavior are checklists and rating scales. A teacher may use a checklist to note the frequency of a behavior, to compare it with other behaviors, or to record a change. Checklists may also help in identifying a child's interests. For example, you might prepare a list of potential activities in a classroom and then check the frequency and duration of use of each activity by a child or by a class. Similarly, checklists may be used to describe personality traits. In this case, a list of behaviors, such as "completes tasks," "seeks teacher's attention," and "offers information or help," may be prepared in advance and checked when the behaviors are observed. The checklist of behaviors may be used randomly, but it is usually more reliable when observations are made at specified times (e.g., during snack time and free play) and intervals. This is a sampling technique that helps eliminate bias. Rating scales, like checklists, are quicker ways to record observations than recording anecdotes. Advance preparation is required to create a scale that accurately describes the dimensions of the behaviors or traits. For example, rating scales for two typical dimensions might be prepared as follows:

| Intensity | Frequency |
|---|---|
| 5—High | 5—Frequently |
| 4—Moderate | 4—Often |
| 3—Average | 3—Usually |
| 2—Slight | 2—Occasionally |
| 1—None | 1—Rarely |

Figure 6.3 is an example of a rating scale for personality factors, and Figure 6.4 is an example of a checklist for observing children's behavior during story time.

**FIGURE 6.3** Child Personality Rating Scale[a]

Name of Child _____

Date of Rating _____

Name of Rater _____

| | Always | Almost Always | Usually | As Often as Not | Some-times | Rarely | Never |
|---|---|---|---|---|---|---|---|
| 1. At ease in social situations | 1 | 2 | 3 | 4 | 5 | 6 | 7 |
| 2. Gets along well with other children | 1 | 2 | 3 | 4 | 5 | 6 | 7 |
| 3. Destructive | - | 2 | 3 | 4 | 5 | 6 | 7 |
| 4. Seeks attention from other children | 1 | 2 | 3 | 4 | 5 | 6 | 7 |
| 5. Concerned about being the "best" | 1 | 2 | 3 | 4 | 5 | 6 | 7 |
| 6. Anxious to please | 1 | 2 | 3 | 4 | 5 | 6 | 7 |
| 7. Has a long attention span | 1 | 2 | 3 | 4 | 5 | 6 | 7 |
| 8. Has unique (original) ideas | 1 | 2 | 3 | 4 | 5 | 6 | 7 |
| 9. Alters routines and approaches to tasks when appropriate | 1 | 2 | 3 | 4 | 5 | 6 | 7 |
| 10. Recognizes needs of others | 1 | 2 | 3 | 4 | 5 | 6 | 7 |
| 11. Avoids close contact with teacher | 1 | 2 | 3 | 4 | 5 | 6 | 7 |
| 12. Avoids close contact with other children | 1 | 2 | 3 | 4 | 5 | 6 | 7 |
| 13. Well-coordinated in physical activity | 1 | 2 | 3 | 4 | 5 | 6 | 7 |
| 14. Physically active | 1 | 2 | 3 | 4 | 5 | 6 | 7 |

|  | Always | Almost Always | Usually | As Often as Not | Sometimes | Rarely | Never |
|---|---|---|---|---|---|---|---|
| 15. Accepts failure | 1 | 2 | 3 | 4 | 5 | 6 | 7 |
| 16. Likes to talk | 1 | 2 | 3 | 4 | 5 | 6 | 7 |
| 17. Cautious | 1 | 2 | 3 | 4 | 5 | 6 | 7 |
| 18. Behaves like own sex | 1 | 2 | 3 | 4 | 5 | 6 | 7 |
| 19. Threatens children | 1 | 2 | 3 | 4 | 5 | 6 | 7 |
| 20. Bosses children | 1 | 2 | 3 | 4 | 5 | 6 | 7 |
| 21. Derogates children | 1 | 2 | 3 | 4 | 5 | 6 | 7 |
| 22. Directs children | 1 | 2 | 3 | 4 | 5 | 6 | 7 |
| 23. Attacks children physically | 1 | 2 | 3 | 4 | 5 | 6 | 7 |
| 24. Threatens teacher | 1 | 2 | 3 | 4 | 5 | 6 | 7 |
| 25. Insists on own ideas | 1 | 2 | 3 | 4 | 5 | 6 | 7 |
| 26. Submits to children when challenged | 1 | 2 | 3 | 4 | 5 | 6 | 7 |
| 27. Avoids rough activities | 1 | 2 | 3 | 4 | 5 | 6 | 7 |
| 28. Follows teacher's directions without resistance | 1 | 2 | 3 | 4 | 5 | 6 | 7 |
| 29. Seeks to be near teacher | 1 | 2 | 3 | 4 | 5 | 6 | 7 |
| 30. Seeks physical contact with teacher | 1 | 2 | 3 | 4 | 5 | 6 | 7 |
| 31. Seeks help from teacher | 1 | 2 | 3 | 4 | 5 | 6 | 7 |
| 32. Completes activities | 1 | 2 | 3 | 4 | 5 | 6 | 7 |
| 33. Gets intrinsic satisfaction from his work | 1 | 2 | 3 | 4 | 5 | 6 | 7 |
| 34. Overcomes obstacles by himself | 1 | 2 | 3 | 4 | 5 | 6 | 7 |

[a]Circle the most appropriate number.

**FIGURE 6.4**  Story Time Observation Checklist

Date of Observation_____ Observer_____

Observer is watching *three* previously designated children. Rating is made immediately
following the story.

| 1. *Attention to story* | Child #1 | Child #2 | Child #3 |
|---|---|---|---|
| a. Completely inattentive (very distracted, disinterested) | _____ | _____ | _____ |
| b. Slightly attentive (quite distractable) | _____ | _____ | _____ |
| c. Moderately attentive | _____ | _____ | _____ |
| d. Quite attentive (throughout most of the story) | _____ | _____ | _____ |
| e. Exceptionally attentive (virtually nondistractable) | _____ | _____ | _____ |

| 2. *Nature of comments or questions* (tally number of each below) | Child #1 | Child #2 | Child #3 |
|---|---|---|---|
| a. Enumerative comment (e.g., "That's a ball.") | _____ | _____ | _____ |
| b. Associative, nonrelative comment (no obvious logical connection to story) | _____ | _____ | _____ |
| c. Associative relevant comment (logically pertaining to story) | _____ | _____ | _____ |
| d. Enumerative question (e.g., "What's that?") | _____ | _____ | _____ |
| e. Casual question (e.g., "Why do . . . ?") | _____ | _____ | _____ |
| TOTAL | _____ | _____ | _____ |

## Recording the Time and Place of Observations

Behavior occurs in the context of a situation or a setting.
Whether the observation is a systematic sampling of behavior or a
random selection, whether it is recorded on a checklist or on a
rating scale, it is essential to record the date of the recording, the
child or children being observed, the time and duration of the observation, and whatever is happening at the time of observation
(e.g., what the teacher is doing) so that the episode can be clearly
understood.

## How Does a Director Encourage Teacher Observation?

Workshops with staff are the best way to initiate teacher observations. Begin with what is already being done rather than imposing a new approach. Some of the teachers might already have favorite techniques, and perhaps there are ways these could

**FIGURE 6.5** A Coping Analysis Schedule for Educational Settings (CASES): Brief Form for Quick Reference

1. *Aggressive behavior:* Direct attack—grabbing, pushing, hitting, pulling, kicking, name calling; destroying property—smashing, tearing, breaking.
2. *Negative (inappropriate) attention-getting behavior:* Annoying, bothering, whining, loud talking (unnecessarily), attention-getting aversive noise-making, belittling, criticizing.
3. *Manipulating and directing others:* Manipulating, bossing, commanding, directing, enforcing rules, conniving, wheedling, controlling.
4. *Resisting authority:* Resisting, delaying, passive-aggressive behavior, pretending to conform, conforming to the letter but not the spirit, defensive checking.
5. *Self-directed activity:* Productive working, reading, writing, constructing with interest, self-directed dramatic play (with high involvement).
6. *Paying rapt attention:* Listening attentively, watching carefully, concentrating on a story being told, a film being watched, a record played.
7. *Sharing and helping:* Contributing ideas, interests, materials; helping; responding by showing feelings (laughing, smiling, etc.) in audience situations; initiating conversation.
8. *Social interaction:* Mutual give and take, cooperative behavior, integrative social behavior; studying or working together where participants are on a par.
9. *Seeking support, assistance, and information:* Bidding or asking teachers or significant peers for help, support, sympathy, affection, etc.; being helped; receiving assistance.
10. *Following directions passively and submissively:* Doing assigned work without enthusiasm or great interest, submitting to requests, answering direct questions, waiting for instructions as directed.
11. *Observing passively:* Visual wandering, watching others work, checking on noises or movements, checking on activities of adults and peers.
12. *Responding to internal stimuli:* Daydreaming, sleeping, rocking or fidgeting (not in transaction with external stimuli).
13. *Physical withdrawal or avoidance:* Flight, moving away, hiding, avoiding transactions by movement away or around.

*Note:* Categories *5* through *10* are further coded as *a* or *b* in structured settings to indicate appropriate or inappropriate behavior (based on social expectations for the setting). Example: *5a* would be recorded when a child was painting during art period (when painting was one of the expected activities). Painting during story time or in an academic setting would normally be coded *5b*.

*Source:* Robert L. Spaulding, *CASES* (Durham, N.C.: Duke University, Educational Improvement Program, 1966). © 1966 Robert L. Spaulding, San Jose State University, San Jose, CA 95192. Reprinted with permission of the author.

be expanded or made more precise. Then other staff members might adopt these techniques.

If there is more than one teacher recording in a room, observations may be shared, or one teacher could be given a specific time for observations while the other works directly with the class. If both teachers are able to observe simultaneously on occasion, this provides a good basis for assessing the reliability of observation (i.e., interobserver agreement).

Having resource books on observing children available for use encourages teachers to learn new methods and to understand the rationale for observation. If staff members use the same resources, they can share ideas at meetings and support one another in trying out the observational techniques. Some suggested books to have on hand are listed in the references at the end of this chapter.

These books also provide some techniques for interpreting the data that are collected. For example, you may wish to create charts or graphs to analyze frequency data statistically. Coding the observations is another way to increase your understanding of the behavioral statements. With coding, each behavior can be placed in a predetermined category (e.g., dependent, constructive, social) and given a category code number so that patterns and frequencies can be observed. Spaulding (1966) has devised a universal coding system for classroom behavior. Figure 6.5 describes Spaulding's coding categories.

### Suggested Activities

1. Note the developmental needs of children identified in Figure 6.1.
   a. Are there others that you would add to the list?
   b. Observe in an early childhood classroom. See how many of these needs you can identify.
   c. Note how the program does or does not take these needs into account.
2. Develop your own category system for classifying observations in an early childhood classroom.
   a. Try your system out in several classrooms on several occasions.
   b. Note how the observations correspond (reliability).

3. Identify a child in the classroom that you would like to observe closely. Do a case study based on systematic observation. Answer the question, "Are the child's needs being met in the classroom?"

## References and Further Readings

Almy, M. *Ways of Studying Children.* New York: Teachers College Press, 1959.

Boehm, Ann E., and Weinberg, Richard A. *The Classroom Observer.* New York: Teachers College Press, 1979.

Cartwright, C., and Cartwright, P. *Developing Observation Skills.* New York: McGraw-Hill, 1974.

Charles C. M. *Teacher's Petit Piaget.* Belmont, Calif.: Fearon-Pitman, 1974.

Cohen, D., and Stern, V. *Observing and Recording the Behavior of Young Children.* New York: Teachers College Press, 1978.

Colby, John. *Maternal Care and Mental Health.* Monograph Series No. 2. Geneva: World Health Organization, 1951.

Erikson, Erik. *Childhood and Society.* New York: Norton, 1950.

Fraiberg, Selma. *The Magic Years: Understanding and Handling the Problems of Early Childhood.* New York: Scribner, 1955.

Gordon, I. J. "Reaching the Young Children Through Parent Education." *Childhood Education 46,* February 1970, 247–249.

Grossman, Bruce, and Keyes, Carol. *Helping Children Grow: The Adult's Role.* Wayne, N.J.: Avery, 1978.

Harlow, Harry. "The Nature of Love." In Morris L. Haimowitz and Natalie Reader Haimowitz, eds., *Human Development: Selected Readings.* New York: Crowell, 1973.

Heighberger, Ruth, and Schram, Carol. *Child Development for Day Care Workers.* Boston: Houghton Mifflin, 1976.

Jackson, Philip, and Wolfons, Bernice. "Varieties of Constraint in a Nursery School." *Young Children 23*(6), September 1968, 358–367.

Jacobson, A. L. "Infant Day Care: Toward a More Human Environment." *Young Children 33*(5), July 1978, 14–23.

Keyes, Carol, and Grossman, Bruce. *Families and Schools: An Ecological Study.* Unpublished manuscript, 1979.

Levenstein, P. "Cognitive Growth in Preschoolers through Verbal Interaction with their Mothers." *American Journal of Orthopsychiatry 40,* 1970, 426–432.

Piaget, Jean. *The Psychology of the Child.* New York: Basic Books, 1969.

Provence, S. *Guide for the Care of Infants in Groups.* New York: Child Welfare League of America, 1967.

Rabinoff, Bunny, and Prescott, Elizabeth. "The Invisible Child: Challenge to Teacher's Attentiveness." In *Joys and Risks in Teaching Young Children.* Palo Alto, Calif.: Pacific Books, 1978.

Rheingold, H.; Gerwitz, J.; and Ross, H. W. "Social Conditioning of Vocalizations in the Infant." *Journal of Comparative and Physiological Psychology 52*, 1959, 68–73.

Rogers, Carl. *On Becoming a Person.* Boston: Houghton Mifflin, 1961.

Rosenthal, R., and Jacobson, L. *Pygmalion in the Classroom: Teacher Expectations and Pupils' Intellectual Development.* New York: Holt, Rinehart and Winston, 1968.

Satir, Virginia. *People-Making.* Palo Alto, Calif.: Science and Behavior Books, 1972.

Spaulding, Robert L. *CASES.* Durham, N.C.: Duke University, Educational Improvement Program, 1966.

Spitz, Rene A. *The First Year of Life.* New York: International Universities Press, 1965.

Weiner, Irving B., and Elkind, David. *Child Development: A Core Approach.* New York: Wiley, 1972.

White, B.; Castle, P.; and Held, R. "Observations of Visually-Directed Teaching." *Child Development 35*, 1964, 349–364.

Wolfgang, Charles H. *Helping Aggressive and Passive Preschoolers through Play.* Columbus, Ohio: Merrill, 1977.

# Chapter 7
# Meeting
# Children's
# Special Needs

## DIFFERENT BACKGROUNDS, DIFFERENT ABILITIES

### Children from Single-Parent Households

As the number of children from single-parent households increases, it is essential that we broaden the view of the family that we present to the children. The teaching staff may sometimes need to be warned against assuming that all children come from standard two-parent households. In fact, at least 25 percent of the children may come from single-parent homes, and others are likely to have stepparents as well as natural parents.

In the classrooms, the choice of books dealing with families should not exclusively reflect the nuclear family. Storybooks should represent a variety of family constellations. When you are purchasing books or assisting teachers in selections, books that describe single-parent households, parental visits, stepparents and stepsiblings, and divorce situations should be included. Certainly, class discussions should allow children to describe visits with non-custodial parents and to explore such issues as divorce and parental remarriage. Some authorities regard the years from 3 to 6 as the worst age for children to experience a parental divorce (Turnow 1977). Although teachers are not therapists, they can be helpful to young children by encouraging open expression of feelings about absent fathers, new parents, new stepsiblings, and so forth. It is reassuring for the children to discover that others have lost parents to divorce and that they are not alone in such losses.

A psychiatrist or psychologist may be called in as a consultant if the discussions suggest a need for professional help. As we noted earlier, many child guidance clinics and mental health associations will provide professionals to conduct workshops on this topic with the teaching staff.

On a very practical level, it is also useful to keep in mind that the traditional celebrations of Mother's Day and Father's Day, which may involve making presents, can be a problem for children with absent parents. Some children could make Father's Day gifts for their grandfathers, perhaps. Caution should also be advised in teacher's discussions with children when references to mothers and fathers assume a traditional home situation. It is important to keep in mind the actual family constellation of each child being addressed. Furthermore, for children whose fathers are absent from the home, the presence of a male teacher or assistant is particularly desirable. In the references at the end of this chapter, we have included some books about divorce for young children. A good resource for books on such specific topics is *The Guide to Children's Books in Print* (1983).

### Children Who Are Bilingual

The most important reason for the rise of bilingual education today is the generally poor school performance of non-English-speaking children. This problem can be noticeably lessened by using a child's own language along with English. This approach seems to have a positive effect on the child's ability to master skills such as reading, and it also improves his self-concept and his attitude about school.

Advocates of bilingual education point out that, in addition to assisting non-English-speaking children in the ways discussed, offering children education in their native language as well as in English demonstrates respect for the children's culture and for diversity in our society. It also allows the children an opportunity to become articulate and literate in more than one language and to learn about other cultures.

People from other cultures might be expected to feel somewhat out of place and even frightened in the cultural setting represented by an English-speaking classroom atmosphere. This is certainly likely to be true for a young child. In addition to differences in language, the child will be confronted by differences in food, dress, and customs at the same time he is being separated from his family. To reduce this initial anxiety, it is helpful for you, as the center director, to meet the child with his mother and/or father somewhat more extensively than you would ordinarily. If you do not speak the family's native language, you should have a bilingual teacher present. This enhances communication and it makes the child and the family feel more comfortable.

The move into the classroom can be facilitated in the same way. If the bilingual teacher is not the regular teacher, then it is advisable that she introduce the child into the classroom and help make the connection to the regular classroom teacher. The bilingual teacher can also assist the classroom teacher in learning simple greetings and other vocabulary to offer the bilingual child in his native tongue.

The classroom teacher can learn some of the foreign language from the child himself. For example, if a child points to an object and says "that," the teacher might say, "Yes, tell me what that is called." If the child responds in his native tongue, the teacher can then repeat the phrase or word and then offer the same expression in English, asking the child to repeat it. The teacher has thus created a reciprocal process, which is most effective in building trust between the teacher and the child and in helping the child learn a new language.

There are also more direct ways to introduce English to the non-English-speaking child, including the process of meeting the child's needs for a drink or a toy or simply the response to a request for help. In the latter case, if the child is apparently seeking assistance, the teacher might reply, "Would you like some *help*?" or "Would you like that *truck*?" emphasizing the key word and waiting a bit until the phrase is repeated or, if not, repeating it herself as she responds to the child's request. Still another, less direct way that a teacher might encourage language learning in a bilingual child is in her nonverbal support. Education is most effective when the teacher is first able to establish a warm relationship with the child. This is true with any young child, of course, but is particularly important with the bilingual child. When the child is relaxed, he is much more likely to want to communicate and to imitate the teacher's language.

What do you do if a non-English-speaking child is enrolled and no bilingual teacher is available? Nonverbal gestures work for a while. A recent experience at our campus center showed us, however, that nonverbal communication is not sufficient after a time. We had no bilingual texts for early childhood that provided the phrases the staff needed, so we began to write down all the phrases we felt we needed to communicate. Then we found a bilingual parent who volunteered to translate the phrases for us and to spend some time in individual instruction with the child. A second experience came several years later, when two Japanese children came to the center. Again, we prepared a list of phrases, and a parent who had just returned from Japan translated them for us. His child, who had attended the center and was now in kindergarten, came to help us communicate with the Japanese children for the first few days.

### The Developmentally Disabled Child

Early identification of developmentally disabled infants and toddlers and placement of these disabled children in appropriate programs have become the goal of an increasing number of state and federal programs. As a result, more and more new programs are being developed for these very young children. In some cases, the programs are specifically directed at the retarded, neurologically impaired, physically handicapped, or autistic child. In other cases, special classes are offered in early childhood centers or opportunities are developed for mainstreaming the child.

Although there are specific factors to be considered by administrators and teachers in each situation of working with a developmentally disabled child, there is a special orientation that would apply in most cases. In an earlier book (Grossman and Keyes 1978), we outlined a number of basic hints that are important for teachers and administrators to keep in mind. We shall review them briefly here, with a special view toward the implications for administration.

## LEARN ALL YOU CAN
## ABOUT THE PARTICULAR DISABILITY

The entire staff should be informed about the child's disability and how he is likely to deal with it. For example, how does the child compensate, and what types of experiences are likely to be particularly frustrating for him? A child who is emotionally disturbed, for example, may become upset for no apparent reason and may be subject to temper tantrums or to expressions of extreme rage or withdrawal. It is also crucial to learn about any existing allergic conditions. Such information should be sought in some detail by the director or by whoever interviews the parents initially. It may also be obtained from the application. Once these factors are known, the child should be observed closely. To the extent that you and the staff are able to anticipate problems, they are less likely to be traumatic to the disabled child.

What modifications might you and the teaching staff need to make to accommodate a particular disability? For physical disabilities, the needs may be quite apparent. For children in wheelchairs, ramps may need to be built and furniture rearranged to provide extra room. You may also have to allow for more assisted physical activities, such as massage or guided exercise. For deaf or hard-of-hearing children, it is important to remember to face the children as you speak and to make more physical gestures. For autistic or withdrawn children, programming and staffing may require adjustment to provide for more external stimulation.

### LEARN ABOUT A CHILD'S SPECIAL NEEDS

You need to know which children are likely to have seizures and what to do about them. You also need to be aware of each child's special dietary needs or special need for rest. For a child with a physical handicap, you may need to know how to adjust special aids, such as braces or hearing devices. For an emotionally disturbed child, you may need to know about excessive fears. Again, it is important to obtain this information from parents when a child enters your program or, with parental consent, to consult with the child's physician. We should add here that toilet use is often a special problem for the developmentally disabled child. Intellectual, emotional and physical development can effect a child's toilet skills. For example, a child with delayed speech will likely have difficulty communicating his toilet needs. This may be frustrating to the teaching staff, in which case they may require some additional support from you or from an outside consultant. Behavior modification has been successfully employed to facilitate the toilet training of retarded and autistic children, and structural modifications, such as railings, may be needed with physically handicapped children.

The focus here should be toward increasing the independence of the developmentally disabled child. If a child has been treated as dependent or disabled at home, it is often very difficult for him to change those ideas about himself. It is also very difficult to change his parents' views and habits. A combined program of parent education and intervention with the child, with opportunities for independent self-help in the classroom, can be quite effective. In this regard, teachers also need support and reminders in their efforts to resist doing everything for the handicapped child rather than allowing the child to develop his own skills. A first step, which is impressive to parents of developmentally disabled children, is helping the child learn to hang up his own coat.

### WORKING CLOSELY WITH PARENTS

Working closely with the family is particularly important when dealing with developmentally or otherwise disabled children. The parents usually have very real concerns about their children's well-being and their competence. They may also have some guilt about placing the child in your hands or they may feel competitive in this regard. Many of these parents are dealing with feelings about possibly having caused their child's disability by some defect in themselves, their behavior, or even their attitude. If your staff does not include a psychologist or social worker who can work directly with parents on a one-to-one basis or in small groups, you, as director, may be required to do much of this work with parents. If your center is devoted exclusively to children with such problems, you should have a staff member who is properly trained to handle this work. You cannot hope to be effective with developmentally or otherwise disabled children without also doing some extensive work with their parents.

### SOME TIPS FOR MAINSTREAMING

Introducing one or more disabled children into your center requires some additional attention. The teacher to whom the children are assigned may be offered some special preparatory education or may be asked to attend workshops related to the disability in question.

It is usually best to include more than one disabled child in a mainstreaming situation. This helps keep the disabled child from feeling odd, although that may not be avoided entirely. It is also helpful to enlist the aid of the other children in integrating the disabled child into the classroom. In that way, they will feel more involved and less resentful of the special attention that may be required. It is also a good idea to work with the parents of both the disabled and the nondisabled children before attempting to mainstream. This is where the director of a program can be particularly helpful in increasing a classroom teacher's effectiveness at integrating the developmentally disabled child into the classroom.

We have also had the opportunity to employ several disabled aides and teachers in our program. We have found that the children and parents are very responsive and accepting, and the experience has led to a more positive attitude toward disabled persons on everybody's part.


### Gifted Children

Since the classroom teacher is responsible for the daily program and for working directly with all of the children, including those that are designated gifted, what role does the director play with these children? Do gifted children, in fact, require special consideration?

An early childhood center must take into account all types of children's special needs. The classroom environment may well be stimulating enough for all of the children and may allow for enough self-pacing so that a gifted child receives sufficient opportunities to explore and to experiment with what is available. It is also quite possible, however, that despite an already enriched learning environment, some gifted children are sufficiently advanced to require additional materials. In that case, the director should be able to supply those materials and make suggestions for activities to challenge these exceptional youngsters. Perhaps a consultant could be hired to help the classroom teachers learn about the identification and handling of children with exceptional intelligence and talents.

Some gifted children experience difficulties relating to other children their age. They may need extra attention and wish to be "center stage." Problems may arise from the gifted child's refusal to participate in group activities. Teachers need support and advice in these instances. Although a gifted child may be advanced in intellectual areas, he may be experiencing the same social adjustment problems as any child his age. As adults, we sometimes need reminding that a very bright 3-year-old is only acting his age when he behaves like a 3-year-old. We should also keep in mind that, like any children, gifted children need limits. Because of their advanced capacities, they may be able to use freedom more constructively than the average child, but it is also possible that they will ask for more of an adult status than they can handle. Beware!

Finally, you should recognize that these special children may need more resources than your center can offer. Parents need to be guided to places that offer specialized opportunities for children with exceptional intelligence or talents. Many local colleges and universities have after-school and Saturday programs that include gifted preschoolers. There is also a national society for parents of gifted children with local and regional chapters, that parents find very useful (National Association for Gifted Children, St. Paul, Minnesota). Among other services that such organizations provide are support groups that give parents an opportunity to meet with other parents who are facing some of the same types of problems associated with gifted children. They may also offer peer groups for the children, where they can be with other children their own age who are as capable as they are and share similar interests.

## SETTING UP A PROGRAM FOR INFANTS AND TODDLERS

In her book *Infant and Toddler Programs*, Cataldo (1983) provides an overview of infant/toddler programs. She describes both the approaches to initiating such programs and some specific programs to use as models. Many preschools have expanded their market to include infants and/or toddlers, often because their enrollment is low or at the request of center parents who have younger children. Some programs offer a parent/child 2-hour session once or twice a week. Others include a part-time toddler session. Sometimes, a room for infants and/or toddlers is set up as a regular part of the day care center operation.

Administrators of preschool programs who intend to expand to infant/toddler care must do research in the area, since infants and toddlers have different needs from preschoolers in terms of setting, adult-child ratio, and curriculum. Sometimes, administrators assume that they can just use the same preschool room and bring toddlers in. This can create problems, however. For example, the furniture may not be the right height; the toys may be too advanced; and there may be too many toys.

Different interest areas must be set up for the younger children. Cataldo (1983) suggests a rattle corner, a reaching center, a sensory corner, a touring cart, an exercise mat, an interaction game area, a water table, pet and doll houses, a creative corner, a music area, a construction center, a curiosity corner, a comfort corner, a language and book center, a diapering area, and a rest area.

Various infant/toddler programs have emerged in the past 10 years. Some are specific infant/toddler programs that care for babies in groups. Some have as their goal the prevention of developmental problems in handicapped babies or high-risk infants. Others are part of comprehensive services to parents and infants.

## Developmental Considerations

The developmental considerations that should be taken into account as you are planning for infants and toddlers include (1) environment, (2) staffing, and (3) program.

### ENVIRONMENTAL CONSIDERATIONS

*A Safe and Attractive Physical Environment.* Infants and toddlers require a safe and attractive physical environment. These very young children thrive on varied, bright stimuli, and they also require proper heating, access to the outdoors, and proper lighting beyond standard safety conditions. In addition, access to water, bathrooms, and a kitchen is essential. Infants, who are crawling, and toddlers, who have a precarious sense of balance, need to be protected from stairs. They also need to be supervised closely so that they do not climb onto furniture, pull down heavy objects by accident, or put dangerous objects in their mouths.

*Additional Space, with Opportunity to Move About.* Keep in mind when planning for infants and toddlers that more space is required than for three and four year olds. Too frequently infants have been confined to cribs and surrounded by "bumper guards" for their own protection. Actually, infant development is enhanced by freedom of movement and an opportunity to observe changing stimuli. Similarly, toddlers benefit from open space in which they can move safely. Of course, good supervision in these situations is essential.

### STAFFING CONSIDERATIONS

*Adult-Child Ratio.* The ratio of children to staff should be approximately two to one or three to one for infants and three to one to five to one for toddlers. Because of the need for additional supervision, for assistance in such activities as feeding and dressing, and for more individualized attention, a larger staff is required for working with very young children than is necessary for 3- and 4-year-olds. The staff should also be more mature and more experienced than is required for 3- and 4-year-olds.

*The Primary Caretaker.* It is vital that the staff be well motivated to work with very young children. As Provence (1967) states: "Infants should be cared for by people who want to care for them, who have something to give, and who can get satisfaction from what the infant gives to them in return." In addition, continuity of care is particularly important. Staff members who have responsibility for the direct care of infants must be as consistently available to the children as possible. This may require long hours and the support of additional staff to supplement and relieve the primary worker. We want to emphasize the importance of arranging the caretaking situation so that one adult is consistently involved with each child. In some centers, assignments are made by tasks, but it is preferable to make the assignment by child; that is, one adult should have the primary responsibility for the total care of each child, rather than for performing a particular task.

Infants and toddlers also need to be protected from visitors and observers. This is not to say that they do not benefit from interaction with other adults, but this process should be monitored by the adult who has a consistent responsibility for the child, with the assistance of the center director.

*Availability of Male Staff Members.* This problem is not as severe as it was when Provence (1967) was first writing, but it is still worthy of consideration. Toddlers in particular benefit from the presence of men on the staff, especially in the caretaking role. Many of the households that are likely to use group care for infants and toddlers are single-parent families, with women predominating. This is also likely to be true in day care and preschool settings, and it requires a conscious effort by the administrator to include men in a program.

### PROGRAM CONSIDERATIONS

*Stimulation.* Stimulation of infants and toddlers, in the form of both physical and verbal contact, should be readily available from caretakers. The adults should be encouraged to talk to the infants as they take care of them. In addition, toys and other types of safe, manipulative, and visually stimulating materials should be within reach. Keep in mind, however, that toddlers and infants also need some quiet time, with minimal stimulation.

*Appropriate Limits.* This is another very important area suggested by Provence (1967) that is often overlooked. Although we are primarily concerned with meeting children's needs in a group care environment, we must also assume some responsibility for teaching these very young children how to recognize and accept limits. This is particularly true when the children have become mobile, but it does not apply only to physical limitations, such as increasingly longer periods of delay. They also need to begin to learn rules about how to behave with others and how to treat materials. This may cause them some anxiety and anger connected with the modest frustrations they experience, but these frustrations are bearable and educational when they are accompanied by adult support and by opportunities to express their feelings. This is where a well-trained, experienced staff is most valuable.

*Being Part of the Real World.* Programs for infants and toddlers tend to be tucked away and protected from everyday life, especially from the world of adults. We agree with Provence's (1967) notion that the children should be included in such chores as meal preparation and cleaning. This is what Montessori refers to as "practical life" (Lillard 1972), and it is consistent with the experience of infant and toddler care in the Israeli kibbutz (Gerson 1978).

## The Relationship with Parents

Although the caretaker-teacher's relationship with parents is important in any early childhood center, it is especially crucial when you are caring for very young children. From the child's point of view, a bridge between home and school is essential. The younger the child is, the more dependent and helpless he is. Therefore, he is most in need of familiar patterns of high-quality and continuous care. From the parent's point of view, entrusting their young child to strangers is likely to be a large step. It is important that, as a substitute caregiver, you support rather than compete with parents. For example, it is advisable to be cautious about criticizing how the child is dressed, fed, and so forth. You and your staff should not emphasize your roles as all-knowing "experts" who are taking over the role of parenting. This does not mean, however, that you cannot share your knowledge and your observations with parents or that you cannot help improve the quality of care at home, if necessary, by listening to parents' concerns and working out problems with them according to their needs and skills as well as the child's.

## Monitoring the Child's Needs

A personal data sheet helps caregivers keep track of the particular needs of each infant or toddler. Figure 7.1 is a sample data sheet for an infant.

## Special Equipment

Special equipment needs for infant/toddler programs vary, depending on whether they are day care centers or mother-child brief programs. For example, for the 2-hour program at the Pace University Parent Center, a low mirror, pads for changing on a counter or floor, low toddler tables, a small refrigerator, a small toddler gym, and an array of infant and toddler toys are sufficient. In an all-day program, more equipment and supplies would be needed.

**FIGURE 7-1**  Infant Personal Data Sheet

**Child's Name**_____

**Parents' Names**_____

**Foods**

_____Table foods

_____Baby food (amount/serving):

| *Vegetables* | *Fruits* | *Meats* |
|---|---|---|
| _____peas | _____applesauce | _____beef |
| _____beets | _____apricots | _____veal |
| _____carrots | _____pears | _____liver |
| _____green beans | _____peaches | _____turkey |
| _____squash | _____prunes in tapioca | _____lamb |
| | _____bananas in tapioca | _____pork |
| | _____plums in tapioca | |

Schedule:

Allergies:

Religious preferences:

**Birth Date**_____

**Enrollment Date**_____ **Attendance**_____

**Sleep**

Any special sleeping needs?

**FIGURE 7.1** *(continued)*

Does the baby need or like to be rocked?

What position does the baby like?

What is the usual routine for putting the baby to bed?

When does the baby usually sleep, and for how long?

**Liquids**

*Milk*

_____Cup                    _____Whole

_____Bottle                 _____Skim

                              _____Formula (brand)_____

_____heated                 _____room temp.              _____cool

Amount/serving_____

*Juice*

_____pineapple              _____grape

_____apple                  _____apricot

_____orange                 _____grapefruit

_____peach

Schedule:

**Daily Schedule**

| 7:00 | |
|------|---|
| 7:30 | |
| 8:00 | |

| 9:00 | |
|---|---|
| 10:00 | |
| 11:00 | |
| 12:00 | |
| 1:00 | |
| 2:00 | |
| 3:00 | |
| 4:00 | |
| 5:00 | |
| 6:00 | |

**Diapering**

\_\_\_\_\_Powder

\_\_\_\_\_Ointment (permission)

**Health**

Any handicaps or abnormalities?

Any daily medications?

Any previous medical history?

**Language**

Does the baby say any words? What do they mean?

What languages are spoken in the home?

**FIGURE 7.1**  *(continued)*

**Family**

| Members of Household | Relationship | Age (if sibling) |
| --- | --- | --- |
| _____ | _____ | _____ |
| _____ | _____ | _____ |
| _____ | _____ | _____ |
| _____ | _____ | _____ |

Any pets?


**Play and Comfort**

What are the baby's favorite games, toys, and things to do?


How do the parents comfort the baby when he is upset?

---

Several good sources for equipment are listed in the references at the end of this chapter. For example, Willis and Ricciuti (1975), in *A Good Beginning for Babies*, note that play material must be safe and durable and must encourage action. In "Furnishing the Infant/Toddler Environment," Jim Greenman (1982) suggests that equipment must be versatile and responsive.

Equipment for infant and toddlers must be judged on the basis of safety (consumer product safety standards) and health; for example, it should be flame retardant, it should have smooth rounded edges, and it should include only large pieces that are easily cleaned and cost-effective. Each infant needs his own crib or cot, blanket, and toys from home. Some centers use infant seats instead of high chairs; others use small tables and chairs. Eating utensils must be dishwasher-safe. There must be a changing table for diapering, child-sized toilets and sinks, and soft furniture.

A recent major concern of early childhood educators has been the health aspects of centers. Highberger and Boynton (1983) discuss techniques for maintaining a clean environment and note that the diapering area is "the most dangerous area and the right environment for growth of micro-organisms" (pp. 3–4). They suggest using a disposable surface that can be thrown away after each child is diapered. Suggested disposable surfaces include squares of newspaper, cut-open paper bags, squares of waxed paper, or sheets of computer paper. All equipment should be cleaned once or twice a week by thorough washing with detergent and rinsing with water. Play equipment must be cleaned daily because the infants mouth everything. Handwashing may be most important, because it will eliminate the spread of disease; liquid soap is recommended as more sanitary. A sanitary checklist should be prepared, and staff members who complete a given task should initial the checklist daily.

A research project was designed to determine the effects of handwashing on preventing diarrhea in child care centers (Black et al. 1981). This 35-week study found twice the incidence of diarrhea in centers where handwashing was not a formal program in comparison to two centers where a handwashing program had been instituted.

The following conclusions are based on other findings from the literature:

1. There must be a careful handwashing procedure for both children and adults.
2. Procedures following diapering must include cleaning all surfaces touched during diapering with a solution of one-half cup of household bleach to one gallon of tap water, kept in a spray bottle in the diaper-changing area but out of the reach of the children.
3. There must be separate feeding and diapering areas.
4. The diapering area must be near a sink.
5. The staff must be trained in health care procedures.

### Competent Infant Caregivers

Many professionals and laypeople are concerned about the proliferation of programs for very young children, especially in light of recent evidence about the importance of parent-child bonding and the enormous significance of the first three years of life (White 1975). In an article in *Young Children*, Armita Lee Jacobson (1978b) reviews the research in this area and concludes that the same parental qualities that tend to maximize the potential of infants and toddlers can be found in day care workers. She offers a list of the most desirable characteristics of people who work with very young children, which should serve as a handy guide for administrators who want to select the most able people to work with very young children (see Figure 7.2).

**FIGURE 7.2**  Characteristics of Competent Infant Caregivers

| *Desired Caregiver Characteristics* | *Cues to the Characteristics* |
|---|---|
| I. Personality Factors | |
|   A. Child-centered | 1. Attentive and loving to infants |
| | 2. Meets infants' needs before own |
|   B. Self-confident | 1. Relaxed and anxiety free |
| | 2. Skilled in physical care of infants |
| | 3. Individualistic caregiving style |
|   C. Flexible | 1. Uses different styles of caregiving to meet individual needs of infants |
| | 2. Spontaneous and open behavior |
| | 3. Permits increasing freedom of infant with development |
|   D. Sensitive | 1. Understands infants' cues readily |
| | 2. Shows empathy for infants |
| | 3. Acts purposefully in interactions with infants |
| II. Attitudes and Values | |
|   A. Displays positive outlook on life | 1. Expresses positive affect |
| | 2. No evidence of anger, unhappiness, or depression |
|   B. Enjoys infants | 1. Affectionate to infants |
| | 2. Shows obvious pleasure in involvement with infants |
|   C. Values infants more than possessions or immaculate appearance | 1. Dresses practically and appropriately |
| | 2. Places items not for infants' use out of reach |
| | 3. Reacts to infant destruction or messiness with equanimity |
| | 4. Takes risks with property in order to enhance infant development |
| III. Behavior | |
|   A. Interacts appropriately with infants | 1. Frequent interactions with infants |
| | 2. Balances interaction with leaving infants alone |

3. Optimum amounts of touching, holding, smiling, and looking
4. Responds consistently and without delay to infants; is always accessible
5. Speaks in positive tone of voice
6. Shows clearly that infants are loved and accepted

B. Facilitates development

1. Does not punish infants
2. Plays with infants
3. Provides stimulation with toys and objects
4. Permits freedom to explore, including floor freedom
5. Cooperates with infant-initiated activities and explorations
6. Provides activities which stimulate achievement or goal orientation
7. Acts purposefully in an educational role to teach and facilitate learning and development

*Source:* Arminta Lee Jacobson, in "Infant Day Care: Toward a More Human Environment." Reprinted by permission from *Young Children* 33, 5 (July 1978): 20. © 1978 by the National Association for the Education of Young Children, 1834 Connecticut Ave., N.W., Washington, DC 20009.

# IDENTIFYING AND MONITORING CHILDREN'S INDIVIDUAL NEEDS IN THE CLASSROOM

How can you keep track of children's needs in the classroom? In addition to collecting personal information about each child, observation (as discussed in detail in Chapter 6), supported by checklists, anecdotal records, diagnostic tests, criterion reference tests, and visibility ratings, can be used to identify and monitor the special needs of the children in your center.

## Activity Checklists

One monitoring technique involves posting children's name lists in each activity area. The dates that the children use the area are recorded next to their names on the name list (see Figure 7.3). You should review the lists monthly. If a child has no dates recorded next to his name for painting, for example, you would

**FIGURE 7.3**  Sample Children's Name List: Painting—December

| Name | Date |
|------|------|
| Melissa L. | |
| Emanuel L. | 3, 5, 8, 9 |
| Mathew M. | 3, 5, 8, 9 |
| Jennie M. | 2, 4, 8, 9, 12, 16 |
| Robert M. | |
| Roger M. | 2, 6, 8, 9 |
| Karen M. | 5, 14, 16, 18 |
| Margaret M. | 5, 14, 16, 18 |
| Lori M. | 3, 4, 5, 8, 9 |
| Melodie P. | 3, 4, 5, 8, 9, 10, 12 |
| Alejandro R. | 3, 4, 5, 8, 9, 10, 12 |
| Michael R. | 3, 8, 12 |
| Jamie R. | 3, 8, 12 |
| Thomas S. | 12, 14, 16, 18 |
| Jessica S. | 12, 14, 16, 18 |
| David S. | 12, 14, 16, 18 |
| Christina V. | |
| Scott W. | 3, 4, 5, 6, 8, 10, 12 |
| Peter W. | 3, 4, 5, 6, 8, 10, 12 |

*Note:* The number of dates recorded varies according to how often the children attend the center.

be prompted to question and investigate (once you are sure that no one forgot to write a date next to the child's name) why he has not painted during that month. Perhaps he does not know how to use the paints or is afraid to get dirty.

### Anecdotal Records

Anecdotal recordings are notes about a child's interactions and behavior at the center. Every staff member is asked to note at least one incident concerning each child in the center each week. This procedure helps you keep track of the children's progress and it also serves as a check for the adults' behavior. If you can't write about a child, it usually means that you have not interacted with or observed that child.

### Diagnostic Tests and Criterion Reference Tests

Diagnostic tests and criterion reference tests can be designed in the curriculum plan as play activities. They serve as a technique for monitoring and assessing the skills the children are acquiring or already have. They show, for example, which children can run, jump, and cut with scissors.

### Visibility Ratings

A visibility rating is another way to identify which children you are interacting with. This technique involves making a list of all the children in the group without looking at a list or enrollment sheet. The last child on the list, or those children who are missing from the lists and anecdotal records, are referred to by Rabinoff and Prescott (1978) as "invisible children," children "who have made no impact on us" (p. 123). We can remember little or nothing about them. Some teachers become indignant at the suggestion that they have overlooked a child, but sometimes they do. Data from the Rabinoff and Prescott (1978) study on invisible children show that some children receive no more than six inputs a day or only negative inputs. If some children are "invisible"—or are being lost in the class in your center—it is important to discover this and to find out why teachers are not interacting with them so that you can plan to reach out to them.

### Careful Observation

In addition to identifying "invisible children," observation and recording helps us identify children with special problems. For example, one child in our group was a quiet, solitary player at ages 2½ and 3. Suddenly, at age 3½, he began to push and hit the other children and thoroughly disrupt whatever activity was going on. At first, the teachers thought it was a developmental change in behavior or some negative experience at home, but a few observations and anecdotal notations of the timing led us to identify entry to the group as the problem. This child had discovered that children were fun to play with, but he did not know how to enter a group. After a series of entries with an adult, the child began to develop the skills of entering and playing with a group of children.

In Chapter 6, we offered several techniques for using systematic observation. These techniques should be very useful to you and your staff in identifying the special needs of children. Clearly, such careful observations have similarly positive effects on meeting the needs of all children, regardless of their special requirements. We offer additional ideas in this area in our discussion of staff evaluation in Chapter 5.

### Suggested Activities

1.  Interview a group of single parents. Attempt to discover from them some of the unique aspects of raising young children alone.
2.  Identify a group of parents whose children are apt to have special needs. Discuss what these needs may be, and design or modify an early childhood program to meet them.
3.  Visit and observe an infant/toddler program or another special program for young children, such as a program for the developmentally disabled. Record your observations and analyze them in terms of meeting the special needs of these children.

### References and Further Readings

Bienefeld, Florence. *My Mom and Dad Are Getting a Divorce*. St. Paul, Minn.: E.M.C. Corp., 1980.

Berger, Terry. *How Does It Feel When Your Parents Get Divorced?* New York: Julian Messner, 1977. (For older children, but may be read to preschoolers.)

Black, R.; Dikes, A.; Anderson, K.; Wells, J.; Sinclair, S.; Gary, G.; Hatch, M.; Gangiosa, E. "Handwashing to Prevent Diarrhea in Day Care Centers." *American Journal of Epidemiology 113* (4), 1981, 445–451.

Cataldo, Christine Z. *Infant and Toddler Programs: A Guide to Very Early Childhood Education*. Reading, Mass.: Addison-Wesley, 1983.

Colby, John. *Maternal Care and Mental Health*. Monograph Series No. 2, Geneva: World Health Organization, 1951.

Day, M. C., and Parker, R. K., eds. *The Preschool in Action: Exploring Early Childhood Programs*, 2nd ed. Boston: Allyn and Bacon, 1977.

Erikson, Erik. *Childhood and Society*. New York: Norton, 1950.

Fowler, W. *Infant and Child Care: A Guide to Education in Group Settings*. Boston: Allyn and Bacon, 1980.

Gerson, Menachem. *Family, Women, and Socialization in the Kibbutz*. Lexington, Mass.: Lexington Books, 1978.

Goff, Beth. *Where Is Daddy: The Story of a Divorce*. Boston: Beacon Press, 1969.

Gordon, I. J. "Reaching the Young Child through Parent Education." *Childhood Education 46*, February 1970, 247-249.

Greenman, J. "Furnishing the Infant/Toddler Environment." In R. Neugebauer and R. Lurie, eds., *Caring for Infants and Toddlers: What Works, What Doesn't*, Vol. 2. Washington, D.C.: Child Care Information Exchange, 1982.

Grossman, Bruce, and Keyes, Carol. *Helping Children Grow: The Adult's Role*. Wayne, N.J.: Avery, 1978.

*Guide to Children's Books in Print*. New York: Bowker, 1983.

Harlow, Harry. "The Nature of Love." In Morris L. Haimowitz and Natalie Reader Haimowitz, eds., *Human Development: Selected Readings*. New York: Crowell, 1973.

Highberger, Ruth, and Boynton, Mary. "Preventing Illness in Infant/Toddler Day Care." *Young Children 38*(3), March 1983, 3, 8.

Honig, A., and Lally, R. *Infant Caregiving: A Design for Training*, 2nd ed. Syracuse: Syracuse University Press, 1981.

Huntington, D.; Provence, S.; and Parker, R. *Day Care: Serving Infants*. Washington, D.C.: U.S. Department of Health, Education and Welfare, 1971.

Jackson, E. H.; O'Brien, M.; Porterfield, Jan; and Risley, Todd. *The Infant Center*. Baltimore: University Park Press, 1977.

Jackson, Philip, and Wolfons, Bernice. "Varieties of Constraint in Nursery School." *Young Children 23*(6), September 1968, 358-367.

Jacobson, A. L. "Reaching the Young Child through Parent Education." *Childhood Education 30*, 1978a, 33.

Jacobson, A. L. "Infant Day Care: Toward a More Human Environment." *Young Children 33*(5), July 1978b, 14-23.

Karnes, Merle. *Activities for the Baby's First Eighteen Months*. Circle Pines, Minn.: American Guidance Service, 1979.

Keister, M. *The Good Life for Infants and Toddlers*, 2nd ed.

Washington, D.C.: National Association for the Education of Young Children, 1977.

Keyes, Carol, and Grossman, Bruce. *Families and Schools: An Ecological Study*. Unpublished manuscript, 1979.

Levenstein, P. "Cognitive Growth in Preschoolers Through Verbal Interaction with their Mothers." *American Journal of Orthopsychiatry 40*, 1970, 426–432.

Lillard, Paula P. *Montessori: A Modern Approach*. New York: Schocken, 1972.

Neugebauer, R., and Lurie, R. eds. *Caring for Infants and Toddlers: What Works, What Doesn't*. Washington, D.C.: Child Care Information Exchange, 1980.

Neugebauer, R., and Lurie, R., eds. *Caring for Infants and Toddlers: What Works, What Doesn't*, Vol. 2. Washington, D.C.: Child Care Information Exchange, 1982.

O'Brien, M.; Porterfield, J.; Jackson, E. H.; and Risley, T. *The Toddler Center*. Baltimore: University Park Press, 1979.

Osofshky, J. D., ed. *Handbook of Infant Development*. New York: Wiley, 1979.

Perry, Patricia, and Lynch, Marietta. *Mommy and Daddy Are Divorced*. New York: Dial Press, 1978.

Piaget, Jean. *The Psychology of the Child*. New York: Basic Books, 1969.

Provence, S. *Guide for the Care of Infants in Groups*. New York: Child Welfare League of America, 1967.

Rabinoff, Bunny, and Prescott, Elizabeth. "The Invisible Child: Challenge to Teacher's Attentiveness." In *Joys and Risks in Teaching Young Children*. Palo Alto, Calif.: Pacific Books, 1978.

Rheingold, H.; Gerwitz, J.; and Ross, H. W. "Social Conditioning of Vocalizations in the Infant." *Journal of Comparative and Physiological Psychology 52*, 1959, 68–73.

Rogers, Carl. *On Becoming a Person*. Boston: Houghton Mifflin, 1961.

Satir, Virginia. *People-Making*. Palo Alto, Calif.: Science and Behavior Books, 1972.

Sparling, J., and Lewis, I. *Infant Learning Games: Resources for a Parent Child Partnership*. New York: Walker, 1979.

Spitz, Rene A. *The First Year of Life*. New York: International Universities Press, 1965.

Turnow, Rita. *Daddy Doesn't Live Here Anymore*. Chicago: Great Lake Living Press, 1977.

Vigna, Judith. *Daddy's New Baby*. Niles, Ill.: Albert Whitman, 1982.

Weissbourd, B., and Musick, J., eds. *Infants: Their Social Environment.* Washington, D.C.: National Association for the Education of Young Children, 1981.

White, B. L. *The First Three Years of Life.* Englewood Cliffs, N.J.: Prentice-Hall, 1975.

White, B.; Castle, P.; and Held, R. "Observations of Visually-Directed Teaching." *Child Development 35,* 1964, 349–364.

Willis, A., and Ricciuti, H. *A Good Beginning for Babies.* Washington, D.C.: National Association for the Education of Young Children, 1975.

# Chapter 8
# The Humanistic
# Orientation
# and Parents

How does the humanistic framework guide our work with parents? Parents need to be included in center activities for many reasons, not the least of which is that they are people with feelings (sensitivities, insecurities, prejudices, etc.), with philosophies and goals, with hopes for their children and for themselves, and with needs that they hope to fulfill by involvement in your program. You don't get to know these things by keeping the parents at arm's length, as many schools attempt to do.

Parents have the ultimate continuing responsibility for their children. They also have prerogatives and responsibilities as parents. We don't do them or their children a service by taking over their roles or by leaving them out. Sometimes, parents are all too willing to give an early childhood center the major responsibility for the education and even the health and emotional welfare of their children. We need to get to know these parents especially. We need to help them discover their own parenting potential.

Parental involvement is an important part of an early childhood program. This involvement means *being a part of* and it means *doing*, both of which make the learning associated with these activities especially meaningful. Parental involvement contributes to parents' self-esteem by helping them become better equipped to fulfill their roles and by acknowledging that they have something to contribute as well as something to learn. Parents' contributions to school life are helpful in at least two other respects: they demonstrate to the children the caring and competencies of their parents, and they make it possible for schools to function more effectively by supplementing paid personnel.

## CONCERNS OF PARENTS
## AND PROGRAMS FOR PARENTS

Ellis Evans (1976) makes the point that parent programs may be placed on a continuum ranging from token involvement, such as having a parent as a guest speaker once or twice a year, to community control, whereby parents are directly involved in all policy decisions made about school life. What options are available within these two extremes? What purposes does each option potentially serve for the children, the parents, and the school?

Before attempting to construct a program for parents, it is useful to look at the issues parents must confront in today's society. An effective program for parents should address these issues. As educators, we should not lose sight of the fact that we are part of society; that is, our contribution to the lives of parents and children is part of the dynamic interactive process in which three components—parents, child, and society—have an effect on each other and continually alter the balance between them.

### Concerns of Parents

Parental concerns fall into two categories: (1) those related to child rearing and (2) those that are specific to parents themselves. As implied earlier, these issues and concerns are not independent of one another: In fact, they usually overlap considerably and even interact. Optimally, programs for parents should be designed to offer information and services in both areas.

#### CHILD-REARING CONCERNS

Child rearing is often difficult for young couples. In many cases, young parents are isolated from their own parents, to whom they might otherwise turn for assistance. In addition, new parents are likely to have had little prior experience in caring for young children and little preparation for the stresses of parenthood. Many young parents turn to experts for advice, through reading and direct contact, but they may find the advice confusing, contradictory, or difficult to follow without additional support.

The programs for parents offered by early childhood centers can help young parents examine alternatives and work out approaches that are consistent with their own needs and values. Such programs can also help parents learn more about the developmental needs of their children.

Many young parents require support and encouragement in their parenting role. Adolescent parents, in particular, have unresolved developmental problems of their own for which they require help before they can meet the needs of their children. Single parents are likely to have special needs in addition to the common concerns of all parents of young children. How can parent education help? As we will discuss in some detail here, workshops and meetings contribute substantially to young couples' confidence as parents, and this self-confidence is an essential ingredient for effective parenting.

### THE PARENTS' OWN NEEDS

Although programs for parents are not a substitute for counseling, they can alert young couples to resources for mental health services and orient them toward self-help when appropriate. Having children can put a great strain on a marriage and can affect the personal development of the parents. Older parents of young children, some of whom may be giving up careers to care for their children, have many personal adjustments to make. How to meet the needs of children, how to handle the discrepancy between the ideal and the actual, and how to share responsibility for child care are some of the issues faced by parents that can be addressed in a parent education program. Such problems may be triggered by child-rearing issues, but they also relate to the parents' own personal development and adjustment difficulties. Factors such as poverty, isolation, divorce, single parenthood, and increased opportunities for women outside the home complicate the lives of young parents and inevitably affect their children's adjustments. Programs for parents give these young parents opportunities to share their experiences with others, to become more aware of their own feelings, to learn constructive methods of problem solving, to learn how to work with institutions, to discuss their concerns in a supportive atmosphere, and generally to feel less isolated and more effective. Put in yet another way—they learn to become good parents and still be individuals in their own right.

### THE COMPLEXITY OF MODERN LIFE

We referred earlier to the complexity and style of modern life as possible contributors to adjustment problems faced by parents and children. We, and others (e.g., Bronfenbrenner 1973; Kenniston 1977), have observed that our lives have generally become more transient and less secure as a result of increased mobility, a deemphasis on tradition, and rapid technological change.

Family life seems to be caught up in a wave of change and speed as it is isolated from community, religious, and extended family bonds that at one time were a source of permanence and meaning for parents and children. The high incidence of divorce and single-parent families is both a symptom of this change and impermanence and a cause of it. However, we do not mean to imply that all this change is bad. Obviously, our values are changing regarding the role of women and regarding our attitudes about racial and ethnic pride, work and leisure, cooperation and competition, and so forth. These changing values require that we take another look at how we are raising and educating our children to make the choices and meet the demands that lie before them.

We may feel overwhelmed when we stop to consider that we are preparing our children for a future of which we ourselves are uncertain. This is especially so if we take into account still other factors of modern life, including the possible dangers from nuclear armaments, pollution, noise, and the disturbing ecological effects of our progressive loss of contact with nature. These contemporary forces have put family life under great strain. Urie Bronfenbrenner (1974) sums it up as follows:

> Specifically, when the circumstances and the way of life which they generate, undermine relationships of trust and emotional security between the family members, when they make it difficult for parents to care for, educate and enjoy their children, when there is no support or recognition from the outside world for one's role as a parent, and when time spent with one's family means frustration of career, personal fulfillment, and peace of mind—it is then that the development of a child becomes adversely affected.

## Programs for Parents

In our work with parents, certain needs have become apparent, including (1) the need to counteract their isolation and guilt by sharing their problems with others who are facing similar dilemmas; (2) the need to discuss those concerns in a supportive atmosphere, free from the threat of judgment by others; (3) the need to sort out the advice from experts and others, with which they have often been bombarded; (4) the need to be better informed about the developmental needs of their children; (5) the need to learn constructive techniques for problem solving and managing the home environment; and (6) the need to be more aware of their own feelings and needs as individuals.

We view our parent programs as an *interactive process* in which all participants assume an active role. As James Hymes (1974) has noted:

> In times long past there was no need for parents and teachers to plan ways of working closely together. Home and school were one. The teachers were the mothers and fathers, the older children, uncles, aunts and grandparents, all under the same roof. . . . The curriculum was the life of the family and the life of the community. . . . But it is gone today. . . . Nothing automatically guarantees that home and school will not be in conflict, each pulling for its own separate concerns.

Hymes suggests that parents and schools need to work together for a new unity, what he terms a "man-made bridge—a link to enable us . . . to achieve unity for children which once existed naturally."

The family is, after all, the primary social institution in the early development of the child, both in terms of its initial impact on the developmental process and its continued influence on the emotional and intellectual life of the child. It has become increasingly evident to most observers of early school intervention programs that the family is the most effective and economical system for fostering and sustaining the development of the child (Biber 1970). Bronfenbrenner's words are echoed by Biber (1970), who suggests that "to work with the child alone is to invite failure and frustration" and by Schaefer (1973), who concludes that "ideally, professional education will provide support for family education of the child. . . . Schools are necessary but not sufficient for the education of the child." White (1974) and Shipman (1976), among others, have made similar points about the importance of enhancing the role of parents. In recent years, parent programs have mushroomed—some as parts of early childhood centers, others as separate programs. Those that are separate could conceivably be designed as part of an early childhood center if parental involvement was part of the philosophy of the center.

Some programs—such as PACT (Parents and Children Together), sponsored by the Family Service Association—provide
family education, individual counseling and recreation, and discussions on prenatal care, nutrition, child development, and
parenting techniques. These programs are usually held in community agency facilities. In some parent-child programs held in
hospitals, mothers return with their babies to share ideas; talk with
doctors, nurses, or social workers; and have parent-child home
visits arranged. Some programs are held at universities. For
example, the Pace University Parent Services Center was planned
as a place where parents can come for support in their parenting
role by sharing ideas and concerns with their peers, discussing
recent research with professionals in seminar groups, and practicing skills with their children among peers. Some sessions are
held for parents alone. These sessions are more topical, rather
than emerging from group needs; as do some of the parent-child
sessions.

The limited availability of funds for early childhood centers
has often necessitated using parents in a variety of capacities to
supplement small staffs. In contrast, public schools have generally
depended less on direct parental participation and in many cases
have actually discouraged it. At this time, the mood and thinking
about parent involvement has improved, as educators (both public
and private) have recognized (1) that parental help can ease the
financial burden of escalating school budgets; and (2) that parental
help can enable teachers to conduct more open and individualized
classrooms, where children can have more direct access to materials and to adult assistance than is possible in a classroom where
learning activities are grouped for supervision and direction by a
single teacher.

Parents have begun to be aware of their role in the education
enterprise. They have discovered the importance of their contributions to their children's attitudes about discovery, exploration,
and learning—both in and out of the classroom (e.g., parents'
attitudes and reactions to children's getting messy, exploring the
kitchen cabinets, investigating their own bodies, etc.). Many
parents have also become aware that it is important not to delegate their parental responsibilities to the education specialists. The
humanistic centers of which we speak recognize and teach the
value for parents, children, and teachers of parents' full and
genuine involvement in the educational process at school and at
home.

## ENROLLMENT PREPARATION
## AND PROCESS

Where does work with parents begin? The actual enrollment process is often our first contact with a parent. The process begins with a parent's phone call or letter asking for information about the school. Centers have various procedures for responding to these initial requests. Some simply send out a brochure about their school. In other centers, the director may have a personal telephone conference with the parents to discuss the school. Another procedure often used is a formal open house for groups of parents, either as a recruitment effort or as the center proceeds to enroll families. At each group session, center personnel talk about the various facets of the program, the philosophy of the center, the curriculum for children, and parental involvement. Current users of the center are also often present.

### Parental Visits

Some centers encourage parents to make a first visit to the center without their children so that they can spend sufficient uninterrupted time examining the program and discussing their needs and the center's policies. Keep in mind that a center visit, especially the initial one, can be confusing and even frightening for parents. It may be helpful if you provide parents with some guidelines to help them to decide whether your center is an appropriate choice for their child. For example, you might discuss what your center offers in terms of hours, food service, transportation, and other practical services. You might also help parents by describing your teaching staff and educational program and offering some pointers about what to look for while observing the program in action.

In addition to an orientation and a guided observation, it is useful to conduct a private interview with each parent. The interview should be informal (perhaps including coffee) and uninterrupted, if possible. Parents should be encouraged to ask questions, to raise any concerns about their child's participation, and to discuss any particular needs of the child that should be taken into account in placement and planning.

It is helpful for directors to ask questions also. Why does this parent want to come to this particular center? How did she hear about it? What does she want from the program for her child? What does she expect from it for herself? Listening to a parent's answers can often give you insights into her perceptions of her children's needs and of what children's programs should be like, as well as her thoughts about whether your school can meet those needs. After the interview, the parent can be given a registration packet and information about returning for a visit with her child as soon as she makes up her mind about enrolling the child in the program.

### Parent Orientation

Once the children have been enrolled, an early orientation meeting for parents is advisable, particularly if you believe that the school and the home are partners in the child-rearing effort. Not only is an orientation meeting a chance for the parents to find out about the program, it is also a chance for them to meet the personnel of the center, often in an informal setting. Some schools give group orientations and discuss parents' role in the center, such as parent committees, parental opportunities, and policies and procedures. Some schools assign peers—parents who are veterans of the center—to assist new parents.

### Handbooks

Handbooks should contain all of the orientation information; they serve as a written account of the information about your center that is presented at the orientation meeting. A handbook is also helpful when orienting parents whose children have not entered the center at the start of the year. At our own campus center, which had children entering on a continuous basis, we found a parent handbook to be especially valuable.

Our campus child care center parent handbook developed out of a need to communicate special and ongoing policies to several hundred parents over a few years. It contained the following information:

Description of the center
Philosophy and attitude regarding parents

Medical and emergency procedures
How birthdays are handled
Arrival and dismissal procedures
Procedures for notifying school in case of illness
Absence
Daily attendance procedure
Parental visits
Clothing for school
Emergency clothing
Fund-raising
Special services
Goals of the center
Policies for registration
Enrollment and previsits
Policies regarding toilet training
Holiday gift giving
Introduction of the child to school
Meals and snacks
Newsletter
How bills are calculated
Payment procedures
Parental evaluation comments
Other suggestions

## ONGOING CONTACT WITH PARENTS

### General Meetings

Early childhood programs have developed various ways of working with parents. A general meeting is a convenient way to introduce parents to the staff, the school's philosophy, anticipated programs, and so forth. You might provide a brief program, followed by an informal period for parents and teachers to get together over coffee and become better acquainted. General meetings also are a way to present information of broad interest to parents.

#### TOPICS
Some of the topics we have found to be of general interest to parents include discipline, developmental stages, the role of fathers, sibling rivalry, communicating with children, children's

fears, preparing for later grades, sex education, children and television, and developmental disabilities in early childhood.

### FORMAT

General meetings are usually too large to allow much interaction between the parents and the school personnel. Their size can be kept reasonable, however, to allow for more give and take and attention to individual parents' interests. For example, in a large school, meetings might be held for a limited number of classes at one time or might be devoted to specific topics so that only parents with those particular interests will attend.

Having a guest speaker (e.g., a pediatric dentist, a health officer) is the most common format, but films or presentations by panels of parents, teachers, or other professionals, or even skits prepared by parents, are also effective.

Some kinds of information, such as orientation material, are more efficiently presented at one time to a large group. On other occasions, general meetings may be used to bring together all of the parents and teachers to solve common problems (e.g., fund-raising, planning special events, and creating a sense of togetherness).

Getting parents involved through songs, crafts projects, or discussions can be useful, even with relatively large groups. Usually, such meetings are followed by a brief social time in which more individual contact is possible.

### SOURCES OF SPEAKERS

Local mental health associations, child guidance clinics, colleges and universities, social service agencies, cooperative extension programs, professional societies, and libraries are all good sources for films and speakers. It is also helpful to belong to local early childhood professional groups (e.g., associations for directors or cooperative school groups) where information on interesting meeting topics, speakers, and other programs may be shared. Don't forget that parents themselves may have expertise that can be of interest and value for presentation at a general meeting.

## Workshops

### NATURE AND PURPOSE

Workshops for relatively small groups focus on specific needs of parents or are used as follow-ups to a discussion begun at a larger meeting. They allow for a more intimate exchange of feelings and concerns than is possible in a large meeting, and they are even more likely to prompt a parent to share genuine concerns than a one-to-one meeting with the teacher, which may be somewhat intimidating to some parents. In a small workshop group, parents with special concerns may find that they are not alone in their experience—that other parents have experienced the same feelings. Parents can present problems faced by all of the parent group members. A workshop can also be conducted around a new book on child rearing that all of the parents have read. We have compiled the following list of workshop topics that we have found to be of particular interest to parents of young children:

Crafts, cooking, and other educational and recreational activities to do at home
Problems of single parents
Dealing with death and divorce
Women working outside the home
Independence training for children (dressing, feeding, etc.)
Nutrition
Discipline
Stepparenting
Adoptive parenting

The workshop format may be used to meet the needs of any group of parents whose children are enrolled in your center. Let's take single parents as an example. It is very likely that at least a few children of single parents will attend your center. If that is the case, you may be able to set up a special workshop for this particular group of parents. Topics such as discipline and developmental concerns (e.g., negativism, dependence) take on special meaning to a parent who is raising a child alone. Other issues likely to be of particular concern to single parents include dating, feelings toward men or women, the need for same-sex role models, dealing with anger, child care, and visitation. It is useful for single parents to discuss these and other topics in groups especially created for them. Since more single parents are working, these meetings should probably take place at night, which might best be handled by rotation of staff, extra staff pay as an incentive, or the use of outside consultants, but the extra cost and effort is well worth it in terms of the value for the parents and the children.

Because of the limited financial and emotional resources of single parents, support groups such as Parents Without Partners may be recommended. In the absence of such a resource, you may be able to begin such a parent operation through your own child care facility. Services such as babysitting, family outings, and social events for single parents could be offered. This might be done in cooperation with local mental health or community action groups or through a religious organization. Such a program might also qualify for funding from a variety of sources (see the discussion of funding in Chapter 10). Similar special-interest workshops may be created around many of the issues cited in the list of workshop topics presented earlier.

### ACTIVITY WORKSHOPS

Activity-oriented workshops have a special impact because of the opportunity they provide for parental participation. For example, in crafts workshops parents may engage in fingerpainting, collage, puppet-making, and a variety of other activities enjoyed by their children at school. The crafts workshops may also be built around activities for parents to do at home with their children, including birthday and holiday party ideas. These workshops allow parents to experience directly the types of activities their children enjoy. They are also a marvelous way for parents to relax and get to know one another better. In the process, they also frequently learn more about themselves (e.g., their reactions to materials) and become more effective at facilitating the creative play of their children.

### SELF-HELP WORKSHOPS

Self-help workshops involve considerable participation in discussions of child-rearing problems. In sharing their ideas, the parents not only gain a deeper insight into solutions for their own parenting problems but also find that others are confronted with similar dilemmas and that they have something to contribute in terms of advice or comfort. We have observed that parents who are invited to share their experiences are able to share their feelings as well and, as a result, to help one another gain feelings of confidence in their parenting skills.

In these meetings, the leader's role is to be accepting and supportive. The teacher-leader serves as a catalyst, facilitating discussion and helping to identify common problems. It is important that neither the leader nor one parent dominates the discussions and that all the parents are guided into helping one another. Advice should be offered in the form of suggestions, which may then be discussed and adapted by participants for their own use.

The leader's model of acceptance and concern will likely be imitated by the other group members and will invite participation of even the most reluctant group members. As the leader, you may need to help parents find resources (e.g., babysitters, agencies, Parents Without Partners), but here again other group members may have resources and actual experience to share. The result is that the participants usually discover their own values, resources, and problem-solving abilities; ultimately, personal growth takes place, which is very gratifying to observe. The idea is not to foster dependence on the school but to help parents to become more self-assured and able to rely on their own experience and resources.

Topic-oriented workshops also have a self-help aspect in that parents usually offer each other encouragement and advice, which you may help them evaluate and use constructively. Topic-oriented workshops may also involve some hands-on experience as parents role-play or practice projects that they can then repeat at home. A good way to ensure larger attendance at workshops and other parent meetings is to provide babysitting services.

### SOURCES FOR WORKSHOP LEADERS

Training for workshop leaders and ideas for workshop topics are often available through local mental health associations, child guidance centers, and other community health groups. In addition, these organizations might have workshop leaders available to lead groups on specific topics. Professional associations (e.g., county psychological associations) may also be a source of workshop leaders or speakers. Films to stimulate discussion are often available from the aforementioned sources as well as from local libraries, early childhood and day care councils, state education departments, and local universities. Parents with particular expertise and experience are another source for workshop leaders. Educators, psychologists, physicians, nurses, and social workers who are parents of children in your center should not be overlooked as resources for workshops. We have also found that for certain topics—such as being single, adoptive, or foster parents— a parent leader for a workshop who has had personal experience in the area is often able to initiate a lively and meaningful discussion.

### PARENT-STAFF WORKSHOPS

Workshops in which parents and staff members get together to complete a project for the school help further parent–teacher relations, increase parents' feelings of contributing to their children's education, and add support to the center's operation. Toy building and construction of curriculum materials make excellent mutual projects.

A publication of the Council for Exceptional Children (CEC), *How to Fill Your Toy Shelves Without Emptying Your Pocketbook*, was prepared by the Southwest Educational Development Laboratory (1976). The booklet describes how to plan a parent-staff workshop for building classroom materials. The authors recommend having all materials for the necessary tasks ready in advance and arranging the material in advance in such areas as woodworking, painting, and sewing. Some of the items that parents and staff have in such projects include art aprons, finger-paint, nailboards, rhythm instruments, lockboxes, "feely" boards, and beanbags.

### Bulletin Boards

Bulletin boards should not be overlooked as a means of parental education. They are a convenient way to keep parents informed about school activities. They also provide direct information of use to parents, such as recipes for materials made in school (e.g., play dough), lists for activities to do at home, pertinent articles about child rearing (e.g., how to handle parent-child separation anxiety at the beginning of the year), and other references to books and magazines that might be of interest to parents. Notices about committee activities, community activities, and community resources such as clinics may also be posted. Still another use for bulletin boards is for displaying children's work. Such display accomplishes many goals, not the least of which is to give parents a sense of the activities taking place in the school.

### A Lending Library for Parents

If the budget of a center allows, it is useful to have a library containing current and recommended books and pamphlets on child care, educational activities, and disease and health information. Such materials can often be obtained free from insurance companies and medical suppliers. Center libraries might include such books as *Parent Effectiveness Training* and *Between Parent and Child* for meeting parents' needs for help in interpersonal relations; *Part-Time Father, The Father: His Role in Child Development,* and *Momma* for single parents; and books about explaining death to a child or how to enhance a child's self-esteem. Figure 8.1 lists some useful publications for parents.

**FIGURE 8.1**  Useful Publications for Parents

**Parenting Newsletters**
*Growing Parent* and *Growing Child*
Dunn and Hargill, Inc.
22 N. Second Street
Lafayette, IN 47902

*Parent Talk*
6402 East Chaparral Road
Scottsdale, AZ 85253

*Parent Resources*
Box 107, Planetarium Station
New York, NY 10024

*First Parent*
P.O. Box 29
Bridgeport, CT

*Totline: Activity Newsletter for Home and School*
Warrent Publishing
P.O. Box 2253
Alderwood Manor, WA 98036

**Parenting Books**
Atkin, Edith, and Rubin, Estelle. *Part-Time Father.* New York: Vanguard, 1976.
Bates, Louise, and Ilg, Frances. *Your Four Year Old, Wild and Wonderful.* New York: Dell, 1978.
Bernstein, J. *Books to Help Children Cope with Separation and Loss.* New York: Bowker, 1977.
Brazelton, T. B. *Infants and Mothers.* New York: Dell, 1969.
Brazelton, T. B. *Toddlers and Parents.* New York: Dell, 1974.
Briggs, Dorothy Corkille. *Your Child's Self-Esteem, The Key to His Life.* Garden City: N.Y.: Doubleday, 1977.
Chase, Richard, and Rubin, Richard R., eds. *The First Wondrous Years.* New York: Macmillan, 1979.
Evans, Judith, and Illfeld, Ellen. *Good Beginnings: Parenting in the Early Years.* Ypsilanti, Mich.: High Scope Press, 1982.
Fraiberg, Selma. *The Magic Years.* New York: Scribner, 1959.
Gardner, Richard A. *Dr. Gardner's Stories About the Real World.* New York: Avon, 1972.

**FIGURE 8.1** *(continued)*

Gardner, Richard A. *The Parents Book About Divorce.* New York: Bantam, 1977.

Ginott, Haim. *Between Parent and Child.* New York: Macmillan, 1955.

Gordon, Thomas. *Parent Effectiveness Training.* New York: Wyden, 1970.

Grolman, E. A. *Talking about Divorce and Separation.* Boston: Beacon Press, 1975.

Grossman, Bruce, and Keyes, Carol. *Your Children, Your Choices: A Parenting Guide for the Early Years.* Englewood Cliffs, N.J.: Prentice-Hall, 1975.

Hope, Karol, and Young, Nancy, eds. *Momma: The Source Book for Single Mothers.* New York: New American Library, 1976.

Lynn, David B. *The Father: His Role in Child Development.* Monterey, Calif.: Brooks/ Cole, 1974.

Kelly, Marguerite, and Parsons, Elia. *The Mothers Almanac.* Garden City, N.Y.: Double-day, 1975.

Pulaski, Mary Ann. *Your Baby's Mind and How It Grows.* New York: Harper & Row, 1978.

Rubin, Richard R., and Fisher, John J. *Your Preschooler.* New York: Macmillan, 1982.

Rubin, Richard R.; Fisher, John J., III; and Doering, Susan G., eds. *Your Toddler.* New York: Macmillan, 1980.

## Some Additional Ways to Involve Parents in Center Life

Some schools invite parents to share lunch and birthday celebrations, cook special foods, or come in to talk about their occupations, hobbies, travels, and other experiences with the children. All of these activities help parents become part of the classroom life.

Some schools have newsletters prepared by the parents. By preparing a newsletter about the school for other parents, the parents get to know each other, share information with one another, participate in the school, and have an opportunity to be in charge of an important school function. As they collect the information, put the newsletter together, and have it printed and distributed, they acquire a variety of experiences and skills that they might not have had the opportunity to develop previously.

A "parent space" at school is another way to promote parent involvement. Perhaps such a space can contain a parent library or a place for coffee where parents can sit and read or talk, thus providing a further link between home and school. Such a space has particular significance for women who may feel isolated from others during the day or who may have special needs in their child-rearing tasks (e.g., single parents or parents who may be prone to child abuse).

## A NEWSLETTER FOR PARENTS

Parents like to know who is minding their children and what their children are doing in school, and they appreciate information about coming meetings and activities. School districts and Head Start programs often publish newsletters for parents. Some programs, such as the Freeport (New York) Center for Early Childhood, publish their newsletters in both English and Spanish. The YMCA/YWCA have begun to sponsor parent programs and nursery schools and generally publish newsletters for their parents.

Schools may put out newsletters every month, bimonthly, or a few times a year. One issue, usually the first, should contain a brief description of the staff members and their backgrounds and favorite activities. Newsletters also contain articles on classroom news to share curriculum activities and rationale with parents. There are often lists of coming trips or reports of past trips. In cooperative schools, newsletters serve as reminders to parents of their participation schedules and possible other functions of which the parents need to be aware. Very often a page for the children is included in a parent newsletter.

Some parent newsletters are published as independent operations (see Figure 8.1). *Growing Parent* and *Growing Child* are two newsletters that focus on age-related topics. *Parent Talk*, published by an author of several books on children who is also a parent, focuses on general topics, such as discipline and punishment, rather than on age-related topics. *Parent Resources* is a newsletter published by a parent support group; it includes such topics as separation, activities, and taking care of teeth. *First Parent* is a newsletter developed by the creators of *First Teacher*; it includes such topics as making toys, taking trips, recipes, and saying goodbye.

## NOTICES OF RESOURCES FOR PARENTS

It is most helpful to inform parents, through a newsletter, bulletin board, or special notices, about activities and services that are available for them and their children. College-sponsored conferences on career development for women and seminars for single parents are the types of activities that should be brought to parents' attention. Notices of cultural activities sponsored by local mental health associations or cooperative extension and library programs are also valuable.

### LETTERS TO PARENTS

Letters to parents may be sent on a variety of occasions. Usually, there is an introductory letter in the beginning of the year that states the policies of the school, its philosophy, and/or general orientation information. Some schools put together a parent handbook in lieu of a series of letters. As we noted earlier, the handbook may contain various materials, including center bylaws, attendance procedures, goals for children, a history of the school, parental responsibilities, payment policies, and fund-raising activities.

### HOME VISITS

Home visits, in which teachers go to the homes of children attending the center, can be used as an extension of classroom programs to deal with various specific problems faced by parents. The focus in these visits should always be to help strengthen the role of the parents, rather than to take over. Sometimes, parents want you to solve the problems with them, but it is more meaningful and effective for you to guide them in working with the children themselves. Teachers who are assigned to make home visits may need to be reminded that the emphasis is on enhancing parents' skills so that they can take a more active role in their children's education. Although specific activities may be taught to the parents, they also learn about their own competence and are able to extend the approach to many other areas of involvement with their children.

## Parental Evaluation of the School

Encouraging parents to evaluate the school provides them with guidelines for detecting good practices that meet their child's needs. Some schools use a formal evaluation sheet or checklist; others provide principles (sometimes based on the CDA) for parents to use as a basis for evaluation in determining whether the school is meeting their child's needs. Learning to evaluate the center not only helps parents to be better consumers, it also encourages schools to maintain sound educational practices. A recent government publication provides a comprehensive review of questions parents should ask in regard to choosing child care (Center for Systems and Program Development 1980).

Figure 8.2 is a sample evaluation form to be used by parents.

**FIGURE 8.2**  Sample Evaluation Form for Parents

In order to help us work toward improving all aspects of our child care center, we are asking you to evaluate certain aspects of its operation:

Care of Your Child:

Curriculum:

Availability of Caregivers for Communication with You:

Flexibility in Terms of Meeting Your Needs:

Clearness of Policies:

Other Activities:

Newsletter:

Fund-raising:

Parent Meetings:

Conferences:

Other:

## Fund-raising

Although fund-raising in early childhood centers primarily serves an economic function, it also fulfills the very important secondary function of drawing parents and school together, encouraging social interaction among the parents, and providing publicity for the school.

### TYPES OF FUND-RAISING ACTIVITIES

One type of fund-raising activity involves home "parties" where parents sell and buy products (e.g., Tupperware). One school made $1,800 selling household items. Other schools sell Christmas cards and gift items. One small school of only 35 families earned $435 by selling greeting cards. Some schools sell T-shirts as a combination fund-raising/public relations event. Other fund-raising activities include art raffles, "white elephant" or tag sales, bowling parties, dinner dances, fashion shows, and potluck suppers.

Some fund-raising activities also provide excellent community activities for children. Parents can have fun setting up carnivals or arts and crafts days for families. Such events involve a considerable amount of effort in setting up, obtaining prizes, manning booths, and so forth; but they are well worth the effort in terms of community involvement and publicity for the school. A children's concert is another way to raise funds, and it gives the young children in the community a nice experience. One school's music specialist contributed her time for a concert; it was not a major source of extra money for the school, but it was a great success in every other way.

Another example of an event that ostensibly was held to raise funds but was much more significant in other ways comes from our campus child care center. Because parents felt a bond with the school through their warm relationships with the staff, they suggested initiating a small fund-raising activity—a bake sale. The sale netted only $53 but it involved the participation of both the parents and the children in doing the baking at home. The teacher got involved when she and the children also baked for the sale at school. Each child make one cookie to eat and one to sell. The children then visited the tables on the college campus where their mothers were selling the cookies and cakes. Everyone was surprised to see that one very shy boy, who had not spoken in class, started talking to the college students as they purchased the baked goods. Soon he was approaching others, encouraging them to buy his cookies. The money earned through this little sale was put to a good purpose; it was used to buy children's books and to start a library for parent education.

In cooperative nursery schools, participation in fund-raising activities is usually required of the parents. Such schools generally have a fund-raising chairperson and a committee in charge of planning and conducting fund-raising events.

### Build-ins

Build-ins are activities in which parents, and sometimes staff members, make things for the school, clean up the school grounds, repair equipment, paint, or do other maintenance together. This type of activity is useful for virtually any early childhood center, but, like fund-raising, it is apt to be required in a cooperative nursery school. Build-ins foster parental identification with the school and staff, allow for social interaction among the families of children who are attending the center, and give the children a sense of continuity between home and school.

In one example of a build-in, parents at one school got together to design and build a useful and unique piece of outdoor equipment. Discussion of this project was initiated at a board meeting, then referred to the general membership for implementation. The fathers, the director, and the staff conferred about the requirements of the piece, made sketches, and checked the design for safety. The plan was approved by the general membership, and the materials were purchased. Some of the fathers, mothers, and children formed a committee to do the actual building. Needless to say, all of the families involved in the project felt a special pride in this piece of equipment.

At another school, one parent designed some attractive wooden toys as samples. He then supervised and assisted many other parents in building these toys. Some were used at school and others were sold at a school-sponsored crafts fair.

## PARENTS AND ADMINISTRATIVE FUNCTIONS

In many nursery schools, parent cooperatives, day care centers, and Head Start programs, parents are involved in administrative functions. Sometimes, parents serve as officers, as in cooperatives, which are parent-owned and operated; in other cases, they serve on liaison committees or on community boards that serve along with the professional staff in directing the school's activities.

Working in an administrative capacity gives parents considerable responsibility for decision making. It is an opportunity for concerned community members to develop and use their competence toward the creation and functioning of an educational endeavor that will serve their own and others' children. Many parents become quite knowledgeable about educational decision making under these circumstances. Perhaps even more important, they often acquire a sense of involvement that carries over into other community activities. We have seen many instances in which the expertise and sense of competence and commitment acquired by parents through their administrative participation in early education programs helps them make a significant contribution to subsequent community functions.

## PARENTS IN THE CLASSROOM: VISITORS AND VOLUNTEERS

### Purpose

For parents who work, attend school, or for other reasons have limited free time, being allowed and even encouraged to make periodic visits to the classroom is an important form of involvement. These visits help the parents by allowing a firsthand glimpse of how the classroom functions and how their child functions within it. Seeing the parents in the classroom is also very exciting for the child and tends to promote the connection between home and school for both parent and child.

Because of parents' work or school schedules, it is helpful to have an open-door policy, whereby visits can take place at any time at the request and convenience of the parents. In some cases, such as when a school is large, it may be necessary to schedule in advance, but the schedule should reflect your awareness of parents' needs, such as making an observation period available on a parent's lunch hour. At the university center, when parents are working or attending classes on campus, they are encouraged to join the children during their lunch break (bringing their own lunch if they like) or between classes. This is also possible in such situations as an industry-owned child care center, where parents are working nearby.

Another way to involve busy, active parents is to have them submit a list of their interests, work experience, and hobbies and then invite them to share these with the children. This process of having the parents visit, help, and share is good for both parents' and children's self-esteem and contributes to children's identification with their parents' working roles. Seeing their own parents in this helping capacity also reinforces the bridge between home and school. Parents who are visiting the classroom may also be encouraged to participate, however briefly, in fingerpainting, block building, and other activities.

As a teacher or director, you should make a parent visitor comfortable and check with her to see if she needs further assistance as the visit continues. Some parents may wish to assist in the classroom on a limited basis when they come for a visit. Other parents may be more comfortable simply observing, at least at first. Visitors are less distracting if they are seated along the side of the room or at a table, rather than standing or sitting in the front of the room as an object of curiosity.

It is important to point out to visiting parents that their child is apt to behave differently from the usual when he is being watched. Some guidelines regarding what to look for while observing their children may help parents note significant behaviors. "Guides for Parent Observation," in a publication of the Austin (Texas) AEYC (1973), provides some questions for parents to ask themselves while observing. Some sample questions are as follows:

1. Observe your child's interaction with other children:
   a. How does he interact (leader, follower, etc.)?
   b. Does he tend to seek out others?
   c. Does he tend to play with others? For how long?
   d. Does he play by himself?
   e. Does he talk with other children?
2. Observe your child playing and working:
   a. What types of activities does he seem to enjoy?
   b. Does his pattern of play and work change as the day goes on?
   c. Does he respond affectionately to the adults?
   d. Does he relate easily with one adult? More than one?
   e. Is he able to communicate his needs to the teacher? To relate his experience to the teacher?

Parents may also be guided to widen their observations beyond the scope of their own child—to look at the program and to observe the available material and its use.

## Parent-Child Activity Workshops

Parent-child activity workshops (we call them open houses) are designed for parents and children to play, experiment, and generally experience together. Most communities offer few, if any, opportunities of this sort. Museums occasionally have some events in which parents and children can do things together, but most of the offerings for children do not actively engage parents (very often children are dropped off to participate alone). Parent-child activity workshops bring parents and children together in a meaningful way and are particularly appropriate for sponsorship by an early childhood center. These workshops or open houses may also serve the secondary functions of publicity or fund-raising for a school. We have held regular visiting days, as described in the parent letter shown in Figure 8.3.

We have also had successful experiences with two other workshops: a science open house and an arts and crafts open house. We offered these workshops on many occasions in a number of settings and in each case found them to be of great benefit and enjoyment to the families who participated.

### SCIENCE OPEN HOUSE
*Purpose.* The science open house that we offered at our center was designed to give parents the opportunity to share science activities with their children. Activities that we have used successfully include a "feely walk," in which children and parents put their bare feet into sunflower seeds, sand, and a spongy substance; a sensory experience, in which they guessed what something was by taste, smell, hearing, or touch; and playing with locks, magnets, electrical circuits, and shadows. Nature exhibits included live animals and plants; stuffed replicas; and samples of rocks, shells, and sea treasures. Water activities included pouring, floating and sinking, mixing colors, and making bubbles. We have also provided opportunities to transform materials, such as combining confectioner's sugar, water, and food coloring to make icing for cookies and squeezing oranges for juice. Finally, parents and

**FIGURE 8.3** Letter to Parents Regarding Visiting Day

Dear Parent:

We are having a play day at school today so that you can see and try out some of the toys and materials that your child/children use while they are here.

The *inside activities* that are available today are:

| | |
|---|---|
| painting | table toys |
| water play | supermarket |
| clay | watching the animals |
| salt | |

The *outside activities* that are available (if time permits) are:

large tinkertoy
large blocks
aluminum climber

Please try to take turns with the materials. As a guide for you: we usually allow four children at the blocks; six at the clay; four at the salt; four at the paint; four in the supermarket; four at the water table; two to watch the animals; four at the big blocks outside; four at the tinkertoys. Since you are participating and are larger than the children, please account for that as you take your turns. Remember to play with and assist your children.

The staff will be available to help.

*Our schedule* will go something like this:

| | |
|---|---|
| 1:00 to 1:30 | Play |
| 1:30 to 1:40 | Cleanup—We hope you will assist the children in putting things back where they go; that is an ongoing part of our day. |
| 1:40 to 1:50 | Records and singing |
| 1:50 to 2:00 | Going home and goodbyes |

Ordinarily we would read a story also, but you may do that as part of your free play time.

Thank you for coming.

*Note*: If you would like to experience and experiment with some of the materials when the children are not with you, let a staff person know and perhaps we can arrange a parents' night with the materials.

children are offered a chance to plant seeds to take home and observe. This serves as a nice reminder of the experience and a follow-up activity.

*What Happens at the Science Open House.* When the parent and child arrive, they are given a prepared map. Arrows to point the way are posted conspicuously, along with big signs reminding them that this is a time of sharing and a chance to find out about some science activities that can be replicated at home. We like to display Rachel Carson's (1956) *A Sense of Wonder*, with a quotation about sharing a child's sense of wonder, for parents to see; this sets the mood for their participation. We also place school registration materials, information about the school, and a sign-in sheet near the entrance.

Each time we have set up this activity, it has been hard work, but the joy and fun the parents and children experience make it very worthwhile. After reading about the idea in "A Sense of Wonder—Parents and Children Together" (West 1974), Keyes (1978) designed her own fair and subsequently published a description of her experience.

Our science open house was open to the public as well as to the families who attend our school. In this way, the wider community was made aware of our program through direct experience with our facilities, staff philosophy, and representative activities.

*Deciding on a Time and Place.* Setting up a science open house is hard work but well worth it if you get a reasonable turnout. To ensure a good turnout, it is important to give some consideration to when and where the open house is offered. It is nice to have the event in your early childhood center or classroom if possible. If you don't have enough room to spread out the exhibits or to accommodate the number of parents and children who might attend, it may be necessary to hold the event in a larger area, which may or may not be connected to your school. Also, be sure to consider the weather; for example, don't have it in midwinter if you are in a northern area.

*Choosing the Activities.* After the dates are decided, determine which activities to include. We generally choose some activities that we've used in the curriculum so that the children can show their parents what to do, and then we add some new ones as special treats. It's important to decide how much room and what supplies are necessary for each activity. Then draw a map to decide where each activity should be located. One strategy has been to arrange sensory exhibits together according to how much time they'll take to do. Locating some shorter and some longer activities next to one another is helpful for the flow of traffic. The maps in Figures 8.4 and 8.5 show two model setups, one for one room and the other for two rooms.

**FIGURE 8.4** Setup for Science Open House in One Room

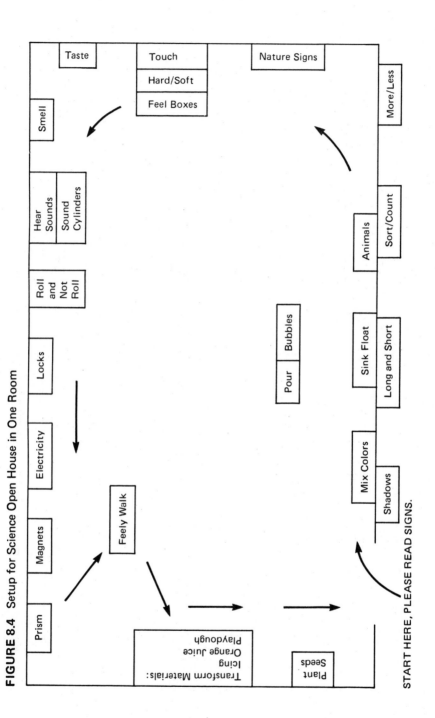

START HERE, PLEASE READ SIGNS.

185

**FIGURE 8.5** Setup and Traffic Flow for Science Open House in Two Rooms

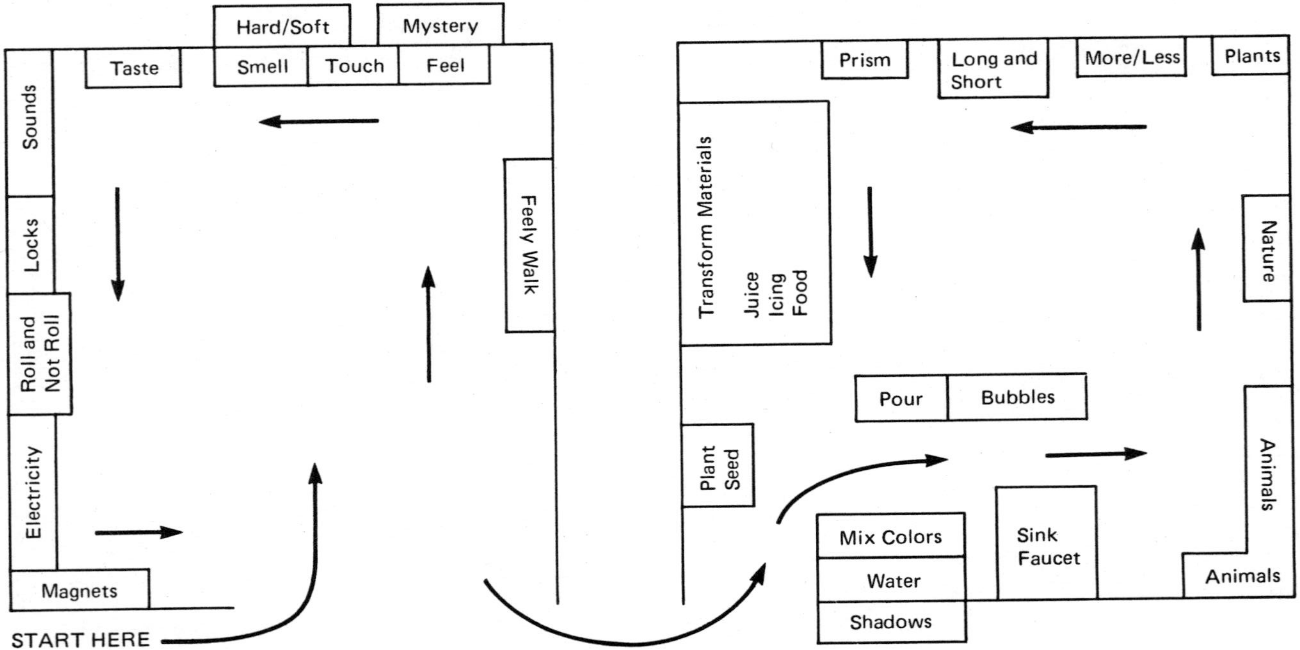

Thank you for coming. We hope you have shared a pleasant time with your child.

186

During the planning stage, it is helpful to ask those who attend your center if they have interesting materials to share for the open house. We have received lava rock, antlers, and even a pineapple plant and a snake one year. This is also a good opportunity to ask parents to help.

As the materials and exhibits are collected, make signs for each activity and exhibit, explaining how to use the materials and asking questions. (For example, near the whale's teeth, the sign might read: "Whose teeth are bigger, yours or this whale's?") The materials should be as self-explanatory as possible, with simple, clear directions. Before the open house, a member of the staff should follow the directions at each exhibit to be sure the signs are easy to understand.

Generally, staff members and volunteers are around at the open house for extra supervision, to keep supplies available, and to interpret instructions when necessary. Some activities are likely to need one-to-one supervision (e.g., making icing and juice), while others just need someone to replace materials as they are used up. This shouldn't be too much of a problem, since parents are expected to do the activities with their own children.

*Publicity.* Notices can be given out to each of the children attending the school, with an invitation to share the experience with other preschool children they know. Announcements can usually be placed in local newspapers in an events-of-the-week column and on some local radio stations as a community service bulletin. Emphasize that parents and children are expected to participate together.

In summary, the aspects of planning and preparation that contribute most to the success of an open house are the following:

1. Clear and easy-to-follow directions for the experiments.
2. Interesting activities for parents and children to enjoy together.
3. Adequate supplies, space, and supervision.

### ARTS AND CRAFTS OPEN HOUSE

After the science open house had been offered a few times, we decided to try to develop another parent-child activity along the same lines. Many schools offer arts and crafts activities in which children are introduced to materials, but it is most unusual to have an arts and crafts event for children and parents to participate in together. The sign we posted at the door on the day of the open house reflects the spirit of the activity:

> PARENTS:
> OUR PURPOSE IS TO GIVE YOU AN OPPORTUNITY TO SHARE SOME CREATIVE ACTIVITIES WITH YOUR CHILD, ACTIVITIES THAT YOU CAN THEN USE AT HOME, WITH EVERYDAY MATERIALS. JOIN YOUR CHILD AND GUIDE HIM/HER IN TRYING THESE ACTIVITIES. THE SIGNS EXPLAIN WHAT TO DO. PLEASE ASK THE ASSISTANTS AND VOLUNTEERS FOR HELP ALSO, IF YOU NEED IT.

*Planning and Preparations.* Again, planning for the open house involved deciding what activities to have, where and when the event will be held, who could be called upon to help, and what materials need be ordered. Directions for each activity were then prepared and put onto signs to be posted at the activity site. Just as with the science open house, we felt it was valuable to pretest each activity and set of directions to see that they were accurate and easy to follow.

After pretesting, a large, brown bag was coded with a number corresponding to the position of the activity in the room, and all the materials for the art or craft, plus the signs and a sample, were put in the bag. This helped in setting up the activity, and it made dismantling easier.

As noted earlier, the arrangement of activities is important. The activities we found successful included texture rubbing, modeling with plaster of paris, sponge painting, making cup puppets, and making play dough. As in the science open house, the parents and children were given maps as they entered the room (see Figure 8.6), and signs were posted about happy sharing and reminding parents to do only what their child was developmentally ready for. Each family was given a bag for their completed projects so that they could take them home. Prior arrangements had been made for drying some of the materials.

The open house was fun for the participants, who enjoyed creating together and discovering craft activities that could be done at home. It also afforded an opportunity to observe parent-child interaction and to help when necessary. It furthered home-

**FIGURE 8.6** Setup for Arts and Crafts Open House

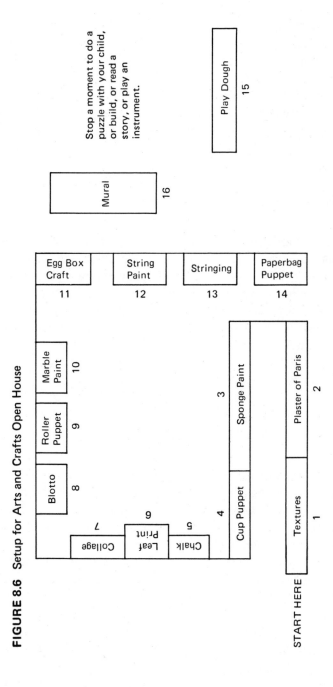

Stop a moment to do a puzzle with your child, or build, or read a story, or play an instrument.

| | |
|---|---|
| Play Dough | 15 |

| | |
|---|---|
| Mural | 16 |

| 11 | 12 | 13 | 14 |
|---|---|---|---|
| Egg Box Craft | String Paint | Stringing | Paperbag Puppet |

| 8 | 9 | 10 |
|---|---|---|
| Blotto | Roller Puppet | Marble Paint |

| 7 | 6 | 5 |
|---|---|---|
| Collage | Leaf Print | Chalk |

| 4 | 3 |
|---|---|
| Cup Puppet | Sponge Paint |

| 1 | 2 |
|---|---|
| Textures | Plaster of Paris |

START HERE

We hope you have had a pleasant visit. Thank you for coming. Please call us or write to us for information.

189

school relations, as had the science open house. We repeated the arts and crafts open house several times with success.

A university, town, or private gallery might be willing to co-sponsor such an event or to have periodic exhibits of special interest to young children, as does our university gallery. If children can see and touch or even do art work themselves in a setting with paintings, drawings, and sculpture displayed, it is very inspiring for them and much more meaningful than the usual gallery or museum visit.

## Parents as Volunteers in the Classroom

There has been a tendency for both public and private schools to increase their use of parent classroom volunteers. Aside from the help that parent volunteers provide, their participation is also an excellent way for these parents to strengthen their parenting skills. They have the benefit of observing the teacher role models and an opportunity to try various parenting and teaching behaviors under the supervision of a teacher. We have found it to be a very effective form of parent education. Parent volunteers are discussed in more detail in Chapter 9.

## Keeping in Touch with Parents

An important aspect of the types of parental involvement we have been discussing is keeping in touch with parents. Parents need opportunities to hear about how their child is doing in school and to discuss problems or exchange information outside the formal parent-teacher conferences. We will briefly discuss two obvious yet significant ways of keeping in touch that are more informal and may be more timely: spontaneous conversations and telephone calls.

When children are being picked up and dropped off, a parent may feel the need to share some information with the director or teacher or to ask a question. At these times, a bit of information may be exchanged about a child's current behavior, or a parent may wish to point out a recent experience that may be affecting the child (perhaps making him tired or upset). We had such an experience a few weeks after the school year started. A little boy who had regularly come and played happily suddenly rebelled against coming—something that might happen for a variety of reasons. In this case, the teacher discovered, while talking for a moment to the parent at the door, that the child's grandmother was telling the mother in front of the child that it was wrong to send him to school. The parent and teacher discussed a possible solution, which was then implemented successfully, and the child returned to his former way of separating and playing happily. Of course, you may not have the time to deal adequately with a problem during such a brief contact with a parent, but it is possible and useful to follow up on information exchanged in such spontaneous conversations through telephone calls or scheduled meetings. You may have other responsibilities at the time that prevent you from giving your complete attention to a problem, or you may wish more privacy or more time to prepare for a discussion. Although these are very legitimate reasons for putting off a discussion, don't forget to express your interest and arrange for a follow-up meeting, no matter how busy you are.

Another way of reaching out in a personal way to parents is through telephone conversations. Sometimes, you might call to share a piece of exciting news about a child's accomplishment. At other times, you might want to share a concern or help a child through a bad time.

In one case, for example, there was considerable competition between two brothers who attended the same school, but it had always been controlled. One afternoon, however, the older boy exploded and poured paint on an assistant, shouted, and became unmanageable. The teacher later telephoned the parents to express concern for the child. The parents were comforted that the staff was so concerned. They suggested what they thought had caused the child's upset—the younger brother's birthday. Together, teacher and parent discussed how to help both boys handle their competition in the future.

Too often, telephone calls from schools and teachers have negative connotations. It is important to keep in mind that a call to share a pleasant bit of news, as well as one to express concern on less pleasant occasions, enhances the communication process between home and school.

## PARENT-TEACHER CONFERENCES

### Purposes

Parent-teacher conferences provide an important link between home and school. The process works two ways: (1) the teacher learns about the child's family life, culture, early development, particular skills, interests, and personality from the parents; and (2) the teacher shares with the parents her observations of the child's reactions to materials, activities, other children, and adults and her suggestions for extending the school's educational program to the home. As a result of these meetings, the child feels the continuity and cooperative alliance that exists between home and school. The child is also able to benefit from the teacher's expertise beyond the classroom. This is the "manmade bridge" mentioned earlier (Hymes 1974).

An informal survey was conducted some years ago regarding strengths and weaknesses that parents perceived in such conferences. Some of the strengths mentioned were that the parents received detailed information on specifics: painting, playing with others, cutting, and social interactions. Parents also appreciated detailed notes on their children that the teacher had written. They generally preferred to be informed of their children's progress in all areas specifically, rather than hearing general comments, such as "He's terrific!" It seems that parents are most pleased when they are convinced that the teacher really knows their children.

### Preparing for the Parent-Teacher Conference

Teachers who have taken notes and who have prepared for the conference can be more specific and detailed in their comments. Anecdotes are particularly interesting and instructive for parents. The following are some ways to prepare for a conference:

1. Review your notes on previous conferences and other contacts you've had with the parents (telephone, written, personal).
2. Collect and review the child's work and observations and any notes you have made about the child since you last saw the parent.

3. Be as well informed as possible about the child's behavior.
4. Give careful consideration to the developmental and educational implications of your observations and other ideas about the child.

### Scheduling Parent Conferences .

Schools may have parent conferences once a year, one each term, or more frequently. We have found that an early conference, in which parents can share information about their child, their family life, their expectations for the school, and so forth, is especially useful. This initial conference is an important step in establishing the teacher's alliance with parents and in generally furthering the communication process. At later conferences, the teacher may share more in-depth information about the child and observations she has made during the year as she continues to share goals and other ideas with the parents.

### Setting the Stage

The key to a worthwhile parent-teacher conference is the development of an interpersonal atmosphere in which parents recognize that your mutual interest in the child prevails and in which they feel comfortable and are willing to share information honestly. This atmosphere is difficult to attain at times, because parents are inclined to approach the situation somewhat defensively. They may wonder what you think of their child. In the case of a preschooler, this may be the child's first extended experience outside the home, which is a special source of anxiety for parents and young children. This is the first chance for a child to be evaluated by a professional in comparison with other children of the same age. The parents usually want to know, "How does my child stack up?"

To set the stage, it is useful to have a comfortable place to meet (ideally, without a desk between you). Greeting the parents with some informal conversation when they arrive also helps them relax. The following are some useful ideas for beginning a parent conference:

194WORKING WITH PEOPLE

1. Say some positive things about the child. This is reassuring and flattering for parents who may be a bit
   worried about how you value their child.
2. Encourage the parents to speak, and listen to what they
   have to say. It is easiest to establish a good relationship
   with parents if you help them voice their concerns and
   share their observations. Listening is a good way to create
   a friendly atmosphere.
3. Communicate a feeling of caring. Let the parents know
   that whatever is said, your primary concern is for the
   child, because you genuinely care about him.

## Forming an Alliance

Once you've established that you are a caring person who is
not passing judgment on them or their child, you can begin to
establish a working partnership with parents. The child is your
mutual concern. What are your shared goals for the child? Do they
correspond? Can you work out differences?

Cultural, socioeconomic, religious, and even personal differences between you and the child's parents may contribute to a difference in priorities or values. Being the teacher does not assure
that you know what is best for a child in the whole context of his
life. A major purpose of the parent-teacher conference is to help
you formulate educational goals in conjunction with the parents,
who are concerned about and responsible for their child's development. It is as great a mistake for you to feel that parents should
completely and passively submit to your view of the child's needs
as it would be for them to feel that you should blindly conform to
their wishes. The issue of reading is a good example. Parents may
enter their child in your program expecting that you will focus
your efforts on teaching him how to read. Rather than completely dismissing their concerns or totally submitting to them, it
is important that you find out where their concerns come from
(e.g., wanting to impress others, desiring to compensate for their
own educational weaknesses, or hoping to prepare their children
to overcome ghetto conditions). It is also important that you respect their point of view while you attempt to make them aware
of the potential value of play and other prereading activities as
more developmentally appropriate and more likely to help the
child realize his educational goals in the long run.

## Conducting the Conference

In addition to the important tasks of establishing an alliance between home and school and sharing her observations of the child's behavior at school, the teacher may learn a great deal about the child from the parents during the conference. To accomplish this objective, some questions to keep in mind during the conference include the following:

1. Are the parents comfortable?
2. How can you help them to be open?
3. What are the parents' attitudes and values that affect their child-rearing practices?
4. What are the problems that the parents have confronted at home (e.g., nutrition, discipline, toilet training)?
5. How do the parents perceive their child?
6. What is the nature of the parent-child interaction?
7. How does the child behave (react) at home?
8. What do the parents expect from the school? How can these expectations be formulated in terms of goals?
9. What sort of nonverbal communication are you receiving from the parents (e.g., body language, facial expressions)?
10. Do you understand what the parents are saying, and do they appear to understand you?

It is useful to keep track of your own feelings and attitudes during the interview. Try to be aware of your own prejudices and values as you attempt to guide and inform parents, and be sure to look for signs of anxiety, anger, or other feelings that might interfere with communication as the conference develops.

## Individualizing Educational Goals

Ultimately, an individualized learning program must take into account the specific strengths and weaknesses of the child toward whom it is directed. As we noted earlier, parents who trust you will be honest about how they feel, about the abilities their child seems to demonstrate, and about some of the deficits the child might need to overcome. You may not totally agree, since you see the child in a context in which he might react very differently (e.g., be more independent, more fearful, etc.) than he does at home. Also, by virtue of your training and potentially greater objectivity, your perception of the child might be different from the parents'. As we pointed out earlier, it is best to avoid an adversarial position, but you should not let the parents feel that you agree with them completely when you do not. A good working relationship should allow for some genuine differences of opinion, which might be resolved through discussions or might remain unresolved until more information is available. All details may not be worked out or shared during the conference, but it is beneficial for parents to realize that you are aware of their child's strengths and weaknesses and that you have taken them into account in your individualized plan for him.

### Establishing a List of Priorities

Given a set of mutually agreed upon goals, it is helpful to establish a list of priorities for the pursuit of these goals. Many times, priorities are determined by developmental sequence, which dictates an order of acquisition of skills. For example, training the child in identification and sorting of objects (classification) should ordinarily precede an attempt to teach counting skills. Other priorities may have to do with parental concerns, with the particular interests of the child, or with the availability of materials. Although you may not be able to share all the details with the parents—and you need to remain flexible—it is useful to discuss with them where you think the emphasis should be placed at a particular time (social skills, gross motor skills, etc.) and get their reaction. If you can agree on priorities, each taking into account the other's position, you have accomplished a great deal.

### Discussing Teaching Strategies

Once you and the parents have agreed upon some additional goals and priorities, you may also wish to discuss with them some of the actual teaching strategies and techniques you intend to employ. As the professional educator, you must take primary responsibility for such choices, but in many cases it is helpful if the parents are able to see how the activities they observe in the class-room are related to your goals.

### Additional Parental Concerns in the Parent-Teacher Conference

Although educational concerns are likely to be your primary focus in a conference, the parents may be dealing with problems at home for which they need help. You are not a therapist, and you may need to refer parents to a mental health specialist for further counseling. However, you can often help relieve some of their stress just by listening without passing judgment. You may also be able to offer some information about child development or activities that might help solve the problems. Be cautious about offering advice, except by way of suggestion (e.g., "This may work, etc.). Remember, also, that parents will not learn to trust themselves if you attempt to supply all the answers (even if you think you have them all). It is important, however, to help the parents articulate the problems they may be having with their child and, through your questioning, help them to discover possible solutions.

### General Guidelines for Working With Parents

Most parents feel guilty. No one is able to live up to her ideals; as a result, everyone is likely to experience some guilt. A little guilt is helpful, in that it can be used to mobilize change in parental behavior when necessary, but guilt can also interfere with parental performance. For example, if parents feel guilty about being too restrictive, they may not be able to set adequate limits for their children. In other cases, guilt can cause parents to be too demanding of their children, whose behavior they view as a reflection on themselves.

Before we leave the subject of parent conferences, it is important to note some frequently overlooked obstacles that prevent parents from even getting to a conference. We've already mentioned work schedules as a potential problem, but we have also encountered problems of dress, language, babysitters, parents' prior experiences with schools, strangeness or formality of the setting, and transportation. When arranging an appointment, it is helpful to call the parents when you suspect they might not be receiving written communications from the school (young children are apt to lose such notices) or when you suspect illiteracy on the part of the parents.

## A FINAL NOTE

In many communities, parents come from backgrounds or cultures that are different from those of the school's director or teachers. It is especially important in such cases to make a conscious effort to overcome the barriers that cultural differences can create and to form an alliance between the center and the parents. To alleviate some of the problems in parent-teacher relations, particularly when there is wide diversity in cultures, some schools have auxilliary teachers to help teach the regular teachers the ways of the community or even to interpret for parents and teachers who speak different languages.

### Suggested Activities

1. In your center, are parents part of the activities? Prepare procedures for parent participation in the activities.
2. Review your center's parent handbook to see if it covers all the topics identified in this chapter. Add any other sections it needs.
3. Prepare a list of community resources available to the parents in your center.
4. Is there a parent evaluation form for the parents? If not, use the one here or design one.
5. Prepare a parent newsletter for your parents.
6. Plan a parent conference.

### References and Further Readings

Austin AEYC. *Ideas for Administrators*. Washington, D.C.: National Association for the Education of Young Children, 1973.

Auerbach, Stevanne, and Freeman, Linda. *Choosing Child Care: A Guide for Parents.* San Francisco: Parents and Child Resources, 1976.

Biber, B. *Goals and Methods in a Preschool Program for Disadvantaged Children.* Unpublished manuscript, Bank Street College of Education, New York, 1970.

Bronfenbrenner, U. Testimony before the Subcommittee on Children and Youth, Senate Labor and Public Welfare Committee, as reported in *Report on Preschool Education,* October 3, 1973, pp. 3-6.

Bronfenbrenner, U. "Is Early Intervention Effective?" In *A Report on Longitudinal Evaluations of Preschool Programs,* Vol. II. Washington, D.C.: Office of Child Development, U.S. Department of Health, Education and Welfare, 1974.

Carson, Rachel. *A Sense of Wonder.* New York: Harper & Row, 1956.

Center for Systems and Program Development. *A Parent's Guide to Day Care.* Washington, D.C.: U.S. Department of Health and Human Services, 1980.

Erikson, Erik. *Childhood and Society.* New York: Norton, 1953.

Evans, Ellis. *Contemporary Influences on Early Childhood Education.* New York: Holt, Rinehart and Winston, 1976.

Gold, Jane, and Bergstrom, Joan M. *Checking Out Child Care: A Parent Guide.* Washington, D.C.: Day Care and Child Development Council of America, 1975.

Gordon, Ira J., and Breivogel, William F. *Building Effective Home-School Relations.* Boston: Allyn and Bacon, 1976.

Grossman, Bruce D. "Closing the Parent-Professional Gap: Toward a Better Working Relationship with Parents of Developmentally Disabled Children." In Barbara Feingold and Carol Banks, eds., *Developmental Disabilities of Early Childhood.* Springfield, Ill.: Thomas, 1977.

Hymes, James I., Jr. *Effective Home-School Relations.* Carmel: Southern California Association for the Education of Young Children, 1974.

Kenniston, Kenneth. *All Our Children: The American Family Under Pressure.* New York: Carnegie Corporation, 1977.

Keyes, Carol. "A Science Open House is Worth Copying," *Young Children 31* (5), July 1976, 346-351.

Levenstein, P. *Verbal Interaction Project: Mother-Child Home Program Manual for Reapplication of the Mother-Child Home Program,* 2nd ed. Freeport, N.Y.: Demonstration Project, 1973.

Morrison, George S. *Parent Involvement in the Home, School, and Community*. Columbus, Ohio: Merrill, 1978.

Schaefer, George. "Development Research and the Educational Revolution: The Child, the Family, and the Education Profession." Paper presented at the annual meeting of the American Educational Research Association, New Orleans, February 1973.

Shipman, Virginia C. "Young Children and Their First School Experience." Princeton, N.J.: Educational Testing Service, 1976.

Southwest Educational Development Laboratory. *How to Fill Your Toy Shelves Without Emptying Your Pocketbook*. Reston, Va.: Council for Exceptional Children, 1976.

West, Suzanne. "A Sense of Wonder—Parents and Children Together." *Young Children 29*(6), 1974, 363-368.

White, Burton, "Reassessing Our Educational Priorities." Paper presented at the Educational Commission of the States Early Childhood Educational Symposium, Boston, August 1974.

# *Chapter 9*
# *Volunteers*

Volunteers in an early childhood program provide varying perspectives and can be a rich source of extra hands and energy. Some centers have student volunteers or student participants who are assigned through youth programs. Some centers have a foster grandparent program, and others use parent volunteers.

In addition to providing extra manpower, these volunteer groups—parents, students, and grandparents—can often provide expertise in music, carpentry, cooking, sewing, and the like, to help the children. In parent-cooperative nursery schools, such help is part of the parents' function. However, parents in other kinds of nursery schools also like to be part of the center life. We have had parents volunteer to run raffles and bake sales. Recently, one bilingual parent volunteered to help a non-English-speaking child learn English. Other parents—including nurses and police officers—have come to describe their work experiences to the children. In some programs, parents contribute their skills in sewing or carpentry. Playground equipment has been constructed by parent groups, and furniture and toys have been repaired.

High school and junior high school students can often be recruited for special projects also. A home economics class prepared a gingerbread house for the children one year. Sometimes, a shop class will build some needed items, or a drama class will present a program. In high schools that offer courses in child development and parenting, the students are encouraged to work with young children. While they are learning, these students bring added hands to the early childhood classroom.

Recently, there has been a focus on inviting senior citizens to become more involved in early childhood centers—to bridge the interpersonal gap between generations. In some cases, foster grandparent grant programs provide funds for senior citizen workers in early childhood centers. In other centers, the children's grandparents may be encouraged to come and spend some time. On some university campuses, groups of senior citizens returning to take courses might be encouraged to contribute some of their experience as a resource for your center.

## SCREENING AND ORIENTING VOLUNTEERS

It is essential that an interview process similar to that used for staff selection also be applied to volunteers. The interview should include a discussion of the philosophy and goals of the center, a tour of the center, and participation with the children. This is particularly important if the volunteers will be coming to the center regularly. Volunteers who will have assigned tasks that do not involve working directly with the children would not require as much preparation as those who will work with the children. The screening will help you identify how much guidance is required for those who are going to work with the children and in the classroom.

Figure 9.1 presents some guidelines for helping volunteers that were developed following discussions with teachers and directors during the Queens College Title XX Day Care Project. Notice that some advance preparation is important. The teachers suggested four types of preparation: (1) list instructions for the location and use of materials; (2) identify support tasks that need to be done at the center and that can be done without direct contact with the children; (3) assign volunteers specific activities for each day, prepared in advance if possible; and (4) list resource materials and guidelines for special situations, such as trips and emergencies.

It is useful for the director to hold a group orientation meeting for volunteers. At that meeting, the volunteers get to know one another and benefit from hearing one another's questions. The director can discuss the philosophy of the center, go over some general guidelines for working with children, and outline the responsibilities of volunteers. The classroom teachers can follow this meeting with a more detailed orientation, including acquainting the volunteers with the children and the routines in the class and holding individual interviews so that the teachers can inquire about particular purposes the volunteers may have in asking to participate and how the teachers may help to accomplish these

**FIGURE 9.1** Helping to Maximize the Benefits of Having Youth Worker and Volunteer Participation in the Day Care Center

*Preplanning by the Teachers*

A. Review tasks youth or volunteers can do with the children.
   1. Preparation of instructions for each task that includes:
      a. Where the material is
      b. How to use the material
      c. The purpose of the material and/or task
B. Review tasks they can do without children.
   1. Arrange furniture
   2. Mount bulletin board material
   3. Label shelves
   4. Prepare instructional games
   5. Prepare materials for trips
   6. Special cleanup

   *Note*: Make sure all necessary materials and guidelines are available for each task.

C. Prepare daily assignments for time period that include:
   1. Activities with children
   2. Activities without children
D. Prepare resource materials, such as:
   1. A list of favorite games of children
   2. A list of favorite songs of children
   3. A list of favorite stories of children
   4. Guidelines for trips
   5. Accident procedures

*Orientation of Youth Workers and Volunteers by the Director*

A. Suggested topics for a group meeting:
   1. Center's goals
   2. What's expected of children
   3. Discussion of youth's perceptions of children:
      a. How do they perceive what children are like?
      b. What are their favorite types of children?
      c. Problems they have encountered before in working with children.
   4. General guidelines for working with children:
      a. Ages of the children, developmental overview
      b. Classroom management, goals and procedures
      c. Principles of learning
         (1) Children learn by imitation; therefore adult models are important. Tell and show how to do it instead of how not to do it.
         (2) Children are sensitive and aware; therefore, when talking to children use normal tones, simple language; avoid using sarcasm.
   5. Job responsibilities:
      a. Hours, lunch, breaks, absences, behavior and guidelines
      b. Assignments: clerical, classroom and actual class assignment

   *Note*: Placing youth workers/volunteers names on the schedule emphasizes their role as part of the classroom team.

**FIGURE 9.1** *(continued)*

*Orientation of Youth Workers by Teacher*

A. Information to obtain before making in-class assignments:
    1. Why did you take this job?
        a. If interest in children is minimal, assign tasks youth can do without children.
    2. What prior experiences have you had with children?
    3. What special talents or skills do you have?
    4. What would you like to try with children?

B. Discuss with youth worker volunteer teacher goals and philosophy:
    1. Philosophy of the center
    2. Classroom management procedures and location of materials
    3. Schedule of the day
    4. The assignments
    5. How to use the materials
    6. Their role as a model, participant and observer

C. Establish daily procedure for the beginning of the day:
    1. Review teacher's plan of the day
    2. Talk to the teacher about the specific daily assignments

*Preparing the Children for Youth Workers/Volunteers*

*Note*: Telling the children about youth workers/volunteers should be done before the volunteers come into the classroom.

A. Tell the children that the volunteers have come to help the teacher and the children.
B. Describe to the children what kind of activities the volunteers will help with.
C. Use names of volunteers often, to familiarize the children with new adults.

*Teacher's Role as Supervisor*

A. Explain and demonstrate positive interaction with children.
B. Explain and demonstrate appropriate supervision of games.
C. Reinforce the volunteers' successful approaches and interactions with children by praise.
D. Advise the volunteers to avoid disciplinary confrontations and to call teacher when conflicts become unpleasant.

*Resources*

Grossman, Bruce, and Carol Keyes, *Helping Children Grow: The Adult's Role,* Avery Publishing Group, 1978.

    *Particular Sections That Are Useful*
    Participation—Chapter 2 (pages 18-22)
    Facilitation of Participation—Chapter 3
    Talking to Children—Chapter 4
    Discipline—Chapter 5
    Working in the Areas—Chapter 6

Schwartz, Sydney, and Joanna Mott, *Workshop in Classroom Management,* Title XX Queens College Project, 1979.

Mott, Johanna, and Sydney Schwartz, *Social Emotional Development and Cognitive Development,* Title XX Queens College Project, 1979.

*Source:* Originally created in the Queens College Title XX Day Care Project, 1981.

ends. Such individual interviews also allow the teachers to discover specific talents and abilities of the volunteers that might be helpful in the classroom. For example, a volunteer might play the guitar, might be bilingual, or might have had gymnastic training.

Next, the teachers prepare the children for a volunteer's participation in their classroom by telling the children the volunteer's name and how she may be able to help them. This helps establish their relationship with a new person and helps them use the resource of this adult appropriately. Once the volunteer arrives, an introduction to the children is in order, with a reminder that this is the person they were told about earlier. This process eases the way for the volunteer and the children and is certainly consistent with the humanistic point of view.

## HEALTH AND SAFETY CONSIDERATIONS

In addition to screening and orientation, several other areas relating to volunteers need attention. Like staff members, volunteers must prove to be in good health before they come in contact with the children. Notification of a relatively recent physical checkup, including a tine test for tuberculosis and up-to-date measles and small pox vaccinations, is often required. Also, although volunteers should be encouraged to meet their commitment to the center with consistency, they should also be made aware of the importance of staying out when they have a cold or any other potentially contagious illness. Like the regular personnel, volunteers should be required to notify the center if they will be absent.

To assure each child's safety, the teacher should review the security measures volunteers need to take on the playground, on a field trip, and even in the classroom. They should be told which children might present special security problems (including students who are apt to wander off, those who take risks in climbing, and those who are on restricted diets). The volunteers should also know the emergency first aid procedures. Despite careful preparation, however, volunteers need to be supervised in matters dealing with the children's safety. You cannot assume that they have the same experience or judgment as a professional or a parent.

## VOLUNTEER ACTIVITIES AND BENEFITS

### Some Possible Volunteer Activities

Volunteers may assist the director, teacher, and assistants in supervising and participating in indoor and outdoor play, in conjunction with policies and procedures established for their participation. In that regard, these volunteer aides must be well trained and supervised, especially if they are to be given teaching responsibilities or are ever to be placed in charge of a group of children or specific aspects of the program. For example, they may be assigned to take a small group of children out for an exploratory walk, to conduct a music session with a guitar, or to supervise woodworking or cooking projects.

The activities the volunteers do with the children depend on their level of training and their prior experience working with young children. For high school and college student volunteers, the nature of their participation also depends on their own teacher-supervisor's expectations. A good beginning activity would be assisting with a group. In that situation, the volunteer can observe the behavior of the leader and, in turn, can be more closely supervised than if she were working alone. On the playground, on a walk, or at a classroom activity, it is best not to rely on beginning volunteers for exclusive coverage.

Volunteers who will be working with individual children can first be given very specific assignments, such as getting a child set up at a painting easel or helping with a table activity. For such individual activities, teachers need to be reminded that volunteers should be rather closely supervised, at least at first. For example, a volunteer might become too involved in a puzzle or a clay project—attempting it herself and losing track of the child she is helping. Beginning volunteers are also apt to make the wrong comments while a child is painting, such as, "What is that?"

Once-a-week conferences with the volunteers are useful, especially if the volunteer is expected to be there throughout the school year. Some participants may be student teachers in training, and they will require opportunities to take over teaching functions. After appropriate preparation, we might set a goal for them of having the experience of actually taking over the lead teacher role at the center for at least a day. This would include preparing the day's curriculum as well as supervising the other teachers in the classroom.

There are many advantages to developing a plan for volunteer involvement at your center. If the process is in effect and running smoothly, it can be of great assistance to the center in terms of extra hands. It is also nice to have young, energetic students, as well as parents or senior citizens, around the younger children; this serves to bring the generations together. Volunteer involvement also enables you to have a wider range of adults than is possible with only a paid staff. You might encourage the participation of some male volunteers, some bilingual students, some persons representing other races and cultures than your staff, and some persons with particular skills or interests that you might tap. For example, we have found that students who play the guitar or who have some dance training are very helpful to the children. We should also not neglect to mention the value of encouraging a disabled person to participate at your center, if possible. This helps toward dispelling any fears or prejudices the children and staff may have toward people who are disabled. Our experience with nonsighted and physically disabled student volunteers has been very helpful in enlightening our staff, the children, and disabled students themselves about the potential of these so-called handicapped persons.

All in all, we feel that volunteers require considerable effort on the part of the director and her staff but that their involvement under planned conditions is well worth the effort.

### Benefits to Students and Volunteers of Working in an Early Childhood Center

#### PREPROFESSIONAL TRAINING

Perhaps the most obvious use of volunteer classroom participation has been to train teachers. Students in introductory education courses may be in the center to observe children interacting with the materials, to observe the teacher, and to observe each other. At a later stage, teachers in training may begin their actual teaching experience at the center, including planning and presenting lessons. However, students other than those who are planning to enter the teaching profession can also benefit from this experience. Students preparing for careers in medicine, nursing, psychology, and social work, among others, can profit from a firsthand acquaintance with young children in a group setting. For example, one of us supervised pediatric dental students who were placed in early childhood classrooms to help them become more comfortable with young children. In this process, the dental students also learned a great deal about the positive handling of children's fears. They gained confidence from observing the teachers and working with the children under the preschool teachers' guidance. We are certain that their later young patients benefited from the graduate dentists' experience, too.

### PREPARENTING

It is useful for young adults in high school and college to obtain some beginning preparation for positive parenting by participating in an early childhood center. We have found that involving future parents in interaction with the children in a child care center makes their readings and discussions, and consequently their learning, much more meaningful than if they had not had the opportunity for such a hands-on experience. Obviously, a center doesn't duplicate the home situation, but it does offer the learners a good role model with an opportunity to develop their own styles of interaction with young children under supervision.

### CHILD DEVELOPMENT

College and high school courses that focus on the psychology of human development frequently place students in an early childhood setting. The reasons are obvious; they underlie the value that such an experience has for the preprofessional student and future parent, as discussed earlier. Understanding the developmental stages involved in the growth of intelligence and in emotional and social functioning is very much enhanced by an opportunity for the students to observe and interact with young children of various ages.

We have also been successful in incorporating visits and participation in the child care center by a number of other students in child-related courses. In a course called "Child Rearing in Today's Society," students were asked by their teacher to view and evaluate the child care center from the perspective of a parent. In a course dealing with children and television, students compared children at play in the center with children watching television at home.

### ANTHROPOLOGY AND SOCIOLOGY

Professors of anthropology and sociology have found that students benefit from observation and participation in early childhood centers for the same reasons mentioned for other students. The difference is that these students may view the situation from additional perspectives. For example, anthropology students may be making some cultural comparisons regarding development or customs. Sociology students may be observing group behavior or role behavior. The early childhood classroom is a natural laboratory, which makes their course reading come to life.

To maximize the potential benefits for course-related participation, it is important that there be a clear understanding among professor, students, and center staff about the purpose and design of the assignment.

## PARENTS AS VOLUNTEERS

Many teachers are still resistant to the idea of using parents as volunteers. Some of their concerns have been that a parent is apt to get distracted by her own child or even disruptive to the child's progress. Teachers have also expressed concern that if parents are used as volunteers, they might tend to evaluate the competence of the staff or director or they might be difficult to supervise.

Despite these potential problems, there are some very significant positive benefits to be derived from the use of parent volunteers in the classroom. These benefits include the value that this type of involvement has for parent education. Their participation in the classroom gives parents the following opportunities:

1. To observe how professionals work with children and model their own behavior after them.
2. To be observed and assisted by the teacher in developing their skills with children.
3. To learn more about children and about how to use materials to stimulate development.

4. To observe their own children in a broader context and from a different perspective than may have been possible before.

In addition, of course, are the benefits derived by the school, including the following:

1. Providing extra help in the classroom.
2. Providing specialized skills and talents that would otherwise be unavailable to the teacher.
3. Freeing the teacher to work with individual children and with smaller groups.
4. Affording the teacher an opportunity to observe aspects of the parent-child relationship firsthand and to help guide parents in their roles.

The positive benefits to be derived from parent involvement in the classroom in many ways depend on the support and guidance given to parents during their participation. Some guidelines for assuring successful parent participation are as follows:

1. Conduct an orientation and/or preclassroom workshop during which the functions and roles of volunteers are described (e.g., role play and hands-on practice). For example, we ask all volunteers, including parents, to read our guidelines on observation and participation before they begin any volunteer activities.
2. Define and offer specific tasks for parents to do, such as helping to prepare materials, supervising sections of the room, working with audiovisual materials, or working one-to-one with children.
3. Take into account parents' particular aptitudes and interests in assigning them tasks.

Despite such precautions, there are some potential problems in using parents as volunteers. Some parents have trouble seeing themselves as effective and responsible educators. They may be unaware of their ability or fearful of making a mistake. For example, some parents react poorly or inappropriately with children verbally, or they may be overcritical or punitive in their actions and need continuous supervision. Other parent volunteers do not react quickly enough or do not transfer learning from one situation to another. In such cases, we recommend holding training sessions for parents.

Some parents have too many personal problems that interfere with their ability to participate effectively. Other parents have difficulty with confidentiality.

Despite the problems that might arise, however, we are convinced that using parents as volunteers in the classroom is an excellent form of parent involvement. If you still have reservations, start small; involve only one or two parents at first to see how it works. Later, you may be able to add more with confidence.

Using parents as volunteers on trips is a specific use of parent volunteers that is fairly common and very useful, but it also needs careful consideration. Using parents as volunteers on trips serves many of the same purposes as using them in the classroom:

1. It gives parents an opportunity to observe and work with positive professional role models.
2. It offers parents a chance to participate on a less regular basis than classroom volunteering usually requires.
3. It demonstrates to parents possible trips and experiences for them to share with their children outside of the school program.
4. It provides extra supervisory help to the staff at a time when it may be particularly necessary.

Just as there are special advantages associated with using parents as volunteers on trips, there are special problems that are likely to arise. Parents might be tempted to talk with one another, which reduces their attention to the children and is generally distracting. In one example of a problem from our own experience, a parent went along on a supermarket trip and wanted to do her family shopping at the same time.

Working with parents on trips is a learning experience for the staff. There are likely to be unexpected happenings as you leave the somewhat more predictable environment of the school setting. To prevent problems, it is best to have an orientation meeting or even a workshop for parents before they serve as volunteers on trips.

## CONCLUSION

As we have noted in this chapter, there are many sources of valuable volunteers for participation in an early childhood center. Their efforts can be enriching to the children as well as being a way to reduce the costs of running a center. It is the director's responsibility to select volunteers carefully and to give them a good deal of instruction, including training sessions if possible. It is also essential that volunteers be well supervised and that teachers be given support in these efforts. With proper selection, training, and supervision, volunteer participation can add significantly to the life of a center. In addition, it can and should be a valuable learning experience for the volunteers themselves.

## Suggested Activities

1. If you are working or participating at a center, identify a possible group of volunteers and write a proposal for their participation.
2. If you are at a center using volunteers, prepare a list of instructions for their possible participation in several activity areas.
3. If your center doesn't have a manual for volunteers, prepare one that they can read before participating. What kind of orientation would you give the volunteers?

## References and Further Readings

Blandt, Ronald S. *Partners: Parents and Schools*. Washington, D.C.: Association for Supervision and Curriculum Development, 1979.

Grossman, Bruce D., and Keyes, Carol. *Helping Children Grow: The Adult's Role*. Wayne, N.J.: Avery, 1979.

Hymes, James I., Jr. *Effective Home-School Relations*. Carmel: Southern California Association for the Education of Young Children, 1974.

Morrison, George S. *Parent Involvement in the Home, School and Community*. Columbus, Ohio: Merrill, 1978.

# Part III
# Management

*Part III contains two chapters that discuss the director's roles as manager and as advocate. Given the varied tasks and often hectic pace of early childhood administration, it behooves a director to learn to organize her time and her tasks. Chapter 10 offers many useful tips in this regard. Chapter 11 points out that a director not only serves as an advocate for the children, parents, and teachers in her own center, but that she can spread her expertise and her concern for children and families into the community at large through her activity in professional organizations and her active role in advocacy groups.*

# Chapter 10
# Managing
# the Program

Once you have set up an early childhood center and the program is under way, it is important to organize your time and tasks and to set priorities so that directing the program is manageable and pleasurable rather than overwhelming. Your goals are (1) to be a competent director who budgets time for all foreseeable administrative activities, allowing a portion of flexible time for spontaneous development and for emergencies; and (2) to combine efficiency and organization while maintaining a humanistic attitude toward children, parents, and staff.

We talked about some of the director's tasks in Parts I and II. This chapter will discuss the definition of your role, the organization of your time, some specific management activities, evaluation, preparation of policies and procedures, record keeping, and fiscal management.

## CHARACTERISTICS OF AN EARLY CHILDHOOD DIRECTOR

An early childhood director must be a capable supervisor, must be able to budget, must have good oral and written communication skills and good interpersonal skills, must be able to plan, must be flexible, and must be a good decision maker who is willing to initiate action (Kostelnik 1982). Rogolsky (1979) points out that some directors may find it difficult to be viewed as authority figures, especially if they are younger and less experienced than some of the staff members. She recommends that directors be aware of the possibilities of tapping the strengths of individual staff members. Sometimes, being in authority can lead to loneliness and isolation, which a director must learn to tolerate.

Hewes (1979) suggests that management of a day care center requires the same qualifications as management of any other enterprise: "A real desire to manage . . . by furthering personal beliefs and value systems and seeing a job well done." Hewes offers some other specific attributes of directors:

A willingness to take responsibility whether things turn out right or not, without watching the clock or calendar too closely or worrying about being overworked.

An ability to analyze what's important without being bogged down in administrivia or leaping from crisis to crisis.

An ability to use the time and talents of others including not only paid staff but also members of the community and the children themselves.

Proficiencies in the competencies necessary for working with children and families so that they can develop understanding of the work being done by staff and volunteers.

Recognition that every manager arrives on the job with an administrative style as unique as a thumb print, with self-awareness and self-confidence that allows openness to change and further learning.

## MOVING INTO MANAGEMENT

There is a considerable difference between being a teacher who is responsible for running a classroom and being a center director who is responsible for an entire program. As we noted earlier, having been a classroom teacher, who is used to attempting to meet everyone's needs, may sometimes interfere with the objectivity required to run a center. Directors often have little administrative training and, in an early childhood setting, may lack the supports that administrators enjoy in a school system (Rogolsky 1979). Raeburn (1977) notes some of the typical changes that occur as one moves from teaching into management. Being an administrator requires a greater commitment to agency policy than was required previously. With increased authority comes increased responsibility, along with greater accountability. Relationships with fellow workers are apt to change with increased status. One is apt to have fewer peers and to be more lonely than may have been true previously. The administrator has broader decision-making powers than a classroom teacher and is also likely to have access to more inside information. There is also apt to be more compensation but less job security and, according to Raeburn (1979), increased opportunity for both praise and criticism. Being an administrator also involves a degree of conflict. In "Thoughts for New Administrators," Robert LaCrosse (1979) makes the point that conflict is a corollary of growth; it is a sign of health in an administrative organization. There are bound to be disagreements about goals and about what he refers to as short-range "checkpoints" on the way to long-term objectives. An administrator must be prepared to acknowledge and work with differences, rather than denying them.

### Some Important Principles for Directors

In addition to the principle that conflict is an inevitable aspect of a healthy system, Kostelnik (1982) suggests other principles regarding directors:

1. The director must develop a broad perspective about her role in the agency and change her focus from unit goals to overall organizational aims.
2. The director alone is ultimately accountable for program quality and productivity.
3. The director must keep in mind the needs of adults as well as children. At times these needs conflict.
4. The role of director involves being someone's boss. Critical to this function is the supervision and evaluation of employee performance.
5. The director is responsible for achieving agency goals through the work of others. Thus, directing involves coordinating, motivating and influencing others to achieve program service, rather than expecting to perform most services oneself.
6. The mark of a good director is not necessarily charisma or personal popularity but rather the creation of an environment in which individuals are mutually engaged in working toward common goals. (p. 12)

Kostelnik (1979) also suggests a number of things a director should do to clarify her role as she moves into her position:

1. Obtain a written description and job requirements before accepting the position.

2. Clarify the persons, boards or committees to whom she is responsible, and the methods of reporting to them.

3. Identify those persons who are directly responsible to you and their job descriptions.

4. Identify the employees (if any) who may have an impact on you and your staff but who are not accountable to you. Meet with them and their supervisors to clarify how your position fits into the overall organization.

5. Obtain facts about wages, benefits, retention, promotion and grievance.

6. Learn all you can about the organizational history and the evolution of the current program. (pp. 13–14)


### Organizing Your Time

How does a director organize her time? Efficiency has to be a top priority of an early childhood center director, yet this efficiency has to be balanced with a good degree of flexibility to handle the many unpredictable events that are likely to occur on any given day. Perhaps a child has an accident, or a teacher is ill, or a parent needs some immediate attention, or the heat is off in the building. These are all extenuating circumstances that are likely to require immediate attention. How does a director protect her time and defend herself against constant interruptions? How does she set priorities? There are some specific activities that will help you perform your job as a director more easily and more effectively while still allowing you to maintain a humanistic orientation. Planning and budgeting your time allows you to be both efficient and humanistic.

Roger Neugebauer (1979) suggests that the most effective use of time results from identifying the tasks that are most vital to the success of the center. Top-priority tasks are identified by outlining the center's goals and listing the tasks required to achieve these goals. He designates these as "A" tasks, in that they have the most significant impact on the center's future. They might include presenting a proposal to the board, interviewing new staff, ordering new curriculum materials, and the like. The second-priority or "B" tasks are "must do" tasks. Less urgent, lower-priority tasks are labeled "C" and "D." Time must be budgeted to accomplish all of these tasks, but the most time should be spent on the high-priority tasks (Neugebauer recommends 4 to 6 hours per day).

Neugebauer also suggests that 30 minutes (we would say "at least") should be set aside at the end of each week to review priorities and to list new tasks. Establishing priorities in this way keeps you from spending excessive amounts of time on trivial tasks and thus not being able to get to the more significant, high-priority tasks.

Zimmerman and Herr (1981) have compiled a list of solutions to "time wasters." They suggest that having a specific telephone hour during which parents are asked to call helps prevent frequent calls to the telephone during the time you should be working with the staff and children. A similar policy may be used to arrange scheduled meetings with parents, rather than meeting with them on a drop-in basis.

### Working Job Descriptions

The planning of activities includes preparing a detailed working job description that includes hourly, weekly, monthly, and yearly descriptions of the activities that you and the staff must do. Planning a schedule takes time, but it is time well spent since it helps you determine what types of activities you need to perform each day and the best times to accomplish each task, and it allows you to be sure that you have taken into account all the activities for which you are responsible. Review your general job description to determine that you have included activities in your plan for each area of responsibility. For example, a director is responsible for overseeing the physical plant as well as for doing the educational planning. What activities would a director engage in to oversee the physical plant? The actual practices should be described in the working job description. A working job description allows a director to set detailed priorities for her tasks and allows others to know the times of the day when the director will be available to interact with them and the times of the day when she cannot be disturbed. The planned schedule can be a rotating one that accommodates early morning observations on one day and evening observations on another. The planned tasks may include administrative tasks, such as report writing, reviewing the budget, and reviewing income and expenditure for the week, as well as telephone follow-ups, class rounds, and meetings with parents. One schedule may be daily, another might be weekly or monthly.

The schedule should detail when reports are due, when meetings (internal and external) will be held, what must be done each week, what needs to be done frequently, what is urgent, and what is high-priority. The director should also make a yearly calendar, which would include such items as contract time, preparation of quarterly reports, inspections, graduation, preparation for the fall, recruitment, and so forth.

It is a good practice to develop a staff schedule. This helps the director note the adequacy of her coverage at any point and the flow of staff movement in relation to the schedule of the children.

Some centers prepare individual program schedules for each room as well as a master schedule for the director's office. All schedules are recorded on the master schedule so that the director can see all activities that are scheduled and identify where there are schedule conflicts. For example, if you have a small outdoor play area, suitable for only one class, it is necessary to use a master schedule to be sure that two classes are scheduled to use it at different times.

### Delegating Responsibility

Like all administrators, early childhood directors need to learn to delegate responsibility. Teachers and parents may be asked to form a committee to schedule parent programs. A staff member or volunteer may be able to assist with orientation and scheduling of new volunteers and even with the routine ordering of supplies. New administrators especially suffer from the plight of wanting to do everything themselves, in which case they usually find themselves bogged down in details and thus unable to give the necessary time to development, evaluation, planning, and supervision. We have discovered, however, that it is still important for a director to be in touch with the daily aspects of the center's functioning and to keep an eye on routine tasks. Efficiency is thus really a question of balance. First, you have to decide what to delegate. It is tempting to delegate low-priority or unpleasant tasks, but in some cases this is not best. We suggest that you delegate one-shot tasks with clear parameters, such as coordinating a fund-raising activity. You may also wish to delegate specific ongoing tasks, such as selecting and purchasing curriculum supplies. Once you have decided on a task to delegate, select the best person to accomplish the task and offer specific instructions.

## POLICIES AND PROCEDURES

Written policies and procedures serve as a reference for center operation. They are used in orientation for new staff members, and in centers where staff or board members change regularly, or suddenly, they allow for a smooth transfer of function from one group to another. In some cases, the regulations of a funding agency also mandate written policies and procedures. Centers often have a master manual of operating procedures that contains all policies and procedures for all aspects of center activity. The manual includes a brief overview of the program, a list of personnel, job descriptions, a yearly calendar of events, and fiscal management activities. A well-developed manual of operating procedures makes it possible for the center to function smoothly and for activities to take place even when the director is not present. It is useful when developing the manual to have various sections reviewed by selected staff and parents and to try out specific procedures to make sure they are easily understood. Some centers strive to have their procedures specific enough so that a person who had never been there before, or who had a minimum background in some of the activities, could follow the written procedures. Some centers keep a master manual containing all policies and procedures in the director's office and specific sections dealing with procedures for particular areas, such as classroom activity or maintenance or evaluation, in each area.

Sometimes, specific policies and procedures from the various sections that relate to staff activity are collected for a staff handbook; and specific policies and procedures that relate to parents can be collected for a parent handbook. Some centers even collect appropriate items for a visitor handbook.

In developing policies and procedures, it is advantageous to begin with the center's goals for staff, parents, and children. Then determine the objectives that are necessary to achieve the goals and the particular practices that must be implemented. Generally, written procedures outline who does what, where, when, and how. There are times when specific procedures are written first, because it is expedient, then collected and compiled into a manual.

What is the director's role in developing policies and procedures? If there are no existing policies, the director would be responsible for developing the appropriate goals and policies. In some centers, a policy and procedure committee is appointed to assist in that process. If a program has already been developed, the director would be in charge of supervising its operation and expanding and/or modifying its features as necessary. As part of her administrative role in that area, she would function as both a resource and a role model in carrying out the policies and procedures necessary to implement the identified goals.

The following discussion provides examples of policies and procedures developed from goals.

### Health Care Procedures

The goals for health in regard to children are to protect, maintain, and improve the children's health by a variety of methods. The following is a sample outline of some health care procedures:

1. *Objectives to Implement the Goals*
   a. Develop guidelines for the acceptable initial health status of children.
   b. Prepare daily health procedures.
   c. Determine what health services are to be offered.
   d. Decide what health education is to be offered.
2. *Practices to Implement Objectives*
   a. Develop guidelines for the acceptable initial health status of children.
      (1) The children who enter the school must have had a physical examination within the past year, with appropriate immunization.
      (2) Appropriate immunization includes (New York State is used as an example):
         (a) One dosage each of diphtheria, pertussis, and tetanus (DPT) vaccine and oral polio vaccine (or Salk after 1968).
         (b) Measles live vaccine (on or after the first birthday), documented measles history, or positive serology test.
         (c) Rubella live vaccine (on or after the first birthday) or a verbal serology test.

(d) Live mumps vaccine (on or after the first birthday) or a verbal mumps disease history as given by the parents.

(3) If a child does not have the required immunization by two weeks, he is not to be allowed to be in school.

(4) Parents must complete a health record for their children before the session actually begins. This health record is to include an emergency card, listing

(a) Child's name

(b) Birthdate

(c) Date of admission

(d) Parent's name

(e) Parent's home and business addresses and telephone numbers

(f) Name, address, and telephone number of person to be notified in an emergency if a parent cannot be reached

(g) Name of other persons to whom the child can be released

(h) Name, address, and telephone number of the child's physician

b. Prepare daily health procedures

(1) Children with active cold symptoms, a fever, or obvious illness must be kept at home.

(2) Children are to be kept at home for at least 48 hours after the temperature is normal.

(3) Children are to be kept at home with a cold until the active cold symptoms are gone.

(4) Children are to be observed daily at school for signs of illness. (Some schools have a nurse who gives an initial check to the children. If there is no nurse, the teacher would be the one to look at a child's general appearance, including posture, skin and scalp, eyes, ears, nose, throat, teeth and mouth, speech and behavior, and note any changes in child's appearance or behavior. Is a child more lethargic or hyperactive than is customary? Does one of the children seem to be listless or have a pallor? If a child has symptoms of illness, some centers call parents right away and ask that they come to take their children home. Other centers have a sick room and isolate a slightly sick child.)

(5) There must be a locked cabinet where medicine can be stored.

(6) The school nurse (if the school has one) will administer medicine, provided that parents have completed a permission form giving details about the medicine, including the child's name, the date, the time of administration, the drug, and the dose.

(7) The person who gives the medicine must also complete a form stating how the drug was given, to whom, by whom, and the time and amount.

3. *Emergency Medical Care for Children*: Emergency medical care policy and procedures are to be prepared and understood by all staff members before a school session actually begins. These procedures must include the following information:

a. Who will take care of a sick or injured child?

b. Who will call the parent?

c. Who will take care of the other children?

d. What information is to be given to the other children?

Regarding these emergency procedures, in one center located on a university campus that has an infirmary, the center's policy is that if someone gets sick or is injured such that a doctor or nurse is needed, one person will stay with the injured child while another staff member arranges for a way to take the child to the infirmary or have a medical person come to the center. In either case, the parents will be called immediately.

When children become ill or are hurt, one of the problems that seems to worry staff members more than the actual emergency is what to tell the other children. Here and in other problem situations (e.g., if we have less staff than usual), we have found that sharing the problem with the children is the most successful policy. A simple, calm explanation that the child is hurt or ill and needs our help and their help tends to keep the other children calm.

### PROVISON OF HEALTH SERVICES

We try to make sure that the children receive all the preventive testing and screening opportunities that are available. In our center on the university campus, we have been able to provide hearing and speech training. Various resources may be available in your community. In some communities, the Industrial Home for the Blind trains volunteers to administer vision-screening programs at early childhood centers. In some communities, there are volunteer groups, school health programs, and clinics that will provide screening and preventive testing, such as tuberculin tests, urinalysis, sickle cell anemia testing, and other measures aimed at helping to prevent and/or diagnose and treat symptoms that interfere with good health for children. It is necessary to develop policies regarding who will do what, when, and where, under whose supervision, and with whose permission in matters related to the children's health.

### HEALTH EDUCATION FOR CHILDREN

In addition to comprehensive health care procedures and policies, health education is important in helping children protect, maintain, and improve their health. Such specialists as dental hygienists, dentists, doctors, nurses, physicians' assistants, nutritionists, fire fighters, and police officers can be invited to discuss health and safety measures with the children. Some of the persons recruited may be parents, grandparents, or friends of children in the center, which makes their presentations especially meaningful to the children. When we have had parents who are doctors, nurses, and police officers come in their uniforms to discuss health and safety, all the children were delighted to see these parents in their professional roles.

### INFORMING STAFF MEMBERS
### OF HEALTH CARE POLICIES AND PROCEDURES

One method of making sure that staff members know about specific health care policies and procedures is to have each staff member read the appropriate manual and sign a list to note that she has read it. Another method is to hold a staff meeting to review health policies in the center, making sure that all the employees understand and are practicing appropriate procedures. Agenda items for such a meeting would include, for example, a review of how to observe a pupil's health and a review of first aid. Specialists who come to visit the children can also be scheduled to meet with the staff to discuss health matters. During their meetings, staff members might develop a checklist for evaluating health conditions in the center.

### Fiscal Management Procedures

An early childhood center is really a small business, and records of financial activity are essential for managing it effectively. Usually, directors of early childhood programs have not had formal training in fiscal management. In parent-cooperatives, parent members often serve as treasurers and handle most of the fiscal matters under the supervision of the director and the board. In other centers, there may be a part-time bookkeeper, or a director may be able to obtain accounting assistance from professional organizations that have volunteer bureaus. In some centers, all management is left to the director. If so, it would be useful for the director to join a group of directors who run similar centers and discuss fiscal policies or to take a day care management course.

Directors are responsible for making sure that there are detailed records of incomes and expenditures. They are also required to project costs and prepare budgets and financial statements for the board of directors, funding sources, and sometimes parents. An accounting system must be developed to keep records of how much money is being spent and received, what financial resources are available, how the operation functions, and what services are provided or must be developed. Of the several documents necessary in an accounting system for an early childhood center, the budget is the most important.

### The Budget

The budget is a financial plan for a center as well as a record of how well that plan is working. Annual budgets actually have several purposes. Besides providing an accounting for advisory groups and regulatory agencies, they are also extremely useful to the director for planning purposes. They help her establish priorities, they provide an economic basis for change, and they generally assure that her center is economically solvent.

Although budgets should not dictate programs, it is unrealistic, in view of increasing costs, not to consider how to maintain and improve services without constantly raising tuitions. It is important for a director to itemize costs precisely and to note which expenses are fixed and which are variable. By definition, fixed costs are items that require regular payment each year, but these days such fixed costs as mortgage or rent, utilities, and some supplies and materials tend to be more costly every year. If tuition is to stay within the range of your families, you will need to consider how to reduce or at least maintain the variable costs. One way to do this is to acquire free labor and materials when possible. Other solutions would be to attempt to reduce waste and to find less expensive sources of supplies. Perhaps spending more for a start-up amount of supplies from a wholesale distributor at the beginning of the year will save a center money in the long run by requiring fewer last-minute retail purchases. Still another solution is to increase income by increasing enrollment or by fund-raising. It is important to keep in mind, however, that increasing enrollment or fund-raising may not always be effective ways to save money if they require the addition of another staff member whose wages add to variable costs (Halpern 1982).

### BUDGET PREPARATION
Budgets are usually prepared annually according to the previous year's figures. The budget must match tuition and registration, and should include a contingency amount for one-third less enrollment than capacity. If the budget is for the first year of a center's operation, the director might consult with other centers in the area that have similar operations. There may also be parents or other members of your board of directors who are skilled in this area.

When budgeting a center for the first time, keep in mind that some of the anticipated costs will not be repeated in subsequent years. Perhaps an even more difficult problem is that enrollment will be the major basis for the income of the center. If you are beginning a program or want to make additions to an existing program, you can sometimes apply for outside funding for the center to offset the initial expenses. As we noted earlier, a needs assessment survey is advisable to see if there is a market for the program in your area. This will also help you determine which services are required in your community, which will help you reach your enrollment goals.

An early childhood program budget includes income and expense items. The income categories, or money received, include tuition, subsidies, reimbursements, donations, fund-raising. The expenditures, or money spent, include such items as salaries, fringe benefits, consultant services, equipment, supplies, rent, utilities, transportation, telephone, insurance, staff development, public relations, food, depreciation, and other costs.

One of the major costs in the center budget is *salaries*. Salary costs vary, depending on the teachers' experience and educational level. They also vary from area to area. It is sometimes helpful to survey salaries offered by other centers; this information can be obtained from experienced professionals in local early childhood organizations. Salary costs also include the director's salary and, if possible, the salary of a full- or part-time secretary. The center may also be charged with the expense of a custodian, although this might be included in the rental fee. If the center provides busing, the cost of a bus driver has to be included. If meals are provided, the cost of a kitchen staff must be considered. The number of paid assistants will vary with class size, which, in turn, is related to the ages of the children attending your center. The younger the children are, the more adults must be present. Also, if you offer a full-day program, there must be a relief staff for the afternoon and early evening.

Another expense is *overhead*, which includes such items as rent, utilities, and telephone. When determining overhead expenses, there are a number of questions to consider. For example, will it cost money to meet new standards created by changes in regulations? Does the center need more space? Do you have to make any major renovations? Are you planning more services that might require additional space or renovation? For items such as telephone, electricity, and heat, you must anticipate increases in the rates that are likely for the following year.

*Equipment* is another costly item, at least in the beginning. Good equipment that is well made and safe is expensive. You must keep in mind when you are trying to cut corners here that equipment made for family use is less expensive to purchase but is not well-enough constructed to last in a center. This consideration is especially important if you are outfitting a playground. You can actually get along quite well without swing sets and slides, but if you buy them, don't get ones that are designed for family use; they simply will not endure regular use by fifteen or more children. As we noted earlier (in Chapter 1), you can get room plans with estimated costs from most of the major manufacturers of early childhood equipment. Once you have made your initial purchase of equipment, you can add purchases, if necessary, in subsequent years. You will probably not have major replacement costs for some time, but each year you must take stock of what you have and its condition so that you can build in the cost of replacement in the next year's budget.

*Supplies* are for the most part consumable; they tend to be used up in the course of the year. The costs of supplies is sometimes difficult to estimate unless you are already familiar with the specific supply needs of the program you offer. These costs, like others, are subject to inflation.

If your program offers food, that cost also needs to be estimated. You may be able to use government surplus foods to help provide nutritious meals at a relatively low cost. You should also plan on *miscellaneous expenses*, including costs of office supplies, mailing, licensing, printing, and so on.

### PETTY CASH

In some centers, payment by check for specific purchases is the only approved way to make purchases, even for small items. This method helps keep tighter control over fiscal management than using a petty cash fund. However, it is often useful to have a small amount of cash available for immediate use. This petty cash gives you the flexibility to fill in needed supplies on an emergency basis, to take advantage of sales, and to handle seasonal costs, such as pumpkins or flower seeds.

It is the director's responsibility to maintain accountability for these funds. One way to maintain control is to keep the cash on account at a relatively modest level and to require reimbursement from the general funds after you have reviewed the expenses of the prior allotment. It is essential to keep a record of the items charged to petty cash to determine the budget category into which these purchases fall. This allows accurate planning for the following year.

### INCOME

The major source of income is tuition. After the costs of your program are estimated, determine your enrollment and calculate the per capita tuition that would enable you to cover those costs. Your tuition charges may be regulated by a social service or government agency. Tuition charges also must take into account the parents' ability to pay and their alternatives, such as at-home babysitters, if your charges are too high.

What happens if your costs are higher than tuition income? One solution is to do whatever you can to reduce costs. If there is still a discrepancy between costs and income, you may have to depend on fund-raising by parents. If so, it is important to make this clear to parents before they enroll their children. Also, as we mentioned earlier, parents may provide labor to reduce overhead.

One way to make tuition costs less of a problem for parents is to arrange a payment schedule over the course of the school year. This requires more bookkeeping, and it does not give you the money to use at the beginning of the year, but it may enable certain children to attend your program who would not be able to do otherwise. Still another way to extend the availability of your program to children whose parents cannot afford the tuition is to offer scholarships. These may involve partial reductions in tuition, which you provide for in your annual budget, or they may be based on outside monies that you have collected for scholarship purposes. Still another way to finance new programs and otherwise make additional resources available for your center is to apply for outside funding, which we will discuss later in this chapter.

### PREPARING A BUDGET
### FOR THE FOLLOWING YEAR

As noted earlier, a record of your center's performance during the current school year is usually the best guide for preparing the next year's budget. If you keep careful records, you can document any changes that might have occurred in your enrollment or expense patterns and make note of any alterations in financial planning that might be necessary in your yearly review of your program. The *Child Care Information Exchange* describes a tool for preparing financial status reports (see Figure 10.1). Four columns are used to represent the financial activity for the month:

**FIGURE 10.1** Sample Financial Status Report

| Budget Item | | Actual | Projected | Amount of Variation | Percentage Variation |
|---|---|---|---|---|---|
| *Income*: | Tuition | $17,000 | $16,000 | +$1,000[a] | +6.25% |
| *Expense*: | Salaries | $10,000 | $9,500 | +$500[b] | +5.26% |

[a]Budget justification: increase in enrollment.

[b]Budget justification: increase in staff to respond to increased enrollment.

*Source:* "Financial Management Assessment Guide." *Child Care Information Exchange,* November 1980, 15–16 (PO Box 2890, Redmond, WA 98073).

(1) actual income and expense; (2) projected income and expense (according to the annual budget); (3) the amount of variation; and (4) the percentage of variation when a variation exists. For each variation from the budget, it is important to write a budget justification that would satisfy anyone's review of the budget. By examining these four columns, you can determine your financial status and decide a course of action.

Another useful budgeting tool is the financial management assessment guide provided in Figure 10.2.

**FIGURE 10.2**  Financial Management Assessment Guide

The soundness of a center's financial management system is determined by the extent to which it meets these criteria:

> *Security*: The system should provide safeguards against accidental or fraudulent loss of assets as well as insure that all financial obligations are met.
> *Efficiency*: The system should minimize time spent on paperwork and procedures.
> *Effectiveness*: The system should provide accurate information to decision-makers on a timely basis.

The following questions are designed to be used as criteria for assessing the major components of a center's financial management system. For assistance, refer to the financial management resources recommended in the "Directors' Bookshelf."

*Establishing a Budget*

1. Does your center annually develop a formal budget which balances projected income and expenditures?
2. Does your center annually establish program goals and strive to allocate sufficient funds in the budget for achieving these goals?
3. Are income projections in the budget realistic—i.e., are estimates of fund-raising, grant and in-kind income achievable; are losses of potential income due to typical under-enrollments taken into account?
4. Have all potential sources of income been explored, such as parent fees, employer contributions, United Way, Title XX, Child Care Food Programs, tax write-offs, etc.?
5. Are expense projections in the budget realistic—i.e., are likely price increases for supplies and services factored in and is provision made for unexpected costs such as repairs and replacements or equipment?
6. Does the budget provide for staff development, staff benefits, payroll taxes, leave time, salary increases, evaluation and future planning?
7. Are funds set aside each year for long-range capital improvements?

*Receiving and Spending Money*

8. Are all monies received documented with duplicate copies of prenumbered receipts?

**FIGURE 10.2**  *(continued)*

9.  Are all monies received promptly deposited into the center's bank account?
10. Have procedures been established for avoiding overdue payments and for collecting those that occur?
11. Are all disbursements made by prenumbered check and supported by valid invoices, receipts, or other documentation?
12. Do procedures for signing checks and withdrawing funds from savings accounts incorporate safeguards to avoid the improper expenditure of funds?
13. Can signed checks always be obtained on time so as not to delay purchases or payrolls?
14. Is the petty cash system secure—i.e., is money kept in a safe place, is documentation maintained for all purchases, and are periodic checks made to verify and balance the fund?

*Recordkeeping and Monitoring*

15. Has your accounting system been designed to meet the specific information needs of the center—i.e., can financial data needed for decision-making and reporting be readily obtained?
16. Is data on income and expenses recorded in such a form that it can be applied directly in preparing tax reports, grant claim vouchers, monitoring reports and annual budgets?
17. Whenever possible, are bookkeeping and checkbook reconciliations performed by someone other than the person who receives money, writes checks, and handles petty cash?
18. Are records maintained of the center's assets and liabilities such as major equipment and appliances, savings accounts, insurance policies, outstanding loans, and tax liabilities?
19. Does the center maintain a written schedule of reports and tax payments due to public and private agencies, and is this schedule adhered to?
20. Are checking account balances reconciled monthly?
21. Is a trial balance prepared monthly?
22. Is a cash flow report periodically prepared and analyzed?
23. Is a financial status report comparing current income and expenditures against the projected budget prepared and analyzed on a monthly basis?
24. When financial problems or opportunities are identified in cash flow and financial status reports, are these situations reacted to quickly?

*Source:* "Financial Management Assessment Guide." *Child Care Information Exchange,* November 1980, 15–16 (PO Box 2890, Redmond, WA 98073).

## Records, Forms, and Reports

It is important that a center director maintain a secure location for legal documents related to the program, such as incorporation papers, licenses, records of inspections by funding agencies, and records of fire, police and health inspections. In addition, there are occasions when formal reports must be written for funding agencies or for sponsors. It is important that the director be able to collect the information for these reports as part of the center operation.

Most centers prepare a registration packet for new parents and for yearly or semester enrollment. A registration packet might contain the following:

1.  A registration form, including name, address, telephone number, age of child, hours or session they plan to use at the center
2.  A permission slip for medical emergencies
3.  A permission slip for trips
4.  A permission slip for photographs of their child
5.  A health form
6.  A medical form to be filled out by the doctor, giving the results of a recent checkup (within 6 months of entry) and a record of immunizations (New York State law mandates that children must have all their immunizations within 14 days of entering school or they will be refused admission to school)
7.  An application form, including information on the child's developmental history, family history, particular characteristics of the child, methods of discipline, what parents expect from the school
8.  A bill for tuition payments and a schedule of payments

These forms enable a director to collect data about the families that may be useful in describing the center's service to its community.

Teachers also keep a variety of records: attendance records, checklists of children's participation in various activities, daily and weekly curriculum plans, results of diagnostic checks of children's skill, anecdotal notes on children's behavior, and records of visitors to the center. These records are also important to the director in preparing reports about the center for parents, boards, funding agencies, and the community.

Attendance records and visitor records provide quantitative information on how many children are being served and how often they come. The visitor records also document ancillary uses of the center, such as for observation and instruction for high school and college students or for meetings of adults.

Staff records provide information on how many persons are employed and, in some cases, the diversity of their backgrounds. At our center, a record showing that the staff is composed of college students demonstrated that our center is used for training students as well as for early childhood program activity. Some centers use a questionnaire or conduct a survey asking parents to indicate why and how frequently they use a center and what they would do if there were no center. The results of such a survey may also help substantiate a center's existance. At a university center, it is particularly useful to count how many parents are taking courses and how many of them would be able to do so if there were no center. Similarly, at an industrially sponsored center or one sponsored by a hospital, for the children of nurses, one could keep track of the hours worked by parents to demonstrate a lower absentee record, or get statements from employees about the positive effect this service has on the children and on their own working time. Evaluation forms from parents and staff also help in determining when the center is performing as it should be and what areas need improvement in its services.

## PROGRAM EVALUATION

Evaluation is an essential part of early childhood program planning; it helps a director monitor the match between goals and practices. It is the director's responsibility to examine continually the correspondence between her goals for her program and the daily interactions between children and teachers in the classroom, between teachers and parents, and between center goals and center activities. For example, if the center decides to provide flexible schedules to fit the work and school schedules of parents or to invite parents to each lunch or play with the children at the center to support their parenting role, it is the director's responsibility to examine these practices and the written policies that they involve. It is also the director's responsibility to see that the center is implementing policies. For example, if your goal is to be as economical as possible, it is necessary to review periodically how effective you have been in finding and using inexpensive resources. At the same time, you might want to evaluate whether the lower-priced materials are of acceptable quality and whether the volunteers who provide free help in the classroom are adequately trained before they work with the children. Where a good match does not exist, a director must modify her program or her goals according to existing circumstances.

Evaluation is often required by a sponsoring or regulatory agency. In some cases, periodic reviews are done yearly; in other cases, they are done quarterly. Common areas for evalution include the functioning of the center as a whole, teacher performance in the classroom, and the functioning of the children. We shall consider here some of the ways these areas can be evaluated.

### Methods of Evaluation

One method of program evaluation involves a checklist on which the director can record results of weekly inspections at her center. A more comprehensive review of a center's functioning might include collecting data on everything from the characteristics of the families served to the relationship between income and expenses. An evaluation of the program might also include a series of questions and scales designed to examine the physical environment, the interpersonal environment, the activities that stimulate development, and the schedule. Harms and Clifford (1980) designed a rating scale for an early childhood environment that covers the following seven areas (*environment* has been defined as "use of space materials and experiences to enhance children's development, daily schedule and supervision provided"):

Personal care routine of children
Language
Reasoning experience
Social development
Fine and gross motor activities
Creative activities
Adult needs

A recent survey (Keyes 1980) assesses centers in terms of whether they provide full-day service, meals, health support services, social services, arrangements for sleep, and year-round service. Assessment of educational features was based on traditional laboratory school features. Observations of teachers' responses to the children were collected to detemine whether the teachers used more instructional behavior than management behavior (according to the category system described in Chapter 5). Facilities were assessed to see if they were designed specifically for the children. Other questions related to how the center was initiated; its fiscal policies and staff policies; orientation, enrollment, and program information; academic activities used by parents; and community evaluation procedures.

Although the program's match with the needs of parents, children, and staff is our primary concern, the support sources for a successful operation—public relations, marketing, and fiscal management—should be reviewed regularly to ensure the availability of these services.

Whereas the evaluation instruments developed by Thelma Harms relate primarily to the program's relationship to the children, the *Handbook of Standards for Preschool Group Day Care Centers* (Gopeer and Entree 1979), developed by the Agency for Child Development, is a guide to such program criteria and indicators as parent involvement, social services, community outreach, health and nutrition, the administrator's governance role, personal practices, fiscal management, and maintenance of records.

A center director can use prepared evaluation instruments to develop a system that provides a review of all aspects of her center. For example, a combination of the Harms and Clifford (1980) rating scales, evaluations from staff and parents, a financial assessment, and a public relations assessment gives the director a way to review all center operations.

A director may want to develop her own instruments based on program scales. For each program, indicators would be developed to measure progress toward goals. For example, the following are some goals related to parent involvement:

1.  Program policies and procedures are to be interpreted and explained to parents.
2.  Parents are to be oriented to the facility and to program goals and policies.
3.  There is to be continuous communication between staff and parents.
4.  There is to be an active parent committee for the center.
5.  Parent education activities are to be carried on by the staff.

What indicators might a director assess in regard to these goals? To judge whether parent education activities are being carried out by the staff, for example, the director should assess the following activities:

1.  Parent meetings
2.  Parent-teacher conferences
3.  Parents' visits to the classroom
4.  The class newsletter, which contains ideas for trips

## Monitoring the Match Between Teachers' Goals and Practices

Continuous evaluation of teachers takes place by virtue of the director's daily contact with her staff. As we discussed in Chapter 5, it is important for the director to be a familiar figure in the classroom, in a supportive rather than a critical role. Evaluation does imply that some judgments are being made, since the director has ultimate responsibility for the program.

The category system described in Chapter 5 can be used to describe and evaluate the match between a teacher's goals and orientation and her behaviors, as well as between a teacher's stated goals and her practices.

## Matching Values and Practices

Values are important to identify because they influence our behaviors and attitudes whether we are aware of them or not. Our ideas about how children should behave, what experiences they should have, and what goals we have for their future are based on our values. It is important that the personnel in the center be aware of the values that support their selection of particular activities, that promote them to say one thing and not another, and that affect the feelings they have when they observe a particular behavior in a child. For example, if one of your school's goals is to help children satisfy their individual needs, do the teachers insist that all children participate in a group activity whether or not they truly want to? If your school has a goal of expanding a child's involvement, is the teacher allowing him enough time to work when he is involved in a task, without breaking in for another scheduled task or housekeeping routine?

In summary, all forms of evaluation, including evaluation of the individual children's progress and evaluation of teachers, serve as checks to help the administrator and the teaching staff see how the center's operations are meeting its goals. It also helps them determine what modifications need to be made to processes or materials for children, schedules, meetings for parents, or programs for the community. Don't be afraid of evaluation. Let it be the basis for change and growth.

## OUTSIDE FUNDING

Many early childhood centers qualify for funding from federal, state, and local sources, especially if the center is run as a nonprofit agency. These funds are sought apart from any fund-raising activities. Usually, they are earmarked for a particular purpose, such as the initiation of a new program.

### Local Sources

Local businesses and associations are the most likely places to seek funding for projects. As we noted earlier, if you are designing a new playground, you might be able to get some in-kind assistance from the telephone company (poles), an electric company (cable spools), or a hardware store or lumberyard. You might also be able to get funds from such local business sources or from a Rotary Club or other similar organization. Community funds such as United Way are often good sources of scholarships for needy children as well as for funding for projects related to the families (e.g., parenting workshops). A local department of social services or department of public health may well fund projects such as child care relief and parent education for potentially abusing mothers, parenting education and mother-child programs for unmarried teenage mothers, or support for single parents. A town government might offer assistance to your center in the form of labor, materials, or funds, since you provide a community service. Local colleges and businesses may be interested in a contract specifying the services of your center for their students or employees. Colleges and high schools may also be willing to provide funds for training child care workers.

Local and regional foundations are another funding source. It would be handy for your center to have on hand a book such as the *Foundation Index and Directory*, but you can usually find this reference at the public library. The book will tell you which foundations give money for child care-related projects, which projects they seem most likely to support, and how much money they usually provide. It will also tell you the requirements for submitting proposals and where to apply.

Once you have identified a foundation that is seeking proposals such as you may wish to design for your center, you should submit a letter of intent that outlines your project, including its purpose and the population to be served. It is useful to call the foundation headquarters to see if your idea is a likely candidate for funding and/or what types of modifications might make it more appealing to the foundation. The letter of intent should be brief in its description of the purpose and nature of your proposed project. It should also tell who you are, emphasizing your credentials and qualifications to do the tasks specified.

Your state department of education will tell you what types of proposals they are seeking. Perhaps they are interested in programs for gifted young children, in parenting programs, or in infant programs. If your interests and abilities coincide with the state priorities, it is advisable to apply.

### Federal Sources

The federal government, through such agencies as the Office of Child Development and the Office of Education, will send you, on request, a published list of their funding priorities, including requirements for proposal submission and deadlines. The federal government funds many programs, directly and through state agencies. As an early childhood center, you might be most successful working at the state level. However, to give you an idea of the many federal agencies offering assistance to families, we suggest that you examine the government publication entitled *Catalog of Federal Domestic Assistance*. This document, published yearly, contains all projects—educational, medical, nutritional, and so forth—that apply to individuals and families. Many of these project ideas can be adapted for implementation at the local level by a child care center.

## What Goes into a Funding Proposal?

If you are asked to submit a proposal to a foundation or a corporation, your emphasis should be on being concise and clear. Avoid the use of jargon. Prepare a cover letter that presents a brief description of your proposal and demonstrates that you have the expertise to do the project outlined and the backing of your board of directors. Suggest a personal meeting with representatives of the funding source or a telephone conversation. Also, if you plan to work cooperatively with another agency, attach a letter of support to your proposal.

The proposal itself may vary in length and in form. For some purposes, it may be part of the letter. Usually, a proposal includes a problem statement that emphasizes the intent of the project to solve some existing problem. The problem statement may be combined with a needs assessment. This is followed by an outline of the objectives of the proposal and a description of the plan (method) for achieving those objectives.

The budget is the next important consideration in preparing your proposal. There are many sources of details on how to prepare budgets, including Nolan's (1980) brief account of the items to be included in funding budgets for early childhood projects. The usual approach is to begin with broad headings, such as the following:

Personnel
Rent
Insurance
Supplies
Equipment
Telephone
Printing
Postage
Travel

Other categories may be included, and each category may have several subheadings. For example, personnel would include salaries for professional staff, secretarial and clerical staff, and maintenance staff as well as calculated fringe benefits. Equipment might include any nonconsumable items, such as blocks or furniture for the classroom, as well as filing cabinets, typewriters, and other office furniture. Similarly, supplies may apply to classroom and office supplies and may even include maintenance items. It is important to consider carefully all the incidental costs that a new program might entail. In the printing category, for example, keep in mind the need for brochures, posters, business cards, stationery, and the like. Travel might apply to the costs of attending workshops and conferences to discuss the projects with other professionals; it might also include transportation for the children. Some other costs that you can anticipate would be bookkeeping and even taxes, if applicable. It is good to keep costs down to make your project more attractive to a potential funding source, but it is also important to be realistic and thorough in your budget planning.

The next step in a proposal is to describe your method of evaluation. Evaluation is a significant component of your proposal, since it will demonstrate how effective your project has been in meeting the needs identified at the beginning. Evaluation might take the form of systematically observing changes in the children's behavior or interviewing parents before and after a project is instituted. Whatever evaluation techniques are used, the criteria for judging changes should be developed at the time of preparing the proposal, and these criteria should reflect as accurately as possible the hypothesized effects of your program. You may also need a brief summary of the proposal, which may go in the cover letter, at the beginning of the proposal as an introduction, or at the end of the proposal, depending on the preference of the funding source.

The federal government and even state agencies usually require elaborate proposals, whereas corporations and foundations usually prefer a three- or four-page document. Keep in mind that the people at a private funding source who will be reading your proposal usually have little expertise and little time. Thus, you should stress the immediate practical value of your plan, and you should do it in as few words as possible. State or federal agencies will send you very explicit instructions for filing proposals. It is advisable to follow these instructions to the letter. It would be a shame to have a good idea but not receive funding because you didn't double-space the proposal!

## Suggested Activities

1. Review the characteristics of successful early childhood administrators described in this chapter. Compare these characteristics with your own personal competencies and personality traits. Assess your strengths and weaknesses in this regard.
2. Review some books on management. How do the principles offered for other organizations apply to an early childhood center?
3. Prepare an annual budget for an actual or hypothetical early childhood center. How did you select items and anticipate costs and income? How do these fiscal decisions reflect your values and goals?
4. Analyze an actual center in progress, using the environment rating scale developed by Harms and Clifford (1980) or one of your own designs. How do the practices noted compare with the goals of the center?

## References and Further Readings

Austin AEYC. *Ideas for Administrators.* Washington, D.C.: National Association for the Education of Young Children, 1973.

Axelrod, Pearl, and Buch, Esther M. *Preschool and Child Care Administration.* Course handout, Mobile Training for Directors of Day Care Centers, 1978.

Cherry, Clare; Hunnes, Barbara; and Kuzma, Kay. *Nursery School and Day Care Management Guide.* Belmont, Calif.: Fearon-Pitman, 1978.

Child Development Association Consortium. *Local Assessment Team Guidelines.* Washington, D.C.: Child Development Association, 1975.

"Financial Management Assessment Guide," *Child Care Information Exchange,* November 1980, 15–16.

Finn, M. *Fundraising for Early Childhood Programs.* Washington, D.C.: National Association for the Education of Young Children, 1982.

*Foundation Index and Directory.* New York: The Foundation Center.

Glick, Phyllis. *Administration of Schools for Young Children.* Albany: Delmar, 1975.

Goldman, Richard, and Anglin, Leo. "Evaluating Your Caregivers: Four Observation Systems." *Day Care and Early Education*, Fall 1979, 40–41.

Gopeer, Nancy, and Entree, Suzanne. *The Handbook of Standards for Preschool Group Day Care Centers.* New York: Agency for Child Development. Human Resources Agency, 1979.

Halpern, Robert. "Surviving Competition: Economic Skills and Arguments for Program Directors," *Young Children 37*(5), July 1982, 25–50.

Harms, Thelma, and Clifford, Richard. *Early Childhood Environment Rating Scale.* New York: Teachers College Press, 1980.

Hewes, Dorothy W., ed. *Administration: Making Programs Work for Children and Families.* Washington, D.C.: National Association for the Education of Young Children, 1979.

Human Resources Network. *User's Guide to Funding Resources.* Radnor, Pa.: Chilton, 1975.

Keyes, Carol. *A Descriptive Study of Campus Child Care Centers in the New York Metropolitan Area.* Ph.D. dissertation, Union Graduate School, 1980.

Kostelnik, Majorie. "Making the Transition from Teacher to Director." *Child Care Information Exchange*, January/February 1982, 11–16.

La Crosse, E. Robert. "Thoughts for New Administrators." In Dorothy Hewes, ed., *Administration: Making Programs Work for Children and Families.* Washington, D.C.: National Association for the Education of Young Children, 1979.

"Money Management Tools—Breakeven Analysis." *Child Care Information Exchange*, April 1979, 6–7.

"Money Management Tools—Fee Collecting Procedure." *Child Care Information Exchange*, January 1980, 15–16.

Neugebauer, Roger. "Managing Time, Your Most Precious Resource." *Child Care Information Exchange*, February 1979, 1–6.

Neugebauer, Roger. "Do You Have Delegation Phobia?" *Child Care Information Exchange*, March/April 1983, 2–4.

Nolan, Mary E. "Finding the Green: Funding Early Childhood Programs." *Young Children 35*(3), March 1980, 14–20.

Office of Management and Budget. *Catalog of Federal Domestic Assistance.* Washington, D.C.: U.S. Government Printing Office.

Raeburn, J. A. "Communication" and "Knowing What You Expect and What is Expected of You." Athens: University of Georgia, Cooperative Extension Service, 1977.

Rogolsky, Mary Rose. "Psychologist Views of the Role of a Day Care Director." *Child Care Information Exchange*, September 1979, 1-5.

*The Corporate Fundraising Director.* Hartsdale, N.Y.: Public Service Materials Center.

U.S. Department of Health, Education and Welfare, Bureau of Child Development Services. *Project Head Start Series.* Washington, D.C.: U.S. Government Printing Office, 1973.

U.S. Department of Health, Education and Welfare, Office of Child Development. *Day Care Series.* Washington, D.C.: U.S. Government Printing Office, 1971.

Zimmerman, Karen, and Herr, Judith. "Time Wasters: Solutions for Teachers and Directors." *Young Children 36*(3), March 1981, 45-48.

# Chapter 11
# The Director
# as Advocate

We have chosen to end our book with a brief chapter that discusses the advocacy role of an early childhood director. We have done so because we view the entire scope of a competent director's work as a form of advocacy. In contrast to an administrator who is primarily concerned with maintaining the status quo, the director-advocate is an agent for change on behalf of children and families.

Although being an advocate requires some idealism, it also takes considerable practical skill to bring the ideals into reality. Advocacy is not simply talk; it requires definite action. In most cases, it also requires persistence. Advocacy involves helping to resolve the incongruity between the needs of children and families and the services and other community supports being provided to them. It takes place in your school with staff and parents. It takes place with your board or sponsoring agency. It also takes place in your relationship with government—local, state, and federal—and in your relationship with business and industry.

## ADVOCACY WITH A BOARD
## OR SPONSORING AGENCY

Advocacy in relation to a board or sponsoring agency is a particularly important part of a director's task, and advocacy in this area involves more than getting additional funds for the center. It includes educating the board and other sources of support about the needs for funds and the programs that you are attempting to initiate or maintain.

Conducting a needs assessment survey is an excellent way to establish a case for the initiation of a new program. Keeping good records of your service delivery is also essential to protect a program against a loss of support. We have found that, in some cases, the people who have ultimate administrative or financial responsibility for an early childhood center are not knowledgeable about early childhood education and inadvertently withhold needed funds. In other cases, these people may have different priorities from the director and her staff, who are likely to be more knowledgeable and who are responsible for providing daily services to the children and their families. In your advocate's role, persistence and determination are required regarding what services are minimal. You must establish a point beyond which compromise is not possible.

## ADVOCACY WITH BUSINESS AND INDUSTRY

Outside the immediate realm of your center, there are several other areas to consider in your advocacy role. An important and yet often neglected area is private industry. Company policies—such as daily work schedules, requirements for working weekends or overtime, travel requirements, and sick leave allowances—often work against family life.

Where might you be able to advocate for change? Many companies have found that they can allow employees with school-age children to leave before the traditional 5 P.M. end of the work day if the employees make up the time by shortening their lunch hours, by coming in earlier, or by maintaining their full-day productivity levels in less time. Companies have also been successful in decreasing absenteeism and increasing productivity by hiring workers on a three-quarter-time schedule. Such schedules have been helpful for many working parents.

Some private industries have sponsored free or low-cost day care centers in or near company facilities. This arrangement has proved to be very beneficial to the employer as well as to the workers.

It is important to prod the social conscience of private industries so that they make allowances in work schedules for parents with young children, not pressuring them to travel extensively or work on weekends. We also think it appropriate to advocate the

Swedish sick-pay system, which pays employees for time off when their children are sick. Those who have directed or worked in day care centers know how difficult it is for parents when their children are sick; they are afraid of losing their jobs if they stay out to care for their children.

## ADVOCACY WITH GOVERNMENT

Perhaps the most obvious form of advocacy that an early childhood director can engage in involves the government and other community resources. Early childhood educators and others in this country who are concerned about children have become increasingly aware of the urgency of raising the consciousness of community leaders and government officials about the needs of children and families. There is a great deal of evidence—in terms of government assistance to families, support for day care, preventive health care for children, and the negative effects of poverty, ranging from diet to education—that our country has failed to apply its enormous resources adequately to these problems (Edelman 1979; Kenniston 1975; Solinit 1976; Zeigler 1976). It is also clear that day care and early childhood professionals need to join with each other and other advocates to force government attention toward meeting these needs (Edelman 1979). Administrators can begin at the local and state levels to contact legislators and to process programs. They can and should get parents and parent groups involved in this advocacy process as well. One significant national organization that is spearheading such action is the Children's Defense Fund. Local and state day care councils are other places to exert advocacy efforts. Certainly, the parents and staff at your early childhood center need to be aware of these issues. They should be encouraged to help in the advocacy process.

In a recent article in *Young Children*, Lana Hosteller (1981) points out that advocacy is a natural outgrowth of the necessary professionalization of early childhood workers. Why, then, have many child care workers not actively participated in advocacy? For some, it's a matter of status ("Who are we to have an impact on national policy?"). For others, the reluctance to advocate stems from a fear of self-interest ("If we ask for more programs and more funding, aren't we helping ourselves as well as the children?"). Hosteller (1981) argues that child care workers need to be more assertive about themselves and about the children whom they serve. The alternative—standing by and letting public officials deny services to children and families—is unacceptable.

Ziegler and Finn (1981) agree with many others who have noted that the attempts that have been made to affect public policy have not had sufficient impact. For example, the United States still ranks twelfth among industrial nations in infant mortality. Far too many children are still lacking in regular medical and dental care, and almost two out of five preschoolers are not properly immunized. Unfortunately, the list of things that could be done is very long. What is required to have an impact on public policy? Ziegler and Finn (1981) emphasize the importance of obtaining media coverage. These problems must be brought into public view continually. This means that, as early childhood professionals, we must initiate an active public education campaign. We must also see that our political representatives are reminded regularly of our concerns on these issues. We must lobby to change policy that is inadequate and to create new policies where necessary.

The lobbying should be as broad-based as possible to have the greatest impact. This may mean putting aside some differences and reaching a common point of view in these matters, which has not always been easy. It may well require compromise. Ziegler and Finn (1981) offer some examples of successful lobbying groups for children. In addition to strength, an effective lobbying group must have leverage. They must be aware of when decisions are being made and who in the government may be in a position to affect policy in favor of children. A director and her staff can have an impact in these efforts through national organizations and coalitions. The National Coalition of Campus Child Care is a good example. Although it had an informal existence as a council in the 1960s, it has since gained strength as an advocacy group, and it became formally incorporated as a national group in 1982.

At this time, because of reduced federal and state funding, it is crucial that early childhood directors include economic arguments in their advocacy efforts. It is certainly justifiable to point out that early childhood programs can save a community money in the long run by preventing educational problems that would require expensive remediation at a later point in a child's academic career. Similarly, it may also be argued that high-quality day care and early childhood intervention is one of the best ways to reduce the need for mental health services in the future, in terms of both families and individuals. Certainly, the immediate economic effects of providing quality care for children that frees women for participation in the work force should be articulated by early childhood advocates (Halpern 1981).

## ADVOCACY FOR HUMANISM

From another point of view, Kenneth Goodman (1981) has presented an argument in favor of the immediate need for early childhood educators to lobby for humanism. We cited Goodman at the beginning of our book, since his philosophy is so consistent with our own. Goodman feels that teachers must guard against the pressures that exist to dehumanize the schools with cost-effectiveness, objectivity, and so forth. He calls this an "industrialization" of schools. Among the many commitments that he suggests we make as professional educators is to respect all students by recognizing their unique talents and by accepting and learning more about their various cultures. This commitment may require opposing policies that would overlook these personal and social differences. We must make every effort to see that school is a warm, supportive place where children can learn to respect and support one another and where parents are welcome. Goodman encourages us to fight the use of material, extrinsic rewards and impersonal evaluation. He is fearful that teachers may become technicians, executing packaged curricula in an automated way. He favors evaluations that are holistic—that is, not based on a single dimension—and evaluations that are based on a real and continuing knowledge of students, rather than on yearly testing alone. You may not agree entirely with the extent of Goodman's concern, but he raises important issues for consideration by professionals who wish to hold fast to humanistic and developmentally sound principles in a world of increasing technology.

## PROFESSIONAL ACTIVISM

A significant part of the responsibility of the director of any early childhood center is to participate actively in professional organizations, on her own behalf as well as on behalf of her center. In that respect, she also serves as a role model for her staff. This is another form of advocacy in the sense that membership in such organizations as early childhood councils and day care associations enables her to share ideas informally and to participate in in-service workshops and professional conferences. These groups frequently publicize community events relating to children, advocate for children's services in the community, and sponsor activities. A very good example of such activity was the International Year of the Young Child, sponsored by the United Nations. This event was given publicity and direction by professional children's advocacy groups in many communities.

It is possible to broaden your scope of action and knowledge by participating in a national organization's activities, usually beginning at the local level. For example, as a member of the National Association for the Education of Young Children (NAEYC), you can read and contribute to the association's publications and participate in national and regional conferences. You can involve your staff and parents in all such efforts or bring back materials to share.

## SUMMARY

The humanistic director is specifically an advocate for children. As we have attempted to point out throughout this book, she is an advocate for a point of view that maintains that an early childhood center has the responsibility and the power to contribute to the uniquely human potential available to all of the people it serves (children, parents, and teachers). Clearly, the cause of children must be presented by caring adults to those who have the power to affect their lives—from politicians to parents. Parents require support for their important role in raising children and for their personal development. Similarly, teachers need to be treated as human beings as they pursue their very demanding task of helping young children realize their potential and become the complete persons we wish them to be.

### Suggested Activity

Contact a national, state, or local children's advocacy group. Review the group's literature. Volunteer for participation.

## References and Further Readings

Edelman, Marian. Keynote address, Annual Meeting of the National Association for the Education of Young Children, New York, November 1979.

Goodman, Kenneth S. "A Declaration of Professional Conscience For Teachers." *Young Children 36*(4), May 1981, 15-16.

Halpern, Robert. "Surviving Competition: Economic Skills and Arguments for Program Directors." *Young Children 37*(5), July 1981, 25-50.

Hosteller, Lana. "Child Advocacy: Your Professional Responsibility?" *Young Children 36*(3), March 1981, 3-8.

Kenniston, Kenneth. "Do Americans Really Like Children?" *Today's Education*, November/December 1975.

Solinit, Albert J. "Changing Psychological Perspectives About Children and Their Families." *Children Today*, May/June 1976, 5-9.

Zeigler, Edward F. "The Unmet Needs of America's Children." *Children Today*, May/June 1976, 39-43.

Zeigler, E., and Finn, M. "From Problem to Solution: Changing Public Policy as It Affects Children and Families." *Young Children 36*(4), May 1981, 31-58.

## National Organizations Involved in Advocacy for Children

Action for Children's Television
46 Austin Street
Newtonville, MA 02160

Association for Childhood Education International
3615 Wisconsin Avenue, N.W.
Washington, DC 20016

Black Child Development Institute
6028 Connecticut Avenue, N.W.
Washington, DC 20009

Children's Defense Fund
1520 New Hampshire Avenue, N.W.
Washington, DC 20016

Council for Exceptional Children
1920 Association Drive
Reston, VA 22091

Day Care Council of America
1401 K Street, N.W.
Washington, DC 20016

National Association for the Education of Young Children
1834 Connecticut Avenue, N.W.
Washington, DC 20009

*Report on Preschool Education*
Capital Publications, Inc.
1300 North Seventeenth Street
Arlington, VA 22209

# Index

Action for Children's Television, 251

Activism, professional, 249–250

Activity(ies):
  checklists, 151–152
  opportunities for, 113–114
  timetable of, 45
  workshops, 170
    parent-child, 182–190

Ad journal, for fund-raising, 54

Administrative functions, parents and, 179–180

Adults:
  being surrounded by caring, 111–112
  who enjoy learning, 112

Advertising, low-cost, 48

Advocacy, 245
  with board or sponsoring agency, 245–246
  with business and industry, 246–247
  with government, 247–249
  for humanism, 249
  and professional activism, 249–250

Agency for Child Development, 236

Anecdotal records, 123, 124–125, 152

Anglin, Leo, 99

Annual report, 50–51

Anthropology, students of, as volunteers in centers, 209

Application form, staff, 63

Arts and crafts open house, 187–190

Association for the Blind, 9

Association for Childhood Education International, 75, 251

Association for the Deaf, 9

Attendance records, 233

Austin (Texas) AEYC, 181

Autonomy, 114

Bake sale, for fund-raising, 52, 178–179

Behaviorist theory, 91–92

*Between Parent and Child* (Ginott), 173

Biber, B., 163

Bilingual children, 134–136

Bilingual handbook, preparation of, 98

Black Child Development Institute (*see* National Black Child Development Institute)

Black, R., 149

Block area, 26–27
  flooring, 27
  location, 27
  materials, 27

Board, advocacy with, 245–246

Boynton, Mary, 148–149

Bronfenbrenner, Urie, 81, 162, 163

Budget, 226–227
  and funding proposal, 240–241
  preparation of, 227–229, 230–232

Build-ins, 179

Bulletin boards:
  for parental education, 172
  staff, 88

Bureau of the Handicapped, 8

Business, advocacy with, 246–247

Carnival, for fund-raising, 53

Carpentry projects, 19–20
  (*see also* Woodworking area)

Carson, Rachel, *A Sense of Wonder*, 184

CASES (Coping Analysis Schedules for Educational Settings), 129

Cataldo, Christine Z., *Infant and Toddler Programs*, 140–141

*Catalog of Federal Domestic Assistance*, 239

Category system, for describing adult responses to children's behavior, 89-91, 92, 93, 95

CDA (*see* Child Development Associate)

Census, U.S., 3

Center for Parent Education, 75, 76

Center for Systems and Program Development, 176

Chairs, 38

Chambers of commerce, 9, 11

Change behaviors, stop and, 91-93, 95

Checklists, 125, 128
activity, 151-152

*Child Care Information Exchange*, 230, 232

Childcraft, 17

Child development, 208-209
knowledge and understanding of, by staff, 74

*Child Development*, 75

Child Development Associate (CDA) credential, 12, 98-99, 176

Child-rearing concerns, of parents, 160-161

Children (*see also* Infants and toddlers; Special needs, children with):
developmental considerations about, 112-116
enrolling, 106-109
evaluating progress of, 123-130
identifying characteristics of, 118
identifying needs of, 109-112
according to child's daily experiences, 121-123
and monitoring in classroom, 151-154
matching needs of, with policy and program, 116-123
monitoring responses to needs of, 120-121
multiage centers for, 117-118
notifying, about staff changes, 66
placing of, in class, 108
separation of, from parents, 108-109, 123

supporting individual requests of, 120
visits of, to school, 106-108

Children's Defense Fund, 247, 251

Church classrooms, locating center in, 15

Church-related schools, funding for, 10

Civic organizations:
community support from, 11
funding by local, 9

Classification, training children in, 196

Classroom, setting up:
basic equipment and supplies, 37-45
general principles, 25-26
interest areas, 26-35 (*see also* Interest areas)
room arrangement, 35-37
timetable of activities, 45

Clifford, Richard, 235, 236, 242

Clinical supervision, 91-97

Coding system, for classroom behavior, 129, 130

Cognitive theory, 92

Collins, Raymond, 11-12

Community programs, 51-52

Community support, 10-11

Concert, children's, for fund-raising, 53

Conferences, professional, 74, 75 (*see also* Parent-teacher conferences)

Conversations, parent-teacher:
spontaneous, 190-191
telephone, 191

Cooking activities area, 35
flooring, 35
location, 35
materials, 35

Cooperative nursery schools, 201
funding for, 10

Cooperatives, 179-180

Costs (*see also* Expenses)
fixed, 226-227
variable, 226, 227

Council for Exceptional Children (CEC), 75, 251

*How to Fill Your Toy Shelves Without Emptying Your Pocketbook*, 172

Courses, in childhood and parent
    education, 75, 208-209
Creative arts area, 28-30
    flooring, 29
    location, 29
    materials, 29-30
Criterion reference tests, 153
Cubbies, 38
Curriculum:
    basics of, for staff, 74
    goals, 77, 80-84
    innovations, facilitating,
        85-87
    objectives, 77
    planning and implementation,
        77-87

Day Care Council of America,
    62, 75, 252
*Day Care and Early Education*,
    75
Developmentally disabled child,
    136-139
Devries, Rheta, 77
Diagnostic tests, 153
Diapering area, 149
Diarrhea, effects of handwashing
    on preventing, in child care
    centers, 149
Diary, 125
Didactic instruction, 92
Dinner-dance, for fund-raising, 54
Director, 215 (*see also* Staff;
        Teacher(s)):
    as advocate, 245-249
    characteristics of, 215-216
    delegating responsibility by,
        220-221
    encouragement of teacher
        observation by, 129-130
    and fiscal management
        procedures, 226-234
    and health care procedures,
        222-225
    organization of time by, 218-219
    and personal needs of staff
        members, 87-88
    policies and procedures developed
        by, 221-222
    principles for, 217-218
    professional activism of, 249-250
    program evaluation by, 234-238
    relationship between staff and, 89

role of, in curriculum planning
    and implementation, 77, 79,
    81
transition from teacher to,
    216-217
working job descriptions for,
    219-220
Disabled child
    (*see* Developmentally
    disabled child)
Divorce, 162
    and parental remarriage, 133-134
Dramatic play area (family center),
    27-28
    flooring, 28
    location, 28
    materials, 28

Early Childhood Council, 62
Easter Seal Foundation, 9
Edelman, Marian, 247
Education for Parenthood
    Exchange, 76
Employee files, 67-68
Employment process, 62 (*see also*
        Postemployment procedures)
    application form, 63
    interview process, 63-64
    making final decision, 64-65
    notification of employment, 65
    notifying children, 66
    notifying parents, 65
    recruitment, 62-63
Enrollment:
    preparation and process,
        parents and, 165-167
    and recruitment of children,
        106-109
Entree, Suzanne, *Handbook of
        Standards for Preschool
        Group Day Care Centers*
        (with N. Gopeer), 236
Environment, making sense of, 111
Environment, early childhood:
    defined, 235
    rating scale for, 235, 236, 242
Equipment, materials, and supplies,
    17
    costs of, 228-229
    donated, 19
    government resources for, 20-21
    homemade, 20
    from large discount stores, 18

Equipment, materials, and supplies
    (*cont.*)
    from local professional societies,
        22
    making own, 18-19
    from manufacturers and
        distributors of school
        supplies, 17
    "scrounge" list of, 19-20
    for setting up classroom, 37-45
    from telephone companies, 22
Erikson, Erik, 114
Evaluation, of children's progress,
    123-130
Evaluation, program, 234-235,
    238, 241
    matching values and practices,
        237
    methods of, 235-237
    monitoring match between
        teachers' goals and practices,
        237
Evans, Ellis, 160
Expenses, 227-228 (*see also* Costs)
    equipment, 228-229
    miscellaneous, 229
    overhead, 228
    salaries, 228
    supplies, 229
Exploratory needs, of young
    children, 114
Extending and sustaining behaviors,
    91-93

Family center (dramatic play area),
    27-28
    flooring, 28
    location, 28
    materials, 28
Family Resource Coalition, 76
Family Service Association, 164
*Father, The: His Role in Child
    Development* (Lynn), 173
Feature stories, 49
Federal Interagency Day Care
    Requirements, 11
Financial management
    assessment guide,
    231-232
Finn, M., 248
First-aid, 37
*First Parent*, 175
*First Teacher*, 175

Fiscal management procedures,
    226
    budget, 226-229, 230-232
    income, 229-230
    petty cash, 229
    records, forms, and reports,
        232-234
Fixed costs, 226-227
Foster grandparent programs,
    201
*Foundation Index and Directory*,
    239
Foundations, as funding source,
    9, 239
Freeport (New York) Center for
    Early Childhood, 175
Funding, 230, 238
    for church-related schools, 10
    by civic organizations, 9
    for cooperative nursery schools,
        10
    federal sources of, 239
    for handicapped children, 8
    initial, 7-8
    local sources of, 238-239
    by private foundations, 9
    by private industry, 10
    proposal, contents of, 240-241
    state, county, and town, 8-9
    by universities, 9-10
Fund-raising activities, 52
    bake sale, 52, 178-179
    carnival, 53
    concert or theatrical production,
        children's, 53
    dinner-dance, 54
    to encourage interaction among
        parents, 178-179
    types of, 178-179

Game boards, covering old, 20
Gerson, Menachem, 144
Gifted child, 139-140
Goals, curriculum:
    based on needs of children, 80
    based on values for survival,
        80-84
    individualizing, 195-196
    and practices, monitoring match
        between teachers', 237
    program, 77-78
Goldman, Richard, 99
Goodbye ritual, 117

Goodman, Kenneth, 249
Gopeer, Nancy, *Handbook of Standards for Preschool Group Day Care Centers* (with S. Entree), 236
Government, advocacy with, 247-249
Greenberg, Selma, 19
Greenman, Jim, 148
Grossman, Bruce, 22, 99, 121, 136
Group size, importance of, 12
*Growing Child*, 175
*Growing Parent*, 175
*Guide to Children's Books in Print, The*, 134

Halpern, Robert, 227, 249
Handbook(s):
　for parents, 166-167
　preparation of bilingual, 98
Handicapped children, expanding educational opportunities for, 8 (*see also* Developmentally disabled child)
Handwashing, effects of, on preventing diarrhea in child care centers, 149
Hardware, suggested basic, 38-44
　chairs, 38
　cubbies, 38
　indoor equipment for large-motor development, 38-39
　outdoor play area, 39
　storage units, 38
　tables, 38
Harlow, Harry, 110
Harms, Thelma, 235, 236, 242
Head Start, 8, 175, 179
Health aspects of infant/toddler centers, 148-149
Health care procedures, 222-225
Health and Human Services, Department of, 13, 62
Herr, Judith, 219
Hewes, Dorothy W., 216
Highberger, Ruth, 148-149
Home, transition between school and, 121-123
Hosteller, Lana, 247-248
Houses, locating center in private, 15-16
Humanism, advocacy for, 249

Humanistic orientation, 59, 60, 61, 105, 159, 250
Hymes, James, 163, 192

Imitation, learning from, 115-116
Impatience, of young children, 115
Income, 227, 229-230
Independence:
　balance between dependence and, 109
　of developmentally disabled child, 138
　encouraging, 81-82, 95
Indoor equipment, for large-motor development, 38-39
Industrial Home for the Blind, 225
Industrial sites, locating center in, 16-17
Industry:
　advocacy with, 246-247
　funding by private, 10
Infants and toddlers, setting up program for, 140-141
　competent caregivers in, 149-151
　environmental considerations in, 141-142
　monitoring needs in, 144
　personal data sheet for, 145-148
　program considerations in, 143-144
　and relationship with parents, 144
　special equipment for, 144-149
　staffing considerations in, 142-143
Initiative, 114
Insecurity, child's, 109-110
Interest areas, 25-26
　block area, 26-27
　cooking activities area, 35
　creative arts area, 28-30
　family center (dramatic play area), 27-28
　language arts area, 30
　manipulative materials interest area, 31-32
　music and listening area, 31
　science and pet area, 32-33
　water/sand play area, 33-34
　woodworking area, 34-35
Interferences, to child's exploration, learning, and growth, 120-121

International Year of the Young
Child, 250
Interobserver agreement, 130
Interview process, staff, 63–64
Invisible children, 153

Jackson, Philip, 120–121, 123
Jacobson, Armita Lee, 149–150
Jacobson, L., 124
Job description:
  for staff position, 67
  working, for director, 219–220
Journals, 75
  ad, for fund-raising, 54
  subscriptions to professional, 74

Kammi, Constance, 77
Katz, Lillian, 71
Kenniston, Kenneth, 81, 162, 247
Keyes, Carol, 89, 99, 121, 136,
  184, 235
Kiwanis, 9, 11
Kostelnik, Marjorie, 215, 217–218

LaCrosse, Robert, 217
Language arts area, 30
  location, 30
  materials, 30
Latch boards, construction of, 20
Letters, to parents, 176
Library, lending, for parents,
  172–174
Licensing requirements, 11–12,
  13
Life:
  complexity of modern, 80–81,
    82–83, 162
  experiencing, as worth living,
    111
Lillard, Paula P., 143
Lions, 9, 11
Lobbying:
  groups for children, 248
  for humanism, 249
Location of center, 12
  in church classrooms, 15
  in industrial sites, 16–17
  in prefabs, 16
  in private houses, 15–16
  in public school rooms,
    14–15
  regulations about, 13–14
  in storefronts, 16

Lockboxes, construction of, 20
Log, 125
Lorton, Mary Jane, 11
  *Workjobs*, 20
Lotto, 18

Mainstreaming, 136, 138–139
Manipulative materials interest
    area, 31–32
  flooring, 32
  location, 32
  materials, 32
"Man-made bridge," 163, 192
Manual, staff, 97–98
March of Dimes, 9
Masons, 9
Materials (*see* Equipment,
    materials, and supplies)
Math area (*see* Manipulative
    materials interest area)
McGinn, Joyce, *Primerrily* (with
    F. Rudnick), 20
Medicaid, 13
Meetings:
  formats and times of, 71–72
  with parents, 167–168
*Momma* (Hope and Young), 173
Montessori, Maria, 143
Multiage grouping, 117–118
Music and listening area, 31
  flooring, 31
  location, 31
  materials, 31

National Association for the
    Education of Young Children
    (NAEYC), 48, 75, 250, 252
  Center Accreditation Project of,
    59–60
  Committee for Early Childhood
    of, 78–79
National Association for Gifted
    Children, 140
National Black Child Development
    Institute, 75, 251
National Coalition of Campus Child
    Care, 75, 248
National Council of Jewish Women,
    6
National Day Care Study (1979),
    12, 60, 74
National Head Start Association,
    75

Needs, children's:
  developmental, 112–116
  identifying, 109–112
    according to child's daily
      experiences, 121
    and monitoring in classroom,
      151–154
    matching, with policy and
      program, 116–123
    monitoring responses to,
      120–121
Needs assessment, 3–5
Needs survey, sample, 4–5
Neugebauer, Roger, 218–219
Newsletters, 76, 85
  center, 50
  for parents, 76, 175
Newspapers, public service
      announcements in, 48
News stories, 49
New York State Board of
      Education, 13
New York State Council for
      Children, 75
Nolan, Mary E., 240
Nursery schools, 201
  cooperative, funding for, 10

Objectives, program, 77–78 (*see
      also* Goals, curriculum)
Observation, careful, of children
      with special needs,
      153–154
Observation, systematic, 123,
      154
  director's encouragement of
      teacher's, 129–130
  principles of, 124
  recording time and place of,
      128
  techniques of, useful to
      teachers, 124–128
Observation and supervision,
      staff development through,
      89–97
Odd Fellows, 9
Office of Child Development, 239
Office of Economic Opportunity,
      8
Office of Education, 239
Open house, 182
  arts and crafts, 187–190
  science, 182–187

Organizations, national and
      state-level, 75, 251–252
Overhead, 228

Pace University Parent Services
      Center, 144, 164
PACT (Parents and Children
      Together), 164
Paint, lead-based, 16, 17
Painting, 28, 29, 151–152 (*see
      also* Creative arts area)
Paraprofessionals, 62
Parent(s) (*see also* Parent-child;
      Parent-teacher conferences):
  and administrative functions,
      179–180
  bulletin boards to educate, 172
  concerns of, 160–162
  cultural differences between
      teachers and, 198
  education, 76, 85
  and enrollment preparation and
      process, 165–167
  evaluation of school by,
      176–177
  fund-raising to encourage
      interaction among, 178–179
  handbooks for, 166–167
  home visits to, 176
  and infant/toddler program,
      144
  involvement of, 159–160,
      174–176, 236–237
  keeping in touch with, 190–191
  lending library for, 172–174
  letters to, 176
  materials request letter to, 21
  meetings with, 167–168
  needs of, 161
  and needs assessment, 3–4
  newsletter for, 175
  notices of resources for, 175
  notifying, about staff changes, 65
  ongoing contact with, 167–179
  orientation of, 166
  programs for, 162–164
  publications, useful, for, 173–174
  as visitors in classroom, 165–166,
      180–190
  as volunteers in classroom, 190,
      209–211
  working with, 76
  workshops for, 168–172

Parent-child:
    activity workshops, 182-190
    separation, 108-109, 123
*Parent Effectiveness Training*
    (Gordon), 173
*Parent Resources*, 175
Parent-staff workshops, 171-172
Parents Without Partners, 169, 171
*Parent Talk*, 175
Parent-teacher conferences:
    additional parental concerns in,
        197
    conducting, 195
    discussing teacher strategies at,
        196-197
    establishing list of priorities at,
        196
    forming alliance at, 194
    general guidelines for working
        with parents at, 197-198
    individualizing educational goals
        at, 195-196
    preparing for, 192-193
    purposes of, 192
    scheduling, 193
    setting stage for, 193-194
*Part-Time Father* (Atkin and
    Rubin), 173
Payment schedules, 230
Peabody Picture Vocabulary Test
    (PPVT), 12
Personnel:
    contracts, 66-67
    policy manual, 68-69
Pets (*see* Science and pet area)
Petty cash, 229
Piaget, Jean, 83, 111
Play area, outdoor, 14, 39
Policies and procedures, 221-222
    fiscal management, 226-234
    health care, 222-225
Postemployment procedures:
    employee files, 67-68
    job description, 67
    orientation of new staff members,
        66
    personnel contracts, 66-67
    personnel policy manual, 68-69
Prefabs, locating center in, 16
Preschool Inventory (PSI), 12
Prescott, Elizabeth, 153
Problem solving, 82, 83-84
Professional activism, 249-250

Professional associations
    and societies:
    membership in, by staff, 74
    representatives or consultants
        from, 22, 72
    as source for workshop leaders,
        171
    speakers from, at meetings with
        parents, 168
Program evaluation, 234-235, 238,
    241
    matching values and practices,
        237
    methods of, 235-237
    monitoring match between
        teachers' goals and practices,
        237
Program management, 86
    techniques of, 73-74
Progress, evaluating children's,
    123-130 (*see also*
    Observation, systematic)
Provence, S., 142, 143
Psychological safety, 109-110
PTA, 6, 11, 15
Publications, useful, for parents,
    173-174
Public relations, 47
    assessment, 55-56
    fund-raising, 52-54
    identifying target population,
        47-48
    reaching target population, 48-52
Public school rooms, locating
    center in, 14-15
Public service announcements, in
    newspapers and on radio, 48

Queens College Title XX Day Care
    Project, 89, 202, 203-204

Rabinoff, Bunny, 153
Radio, public service
    announcements on, 48
Raeburn, J. A., 216, 217
Rating scales, 125, 126-127, 235,
    236, 242
Reading, issue of, 194
Records:
    anecdotal, 123, 124-125, 152
    attendance, 233
    forms, and reports, 232-234
    visitor, 233

Recruitment:
  and enrollment of children,
    106–109
  staff, 62–63
Registration packet, 233
Regulations, building, fire, and
    health, 13–14
Remarriage, divorce and parental,
    133–134
*Report on Preschool Education,*
    252
Responsibility, delegating,
    by director, 220–221
Ricciuti, H., *A Good Beginning
    for Babies* (with A. Willis),
    148
Robison, Helen R., 78
  *Designing Curriculum for Early
    Childhood* (with S. L.
    Schwartz), 79
Rogers, Carl, 110
Rogolsky, Mary Rose, 215, 216
Room:
  arrangement, 25, 35–37
  size and shape, 13
Rosenthal, R., 124
Rotary Club, 238
Rudnick, Fredda, *Primerrily*
    (with J. McGinn), 20

Safety, psychological, 109–110
Salaries, 228
Sand play (*see* Water/sand play
    area)
Satir, Virginia, *People-Making,*
    110
Schaefer, George, 163
Scholarships, 230
School District 14 (Hewlett, New
    York), 6
Schwartz, Sydney L., 78
  *Designing Curriculum for Early
    Childhood* (with H. R.
    Robison), 79
Science open house, 182–187
Science and pet area, 32–33
  flooring, 33
  location, 33
  materials, 33
Self-concept, encouraging positive,
    92
Self-esteem, feelings of, 110, 173
Self-help workshops, 170–171

Seminars, 75
Senior citizens, in childhood
    centers, 201–202
Separation, parent-child, 108–109
    123
Shipman, Virginia C., 163
"Simon Says," 115
Single-parent households, 162
  children from, 133–134
Slide, wooden, 19
Society for Research and Child
    Development, 75
Sociology, students of, as
    volunteers in centers, 209
Solinit, Albert J., 247
Sound cylinders, 18
Southern Association for the
    Education of Young Children,
    75
Southwest Educational
    Development Laboratory,
    172
Spaulding, Robert L., 130
Special needs, children with:
  bilingual children, 134–136
  developmentally disabled child,
    136–139
  gifted child, 139–140
  single-parent households,
    133–134
Spodek, Bernard, *Teaching
    Practices: Reexamining
    Assumptions,* 79
Sponsorship (*see also* Funding):
  agency, advocacy with, 245–246
  of center, 5–6
  by types of schools, 6–7
Spools, large wooden, for tables, 20
Staff (*see also* Director;
    Teacher(s)):
  application form for, 63
  basics of curriculum for, 74
  bulletin board, 88
  -child ratio, 62
  choosing, for early childhood
    program, 60–61
  employee files on, 67–68
  and health care policies and
    procedures, 225
  for infant/toddler program,
    142–143
  interpersonal relations between,
    73

Staff (cont.)
  interview process, 63–64
  job description for, 67
  knowledge and understanding of
      child development by, 74
  making final decision about,
      64–65
  needs for various types of centers,
      61–62
  notification of employment of,
      65
  notifying children about, 66
  notifying parents about, 65
  orientation of new, 66
  -parent workshops, 171–172
  personal needs of, 87–88
  personnel contracts for, 66–67
  personnel policy manual for,
      68–69
  recruitment, 62–63
  self-evaluation, 99–101
  teacher as person, 59–60
  techniques of program
      management for, 73–74
Staff development, 71–72
  curriculum planning and
      implementation and, 77–87
  in-service, 72–74
  monitoring and evaluating,
      98–101
  through observation and
      supervision, 89–97
  personal needs of staff members,
      87–88
  professional growth and, 74–75
  staff manual for, 97–98
  working with parents and, 76
Staff selection:
  concerns in, 59–62
  employment process, 62–66
  postemployment procedures,
      66–69
Stalmack, Judith, 85
Stengel, Susan, 77
Stop and change behaviors,
      91–93, 95
Storage units, 38
Storefronts, locating center in,
      16
Supervision:
  clinical, 91–97
  staff development through
      observation and, 89–97

Supper, potluck, for fund-raising,
      54
Supplies (see Equipment, materials,
      and supplies)
Sustaining and extending behaviors,
      91–93
S.W.A.P., 85
Swedish sick-pay system, 247

Tables, 20, 38
Table toys (see Manipulative
      materials interest area)
Target population:
  identifying, 47–48
  reaching, 48–52
Teacher(s) (see also Parent-teacher
      conferences; Staff):
  category system for, 89–91
  credentials of, 12
  curriculum planning and
      implementation by, 77,
      81–87
  evaluation of children's progress
      by, 123–130
  home visits by, 176
  monitoring and evaluating
      effectiveness of, 98–101
  monitoring match between goals
      and practices of, 237
  observation, director's
      encouragement of, 129–130
  as person, 59
  relationship between director
      and, 89
  transition from, to director,
      216–217
  working as team, 72–73
"Telephone," 115
Telephone calls, parent-teacher,
      191
Telephone companies, donations
      from, 22
Television, feature stories on, 49
Tests:
  criterion reference, 153
  diagnostic, 153
Theatrical production, children's,
      for fund-raising, 53
Toddlers (see Infants and toddlers)
Toilet facilities, 14
  difficulties with, of
      developmentally disabled
      children, 137–138

Tuition, 226, 227
  charges, 229-230
Turnow, Rita, 133

United Nations, 250
United Way, 9, 48, 238
Universities:
  consultants from, for in-service
    staff development, 72
  funding by, 9-10

Values and practices, matching,
  237
Variable costs, 226, 227
Visibility ratings, 153
Visitor records, 233
Visits:
  to center
    by children, 106-108
    by parents, 165-166,
      180-190
  home, by teachers, 176
Volunteers, 62, 88, 201-202,
  211-212
  activities of, 206-207
  benefits to, of work in center,
    207-209
  health and safety
    considerations about,
    205
  parents as, 190, 209-211
  screening and orienting,
    202-205

Warning time, 116-117
Water, sources of, 14
Water/sand play area, 33-34
  flooring, 34
  location, 33
  materials, 34
West, Suzanne, 184
Wheelock College, 75
White, B. L., 149
White, Burton, 76, 163
Willis, A., *A Good Beginning for
  Babies* (with H. Ricciuti), 148
Wolfons, Bernice, 120-121, 123
Woodworking area, 34-35
  flooring, 34
  location, 34
  materials, 34-35
Working Mothers Institute, 76
Workshop(s), 75, 168
  activity, 170, 182-190
  leaders, sources for, 171
  nature and purpose of, 168-170
  parent-child activity, 182-190
  parent-staff, 171-172
  self-help, 170-171
  with staff, 129

Yard, fenced-in, 14
YMCA/YWCA, 175
*Young Children*, 75, 149-150, 247

Ziegler, Edward, 81, 247, 248
Zimmerman, Karen, 219